THREE PLAYS:
THE SERVANTS AND THE SNOW
THE THREE ARROWS
THE BLACK PRINCE

THREE PLAYS:

THE SERVANTS AND THE SNOW

THE THREE ARROWS

THE BLACK PRINCE

IRIS MURDOCH

Chatto & Windus

LONDON

PR
6063
U7
S287
1989

Published in 1989 by
Chatto & Windus Ltd
30 Bedford Square
London WC1B 3SG

A CIP catalogue record for this book is available
from the British Library.

ISBN 0 7011 3590 5

Typeset by Rowland Phototypesetting Ltd,
Bury St Edmunds, Suffolk
Printed in Great Britain by
Mackays of Chatham PLC, Chatham, Kent

CONTENTS

To
Lucy and Christopher Cornford

THE SERVANTS AND THE SNOW

A play in two acts

An old isolated country house in winter

Characters in order of their appearance

PETER JACK, a servant.

BASIL, a landowner, the new master.

ORIANE, his wife.

GRUNDIG, a bailiff.

HANS JOSEPH, a servant.

FREDERIC, a valet.

FATHER AMBROSE, a priest.

MARINA, a servant, daughter-in-law of Hans Joseph and betrothed to Peter Jack.

MIKEY, a servant.

PATRICE, a gipsy.

MAXIM, a servant, son of Marina and grandson of Hans Joseph.

GENERAL KLEIN, brother of Oriane. The General should be played by the same actor who plays Patrice.

ACT ONE

An impression of falling snow upon the curtain.
The curtain rises.
The White Drawing Room in darkness. Enter a procession of
servants carrying lamps, then PETER JACK *followed by* BASIL,
ORIANE *and* GRUNDIG. BASIL *and* ORIANE *are wearing out-*
door clothes lightly dusted with snow. BASIL *looks round him with*
puzzlement.

PETER JACK: This is the White Drawing Room, your
honour.

BASIL: The White Drawing Room. How strange. It looks
smaller. You remember the White Drawing Room,
Oriane?

ORIANE: Ooh it's cold.

PETER JACK: We lit all the fires as soon as we knew that
you were coming, but I'm afraid it's still a bit damp.

BASIL: [*raising his voice:* GRUNDIG *is a bit deaf*] I'm worried
about this dampness, Mr Grundig.

GRUNDIG: A place needs to be lived in, Sir. Your late father
didn't occupy this part of the house.

PETER JACK: This wing has been entirely closed, your
honour. Last summer when your honour's father died we
opened it up, but we weren't sure then if your honour was
coming to live here or not.

GRUNDIG: [*examining the walls*] Don't you worry then, it'll
work out. It's a good sound old house.

BASIL: I want that survey done all the same, Mr Grundig.
I'm afraid my father neglected the place.

GRUNDIG: Your father gave up entertaining completely.
Would you believe it, Sir, that we found moss growing on
the floor of the ballroom.

BASIL: Things will be different now! When my wife's
brother the General comes to stay we'll— [BASIL *is taking*
off his coat.] Oriane, won't you take your coat off?

13

ORIANE: No, I'm frozen.

PETER JACK: I'm very sorry, your ladyship, we—

BASIL: It's not your fault, Peter Jack. I'm afraid we're dropping melted snow everywhere and making work for you. I felt I just had to look round at once. Surely you remember this room now, Oriane?

ORIANE: Basil, I haven't been here for nearly twenty years. And when I was here I was always so frightened of your father I could hardly see out of my eyes.

BASIL: God rest his soul. He was a very frightening man.

PETER JACK: Amen! [BASIL looks at him.] God rest his soul.

BASIL: This is a great change in our lives, dear friends, after living for so long in the city—especially for my wife who has never lived in the countryside.

PETER JACK: We were all so happy, your honour, when we heard that you were really coming home at last. We were worried when your honour didn't come to the funeral.

BASIL: Yes, it's taken six months—I wanted to come at once but there were so many things—Oh Oriane, it's so strange!

ORIANE: I know. Your childhood here. Dear Basil. Where are Frederic and Annabelle?

BASIL: I told someone to bring them here. They must be feeling very lost. [To PETER JACK] As I was telling Mr Grundig, we've brought our town servants along with us. Both of them!

GRUNDIG: Well, Sir, you had two servants and now you have two hundred!

ORIANE: Surely there aren't two hundred servants here?

GRUNDIG: There are more than two hundred servants, ma'am attached to the house in various capacities, though of course at this time of year the women and children usually live in the village, still I should say there were nearly two hundred servants now in and around the house. How many would you say, Peter Jack?

PETER JACK: It's difficult to say how many of us there are, Sir, at any given moment.

GRUNDIG: Of course that's not beginning to count the estate workers—

ORIANE: I can't think what so many servants can find to do.

BASIL: It's a very big place, Oriane and if one has never managed property one has no idea—

ORIANE: I'm going upstairs, I'm exhausted.

PETER JACK: I should have said sooner your honour, that Hans Joseph is waiting. He just wanted to welcome you.

BASIL: Hans Joseph? Oh Hans Joseph! Is he still alive? He must be very old. I'm so glad. You must see him, Oriane. Yes, could you fetch him, bring him here at once.

[*Exit* PETER JACK.]

ORIANE: Who is Hans Joseph?

BASIL: Surely you remember? I've told you about him a hundred times, such a wonderful man. He could do everything. He looked after me when I was a child. He taught me to swim, he taught me to fish— He was a sort of ideal father. And Peter Jack was just like my brother. Peter and I are exactly the same age, Mr Grundig. We were children here together, you know.

ORIANE: You don't live here, Mr Grundig?

GRUNDIG: Oh no, ma'am.

BASIL: [*softly in the background as he rapturously examines the room*] Yes, I remember that—and that—

GRUNDIG: My wife and I and our little daughter, we live in the provincial town, just a tiny place, ma'am, not like your great city, but we're proud to have our own little opera house.

ORIANE: I see you're a musical person, Mr Grundig. So am I. Let's go over and see one of Mr Grundig's operas. What about next week? Could you get us a box?

BASIL: Oriane, dear, the town is nearly seventy miles away and no one travels in this weather unless they have to!

You saw what the snow was like.

GRUNDIG: At this time of year one really must regard oneself as a prisoner, ma'am.

ORIANE: I see!

GRUNDIG: Being a family man, I have to be very prudent. I shall wait for some better weather before I try to go home. You were lucky to get here, Sir.

BASIL: I'm afraid it's no opera until the snow melts, Oriane. But you'll find there's plenty to do in the house.

[*Enter* PETER JACK *followed by* HANS JOSEPH.]

Hans Joseph!

[*An affecting encounter.* HANS JOSEPH, *speechless with emotion, kneels at* BASIL's *feet and kisses his hands.* BASIL *is also near to tears.*]

Oh my dear old friend! Get up, please—Let me embrace you. You haven't changed.

HANS JOSEPH: From grey to white, your honour, from straight to crooked, from wise to foolish.

BASIL: No!

HANS JOSEPH: It's so many years. Your honour was a youth, now you are a man. I didn't think to see your blessed face again.

BASIL: I know. I didn't want to stay away—you understand how it was—my heart has always been here. Oh I'm sorry, you remember my wife. Oriane, you remember my old friend Hans Joseph.

ORIANE: No, please. [*She does not want to interrupt the touching reunion.*]

HANS JOSEPH: Welcome home, your ladyship. [*He kneels and kisses her hand.*]

ORIANE: [*not used to this kind of thing*] Thank you, thank you. Please.

BASIL: [*collaring* HANS JOSEPH *again*] Just seeing you brings back so much. Do you remember the mushrooms—that must have been the last time. Peter, you remember that fantastic place with the mushrooms.

PETER JACK: Yes. That must have been quite soon after your honour's marriage.

BASIL: All those years that can never be given back to us.

HANS JOSEPH: There are many years left for you, your honour, my dear, perhaps the best ones.

BASIL: I know you all had a—difficult time with my father. [PETER JACK *and* HANS JOSEPH *exchange glances.*] But everything is going to be so much better now.

HANS JOSEPH: I thought I might die before you came back.

ORIANE: I'm going upstairs.
[*She begins to try to pull off her boots.* HANS JOSEPH *and* PETER JACK *rush to help her.*]

BASIL: Oriane, tu sais il faut les laisser faire des petites choses pour toi.

[ORIANE *waves her helpers away, gets the boots off and puts on a pair of slippers out of her bag. Enter, after knocking,* FREDERIC.] Oh here's Frederic. I thought you'd got lost. Mr Grundig, you've met Frederic. This is Peter Jack, Hans Joseph. Peter Jack is in charge of all the arrangements inside the house, so he'll look after you. Hans Joseph, you know I can hardly believe I'm really here! We'll go hunting just like we used to, won't we, I hope someone has kept the gun room in good order, won't we go hunting?

HANS JOSEPH: I'm too old to hunt anything except the fleas in my beard.

BASIL: Then your son shall take me. Francis James, the great hunter. How is Francis James?

HANS JOSEPH: My son is dead, your honour.

BASIL: Dead. I'm deeply sorry.

HANS JOSEPH: My son married in the house and I have a grown-up grandson.

BASIL: Francis James dead! He must have been quite young.

GRUNDIG: If you'll pardon the liberty, Sir, I think her ladyship should rest.

BASIL: Sorry, Oriane, I'm hopeless.

ORIANE: A musical man is a thoughtful man, Mr Grundig.

PETER JACK: Perhaps later on, your honour, we were wondering if you would care to visit the Servants' Hall. You'll see some familiar faces still there.

BASIL: Of course, I'll come at once!

GRUNDIG: There's no need for you to see them all personally, Sir, you can send a message. You must be tired out too.

BASIL: No, no, I couldn't rest now. I want to see them all, every single one, the old friends and the new. Oriane, you really must come too, just to say hello to them. Isn't it touching that everyone's so pleased to see us?

ORIANE: I should have thought they'd have been getting on pretty well without us.

PETER JACK: We'd better go and warn them, your honour. Some people will want to change their clothes.

BASIL: No, no, they must stay just as they are. Yes, go and tell them, only no special arrangements, I want everything to be *natural*.

[*Exeunt* PETER JACK, HANS JOSEPH *and* GRUNDIG.]

Oh Oriane!

[BASIL *tries to kiss her but she evades him nervously. He notices* FREDERIC.]

Frederic, could you wait outside.

[*Exit* FREDERIC. BASIL *tries again to kiss* ORIANE, *but she still pushes him away.*]

Please come and see the other servants, just for a moment, let them look at you. I know I'm being selfish, but it's such a very special day. I've been waiting for this day for years and years.

ORIANE: I know, dearest Basil, but I can't face them now. I don't want to be "looked at". I'm so tired and the snow has made my head ache so. I'll go and lie down. You know it's you they want to see, not me. I doubt if they really know that I exist.

BASIL: They know all about you! The house will have a mistress again at last.

ORIANE: Hmmm. The house may not have had a mistress but your father had one.

BASIL: Yes, yes, someone said he was living with one of the maids. That's not unusual in this part of the world. My grandfather kept a harem and my great grandfather used to have all the local girls on their wedding night! Oh Oriane, you're not unhappy now that you've arrived? I know you didn't want to come, but—

ORIANE: I delayed you, with my reluctances.

BASIL: I do blame myself for not having come to the funeral.

ORIANE: You mean you blame me.

BASIL: But you did say, once we'd decided to come, that perhaps you would like it after all?

ORIANE: I said I'd try to like it. I will try.

BASIL: You said the snow looked beautiful as we came in the gates. You know, a little sunshine will transform this scene into fairyland.

ORIANE: Fairyland. You're romantic about this house because you spent your childhood here.

BASIL: It's my ancestral place, Oriane. My forefathers owned this whole estate back till—

ORIANE: Of course we are fearfully rich, aren't we, now that your father's died.

BASIL: Yes, but we must think of ourselves here as trustees and not as owners.

ORIANE: You are so serious, Basil. When we were back at home I thought—

BASIL: Oriane, this is home.

ORIANE: Well, when we were back at where we used to live I thought at least it would be fun to be *grand* at last—

BASIL: We don't want to be grand!

ORIANE: We don't deserve to be grand. I thought it would be amusing to impress my brother the General with, you know, but now I just feel frightened of it all, I feel such an outsider, I can't control two hundred servants, I could hardly control Frederic and Annabelle.

BASIL: Everyone here will want to help us.

ORIANE: I'm not sure that I see why they should.

BASIL: Out of love. [ORIANE *laughs sceptically.*] Oh Oriane, when I think of all the years that I've lost, all those meaningless years—when I quarrelled with my father and couldn't come here—

ORIANE: You didn't quarrel with your father. Your father was impossible. He was probably mad.

BASIL: Dear Oriane, if it's any consolation at all to you, I am so deeply happy to return here, to think that I shall run the estate and live in my own real home at last—

ORIANE: A good wife must be consoled by her husband's happiness. I am consoled. I just can't help feeling that everything provincial is somehow unreal.

BASIL: How funny, I feel exactly the opposite!

ORIANE: Of course I can't share your feelings about this place, but— No, it's just—shock—arriving here—things aren't what I expected, they can't be, I don't mean in any special way. I just didn't think about it beforehand, because I kept hoping that maybe we wouldn't come, maybe you'd leave it all to Grundig to manage—

BASIL: Darling, I couldn't leave it to Grundig, he's only a bailiff, he doesn't even live here, and anyway—

ORIANE: All right, all right, I'm not going to start us off all over again, the argument's finished. I'd just forgotten how awfully far away it was and how much snow there was and how big the house is and how many servants—and I'm sure your father's mistress must have been running the place—who was she, is she, anyway, this woman?

BASIL: I don't know who she is and it doesn't matter. My father's world has gone forever, thank God!

ORIANE: It hasn't gone, Basil. We've stepped into it.

[*The Bedroom,* ORIANE *and* FREDERIC *entering.*]

ORIANE: Ooh!

FREDERIC: What is it, Madam?

ORIANE: I thought I saw a rat. Something went away there under the bed just as we came in.

[*They regard each other with dismay.*]

Frederic, would you look under the bed, please.

FREDERIC: I am afraid that I am afraid of rats, Madam.

ORIANE: Go on, Frederic, look under the bed, or I shall have to.

[FREDERIC *reluctantly looks.*]

FREDERIC: There is nothing there, Madam.

ORIANE: I must have imagined it. My eyes are all jumping around after endlessly looking at all that ghastly snow. Are your eyes jumping around?

FREDERIC: Yes, Madam, my eyes are jumping around, too.

ORIANE: Frederic, are there wolves here?

FREDERIC: I don't think so, Madam.

ORIANE: It must be the wind. I thought I heard a sort of howling.

FREDERIC: It's the mastiff guard dogs, Madam. I'm told they are extremely savage and one should not attempt to pat them.

ORIANE: Yes, I saw some enormous creatures chained up as we were coming in. Could you open the shutters please? What's that furry white stuff on the glass?

FREDERIC: Frost flowers, Madam.

ORIANE: Frost flowers? Good heavens, it's frost on the inside of the window. I've never seen that before. Scrape some of it off, would you, so that I can see out. Not much to see. It gets dark so early. It's snowing again, very slowly, with great big flakes. I used to like that when I was a child. All those fir trees going on and on and on. You can close the shutters again. It's so *cold*. These rooms are far too big, no wonder they're freezing. I suppose this *is* our room?

FREDERIC: Yes, Madam, your bags are in there.

ORIANE: Oh yes, I remember that—thing.

[*She looks at a large crucifix hanging on the wall.*]

FREDERIC: Would you like me to take it down, Madam?

ORIANE: No, it's picturesque. It goes with the scene. Well, how do you think you're going to like life in the country, Frederic?

FREDERIC: It's a little early to say, Madam.

ORIANE: Your master is happy, so you must try to be happy too, mustn't you.

FREDERIC: Yes, Madam.

ORIANE: I hope you've brought your books. I know you're a great reader of romances. Perhaps I might borrow them in the long winter evenings. It's so *silent*. I suppose the snow makes this curious sort of silence. I think musical people all really detest silence. Now, Frederic, could you please send Annabelle to me. I think I'll just change my clothes and then lie down for a bit.

FREDERIC: Madam, I'm very sorry, I wasn't able to tell Madam this earlier, but Annabelle is not here.

ORIANE: Not here? My maid, your wife, not here? What do you mean?

FREDERIC: Annabelle decided not to come, Madam.

ORIANE: Why didn't you tell me this before?

FREDERIC: It all happened at the last moment, Madam, and I couldn't get near Madam to tell her as the first conveyance had already started.

ORIANE: She's not coming at all? Why?

FREDERIC: She felt the change would be too much for her, Madam, she's such a city girl. She felt this place was such a long way away and there'd be so much snow and there might be wolves and bears and things and it would all be very gloomy and isolated and she'd miss the gaiety of the town and all the things she's used to. Very silly of her, Madam.

ORIANE: Very. [*Pause*] But she's your wife, Frederic. A

wife should go where her husband goes even if she doesn't think she'll enjoy it.

FREDERIC: I'm afraid she's run away with somebody else, Madam. She's run away with one of His Excellency the General's footmen. They've gone away to some place in the south, beside the sea, I believe.

ORIANE: In the south, beside the sea. It's faithful of you to have come, Frederic.

FREDERIC: Madam knows I am devoted to Madam.

ORIANE: Now you are our only servant. Well, yes—! I must have a maid. Frederic, could you find the brandy, please. There's some in the blue trunk, you know the little blue trunk with the brass nails that has all my toilet things.

FREDERIC: I'm afraid that the little blue trunk is not here, Madam. It was in the conveyance that broke down, you remember, just before we got to that last village. It fell into a snowdrift.

ORIANE: So all my toilet things have gone astray. I must have some brandy all the same. I suppose they keep some. Could you find somebody and ask, please? Oh, it's so cold!

FREDERIC: There doesn't seem to be anybody in this part of the house, Madam, and I don't know the way to the Servants' Hall. We might ring the bell, Madam.

ORIANE: I suppose that thing is a bell. Yes, go on. I can't hear anything ringing, can you?

FREDERIC: Perhaps it rings very far away, Madam.

ORIANE: Try again. I can't hear anything.

FREDERIC: I'm afraid it's broken, Madam. Look, it doesn't connect with anything at the top.

ORIANE: [*near tears*] Well, what are we supposed to do now! Ooh!

[FATHER AMBROSE, *looking like something off an icon, has materialised in the doorway.*]

AMBROSE: I am sorry, I frightened you. I am Father Ambrose.

ORIANE: You must be the local parson, or whatever it's called around here.

AMBROSE: I wanted to welcome you—

ORIANE: How kind of you, your er reverence—

AMBROSE: Please call me "Father".

ORIANE: Father, I feel I should say straightaway—

AMBROSE: I know.

ORIANE: My husband and I are not churchgoers. . . . We are enlightened—sorry—er—modern—for better or worse, if you see what I mean.

AMBROSE: Quite.

ORIANE: I mean we are not religious people in the old-fashioned sense. Well, I suppose that is the only sense isn't it, really?

AMBROSE: Yes.

ORIANE: Sorry, I— We believe in ethics, very strongly, in ethical duties, in virtue, of course, very strongly—

AMBROSE: Of course.

ORIANE: But about religion we are, well, scientific, if you see what I mean.

AMBROSE: I see what you mean, my child.

ORIANE: But I'm sure I speak for my husband when I say we would not wish to interfere with any customary religious observance. We would even wish to give our support, discreetly of course—

AMBROSE: I understand.

ORIANE: We both think that religion has its place, has its role, especially for simple people—

[AMBROSE *is now trying to explain rapidly though obscurely something very important.*]

AMBROSE: Yes, indeed. I simply wanted to say that you are very welcome here. You can be much loved here. This is a moment of—confidence—of which it would be wise to take advantage.

ORIANE: Take advantage?

AMBROSE: I mean—there are loyal affectionate hearts in

this place. If you can respond to them openly and warmly now it may perhaps save trouble later.

ORIANE: Trouble? What trouble? Do you mean politeness buys service?

AMBROSE: I hope that you and his honour will feel able to confide in me should there be—difficulties of any kind.

ORIANE: Naturally we—

AMBROSE: I would observe the sacred silence of the confessional in respect of anything which you thought fit to tell me.

ORIANE: Most obliging, I—

AMBROSE: I trust his honour has not been upset by any foolish rumours among the servants?

ORIANE: Not that I know—

AMBROSE: Please feel that you can come to me at once should anything—unpleasant occur.

ORIANE: But what—?

AMBROSE: I won't detain your ladyship. Receive an old man's blessing. And—*good luck*! [*Exit*.]

ORIANE: What on earth was all that about?

FREDERIC: Shall I help Madam to undress?

ORIANE: No, of course not. Go away, Frederic.

FREDERIC: Yes, Madam. Where to, Madam?

ORIANE: Anywhere!

[*Exit* FREDERIC. ORIANE *looks with puzzlement at the door out of which* FATHER AMBROSE *has disappeared. Then she dissolves quietly into tears.*]

[*The Servants' Hall is shadowily visible. An impression of many people listening as* BASIL'S *voice is heard making a public speech.* BASIL *is enjoying himself.*]

BASIL: My friends, we are all the servants of necessity. We mourn for what is gone, we greet what is to come. This is a time of rebirth and renewal and at this time I would like you all to feel that we are not master and servants so much as fellow workers in an enterprise which concerns us all and which belongs to us all. You have your work and I have mine and it is to our common advantage that this estate should flourish: and when I say "flourish" I have in mind not only new and better methods of husbandry in our wide fields and our great forests. I have in mind equality and shared responsibility, I have in mind a recognition of the dignity of labour and the dignity of the individual. I have in mind everything that is meant by justice. All authority ought in the end to rest upon mutual need, the need for each other which is felt by different members of a happy family. My friends, thank you for your welcome, thank you for your loyalty. I look forward with the warmest anticipation to our joint labours—and I shall endeavour to deserve your respect and your affection. Thank you.

[*Subdued applause, a few muffled and uncertain cheers, a scuffling sound of people withdrawing. The scene lightens and we see a part of the Servants' Hall with* BASIL, PETER JACK *and* HANS JOSEPH. *The cupboard inhabited by* PATRICE *is now obscurely visible on one side, its doors closed. As the scene clears* BASIL *is raising a kneeling servant to his feet.*]

BASIL: No, no, please, please get up. I am only— I am so glad to meet you—and you, and you. [*The sound of withdrawing feet fades away.*] Well, I think that went quite well, don't you?

PETER JACK: [*obviously embarrassed*] Yes, I—think your honour's words were—very welcome.

HANS JOSEPH: [*mumbling, also embarrassed*] Yes, yes, indeed—

BASIL: There were several people I wanted to talk to, faces I dimly recalled—but they seem to have all gone now.

PETER JACK: They are shy, your honour.

BASIL: Now there's someone I remember. Come, please don't be nervous. I want everyone to feel that they can come and talk to me quite freely.

[*He beckons. Enter, precipitately,* MARINA. *She falls at his feet.*] No, no, please don't, please get up.

[*He looks at her, trying to remember.*]

Why, surely it isn't— Yes it is— It's Marina!

MARINA: [*laughing, crying*] Yes!

BASIL: Little Marina, we used to call you. You were a wisp of a girl when I last saw you. And now look how blooming you are and so— Well, I wasn't much older than you were when we called you little Marina. We've both grown up, haven't we? Come then, don't cry.

MARINA: I loved your honour's speech, it was lovely.

BASIL: Marina— Well, well. You and Peter Jack were my good friends when we were all children here together and we must be good friends still, mustn't we? Such a long time ago—you must be a married woman now with children of your own.

HANSJOSEPH: Marina is my daughter-in-law, your honour.

BASIL: Ah, I see—you were married to Francis James. I was so very sorry to hear that Francis James was dead. I give you my deep sympathy. [*To* HANSJOSEPH] I think you said—there was a son?

MARINA: Yes, your honour. I have a grown-up son. His name is Maxim. He is nearly nineteen.

BASIL: You can rely on me to take an interest in the boy. He shall be my huntsman, as his grandfather was before him, eh Hans Joseph? [HANS JOSEPH *looks awkward.*] Well, my dear Marina, it's a joy to see you and if I may say so you don't look a day older than nineteen yourself!

PETERJACK: I feel we should tell his honour, shouldn't we?

[*Uneasy pause between* PETERJACK *and* MARINA.]

MARINA: [*suffocated*] Yes.

PETERJACK: Your honour, Marina and I are betrothed. We are going to be married.

BASIL: You couldn't give me better news! Dear friends of my childhood, let me join your hands.

[*Enter* ORIANE, *with* MIKEY.]

Oriane, Peter Jack and Marina here are to be married. It will be the first wedding in the household since our arrival. We must make it a great celebration. It shall mark the beginning of a new era, a new happiness—

ORIANE: Basil, I couldn't think where you were.

BASIL: [*taking* ORIANE *in at last*] My dear, I thought you were going to rest.

ORIANE: I couldn't rest, I felt so nervous and Frederic has vanished God knowns where to, and I couldn't find the way and it was so dark and there seemed to be no one about at all—

BASIL: They were all listening to me.

ORIANE: Then I met this boy, but I couldn't understand a word he said. Anyway he led me here.

BASIL: I'm so glad you've come. Look, Oriane, I want you to meet Marina, whom I've known ever since we were little children here together. Do you remember meeting her last time?

ORIANE: No, I don't think so.

MARINA: I remember your ladyship. [PETER JACK *nudges her and whispers*.] I wanted to give your ladyship these.

ORIANE: What are they?

MARINA: The keys of the store rooms.

ORIANE: I don't want them. I wouldn't know what to do with them. Thank you all the same. [*To* MIKEY] What's your name?

MIKEY: [*mumble*].

HANS JOSEPH: His name's Mikey, your ladyship. [*To* MIKEY *in a whisper*] Off with you!

ORIANE: Don't send him away, I like the look of him. Don't be afraid of me. [*She beckons.*]

BASIL: That's right, Oriane, nobody must be afraid now. [MIKEY *approaches and kneels.*] No, no, up with you, none of that. We really must reduce this bowing and scraping. Oh I do wish you'd been here, it was such a moving scene, wasn't it, Peter Jack?

ORIANE: And what do you do, Mikey?

MIKEY: [*mumble*].

HANS JOSEPH: He's just one of the kitchen boys, your ladyship. He's a foundling orphan boy. Father Ambrose
found him on the steps of the church.

ORIANE: Oh I had a visit from Father Ambrose. He was
most enigmatic. What is that curious smell?

BASIL: Father Ambrose, I must see the good old man!

HANS JOSEPH: It's our wet clothes drying, your ladyship.

BASIL: Do the servants still practise their religion, Peter?

HANS JOSEPH: In this weather the Servants' Hall gets full
of melted snow. I'm sorry it's a rather disagreeable
smell.

PETER JACK: Yes, your honour.

ORIANE: I wonder if I could have a glass of water?

MARINA: The late supper which your honour asked for is
ready if—

[*Exit* MARINA, *obeying a gesture of* PETER'S.]

BASIL: Yes, that's right, I see the old religious pictures still
hanging there, how well I remember them. See, Oriane,
the old religious pictures.

ORIANE: I wonder if I could have a glass of water?

PETER JACK: Your ladyship, the late supper—

ORIANE: All I want is a glass of water! Please!

[*Exit* MIKEY, *obeying* PETER.]

BASIL: [*still absorbed in the pictures*] Very beautiful, some of
them, quite works of art.

ORIANE: Basil, I think I saw a rat in our bedroom.

[*Re-enter* MIKEY *with the water. He kneels.*]

BASIL: Don't do that!

[MIKEY *is confused, not sure what it is he is supposed not to do.*]

ORIANE: You're a pretty boy. He has such beautiful eyes.
Perhaps I could have him for a little page boy. Don't you
think I should have a page, Basil? [*To* MIKEY] Would
you like that?

PETER JACK: He doesn't know what you mean, your ladyship.

ORIANE: I'd dress you in pretty clothes and pet you and

keep you beside me always. Would you like to be my little page boy?

MIKEY: [*mumble*].

ORIANE: What's that?

[PATRICE *has become visible crawling round the back of the scene in an endeavour to get to the safety of his cupboard unobserved.* HANS JOSEPH *sees him, makes a disgusted noise and aims a kick at him.*]

BASIL: Come, come, Hans Joseph! Who is that unfortunate fellow you're kicking? Please!

HANS JOSEPH: He is not one of us, your honour. He is a gipsy. A parasite and a thief.

[PATRICE *has reached the cupboard and is peeping round one of the doors.* BASIL, *followed by the others, advances toward the cupboard, which now receives full light.*]

BASIL: A gipsy. Yes, I remember gipsies here when I was young. They used to come in the winter time.

HANS JOSEPH: That's right, your honour. They spend the summer on the plains, in the nomad camps, and then when it gets cold they attach themselves to big houses and creep inside like rats and live there by stealing. It's very difficult to get rid of them.

BASIL: They live by stealing?

HANS JOSEPH: Yes, Sir. This one is one of the worst. Whenever we catch them stealing we beat them, but this one is so clever we've never caught him yet.

BASIL: [*amused by all this*] How do you know he steals, then?

HANS JOSEPH: He must, your honour. He can't live on air. Look how fat he is!

BASIL: Well, gipsy, you've heard us talking about you. Come out and show yourself.

[PATRICE *emerges and kneels before* BASIL.]

Get up, get up, look at me like a man. What's your name, gipsy?

PATRICE: Patrice, so it please your honour. [PATRICE *may have a slight Irish accent.*]

BASIL: And what are you doing hiding in that cupboard?

PATRICE: I wasn't so much hiding, so please your honour, so much as living if you see my meaning.

BASIL: Living?

PATRICE: I mean it's where I live, your honour.

ORIANE: [*laughing*] Where you live!

HANS JOSEPH: It's an old empty cupboard, your honour, and no one uses it so the gipsy goes in there at night. But if your honour wishes we'll clear him out—

PATRICE: It's not just me, your honour. Mikey lives here too.

ORIANE: Mikey, do you live in the cupboard too, you poor boy?

MIKEY: [*mumble*].

ORIANE: What?

MIKEY: I live on the top shelf.

ORIANE: He lives on the top shelf!

[BASIL *and* ORIANE *laugh*, PETER JACK *smiles*, HANS JOSEPH *scowls*, PATRICE *looks ingratiating. Still uncertain about* BASIL, *he has sensed a possible ally in* ORIANE *and keeps nodding and smiling in her direction.*]

It must be very cold.

HANS JOSEPH: Gipsies don't feel the cold.

ORIANE: I'm sure Mikey does. You shan't live in that nasty cupboard any more, you shall live with me.

HANS JOSEPH: Your honour's grandfather used to shoot gipsies for sport.

BASIL: Is it true that you live as a thief in this house?

PATRICE: Yes, your honour.

HANS JOSEPH: He admits it, Sir! In that case—

[*He tries to seize* PATRICE.]

ORIANE: Don't hurt him, please. Basil, don't let—

BASIL: Let him go, Hans Joseph. At least he's truthful! We'll have no more violence here. No one is to be beaten. I know this was customary in my father's time, but now—

HANS JOSEPH: We live a very isolated life here, Sir. Force

31

is often the only sanction that we can use. We have to be
our own judges and executioners.

BASIL: From now on we'll have less force and more talk. I
want an atmosphere of trust and understanding. People
can be persuaded without violence. I seem to be the first
person who has had the idea of talking to this poor outcast.

HANS JOSEPH: He's a thief—

ORIANE: Tell them to leave him alone, Basil. Surely we can
spare him the little that he takes.

PATRICE: That's a kind ladyship. You've got a lovely face.

ORIANE: Don't you mean a lucky face? Isn't that what
gipsies say? Can you read palms, Patrice?
[*She holds out her hand.*]

PATRICE: I can see very strange things in your ladyship's
hand.

ORIANE: I hope they're nice things! You must tell me about
them some other time.

[PATRICE *kisses the palm of her hand.* ORIANE *laughs,
pleased. Basil laughs, annoyed.* PETER JACK *is unamused.*
HANS JOSEPH *is furious.*]

BASIL: A rather forward gipsy!

HANS JOSEPH: Your honour, let me deal with this man!

BASIL: [*gesturing* HANS JOSEPH *away*] You are able to live
in idleness, Patrice, because other people work. What
would happen if everybody acted as you do?

PATRICE: But you see, your honour, they don't.

BASIL: You enjoy the benefits of society, but you don't
contribute to it.

PATRICE: Why should I, Sir? Other people contribute out
of self interest because they are ambitious enough not to
mind being slaves. I am not ambitious and I have no
taste for slavery. I steal out of self interest only the little
bit that I need. And there are so many slaves working so
hard that society can easily spare that little bit for un-
ambitious men like myself who prefer to be free.

BASIL: But if society catches you, you may suffer.

PATRICE: Yet even in suffering I remain free.

BASIL: Free! A rather philosophical gipsy. You knelt down in front of me just now.

PATRICE: Mere prudence, Sir. Your honour's father had a very quick temper.

BASIL: I am not my father. But if you are caught stealing in this house we will continue our philosophical discussion. And [*to* HANS JOSEPH *and* PETER JACK] remember what I said just now: no more violence.

[*Enter* MAXIM *carrying a shotgun and a brace of dead birds.*]

Here is another new face, I think.

HANS JOSEPH: Your honour, this is my grandson Maxim.

BASIL: Ah, the son of Marina and Francis James. No, no, please don't— [*Embarrassing moment as it becomes apparent that* MAXIM *has no intention of kneeling.*] Young man, I am glad to see you. I remember your father well.

ORIANE: Another pretty boy. What beautiful eyes these peasant youths have. The way the eye is set, and the cheekbone, so. You see what I mean, Basil?

BASIL: Do you want him for a page too, Oriane? We shall have quite a regiment of pages. Maxim, this is my wife.

[ORIANE *holds out her hand to be kissed.* MAXIM *makes no move towards her but bows stiffly, unsmiling.*]

Well, Maxim, your father was my father's huntsman. How would you like to be my huntsman?

MAXIM: I never kill animals for sport.

BASIL: [*annoyed, but anxious not to show it*] Those are for your supper, I presume. In my father's time those birds were reserved for the master of the house.

HANS JOSEPH: Your honour, I am very sorry, I assure you he knows—

BASIL: No, no, I'm going to abolish all those old game rules anyway—

HANS JOSEPH: I've told him a hundred times—

BASIL: I can value and respect the independence of the young.

[MAXIM *lays the birds at* ORIANE'S *feet.*]

ORIANE: Ooh, they're all covered in blood! Basil, I think I'm going to faint, I can't stand any more of this.

BASIL: My poor darling—

ORIANE: [*to* MIKEY] Go away, don't touch my dress, you're dirty. Basil, please, don't let them come. Where's Frederic?

BASIL: Come, my dear.

ORIANE: Where's Frederic gone to? I want Frederic—

[BASIL, *motioning the others away, leads* ORIANE *off.* PATRICE *collects* MIKEY *and they retire into the cupboard and shut the door. The others move away.*]

[*A different place, a different atmosphere.*]

PETER JACK: [*seizing* MAXIM *who is about to go*] Wait a minute. Marina! Come here, would you.

He doesn't know.

HANS JOSEPH: Yes.

PETER JACK: I think that's quite clear

HANS JOSEPH: Yes. He doesn't know.

MARINA: Isn't he wonderful? I knew he would be.

PETER JACK: You see what I meant, Hans Joseph?

HANS JOSEPH: He is a kind man. Perhaps too kind.

PETER JACK: He has made a very good impression. That is what's important.

MARINA: He's wonderful.

HANS JOSEPH: If only he had come here at once.

PETER JACK: Yes. There would have been less damage to undo. In spite of everything you were glad to see him.

HANS JOSEPH: Of course I was glad to see him, how could I help being glad to see him! But what has happened has happened and has necessary consequences.

PETER JACK: Nothing here is necessary. We are perfectly free. And he is perfectly blameless.

[*Enter* FREDERIC. *The others freeze.*]

FREDERIC: I'm sorry, gentlemen. I seem to be lost. Would one of you gentlemen be so kind as to tell me where my

room is? I arrived in this establishment some hours ago
and have not yet been given the opportunity to, as they
say, freshen up or, as they say, wash my hands. Or am I
supposed to do it in the snow?

HANS JOSEPH: What is your name?

FREDERIC: Frederic.

HANS JOSEPH: Well, Frederic, I think that you will be
living upstairs with his honour and her ladyship, and
not downstairs with us.

FREDERIC: Standoffish lot, aren't you. Not that I care.
The odour of filthy wet garments giving off obnoxious
steam is something you may be used to, but it offends my
rather more fastidious nostrils. Also it's damn cold down
here. I don't mind living upstairs. But what about my
grub?

HANS JOSEPH: Your what?

FREDERIC: Grub. Eats. Scoff. Vittles. To say nothing of
lotions, beverages, poisons various, vino, the hard stuff.

PETER JACK: He means food and drink.

HANS JOSEPH: [*pointing*] They will make arrangements for
you to take your meals upstairs.

FREDERIC: God, and to think that I imagined that at any
rate there'd be fun in the Servants' Hall! [*Exit.*]

PETER JACK: It seems unkind. But it's probably wiser—
in the circumstances.

HANS JOSEPH: That man is a trouble-maker.

PETER JACK: We are perfectly free in this matter.

HANS JOSEPH: Free to do what? Forgive and forget?

PETER JACK: Forgive anyway.

HANS JOSEPH: Forgive the unforgivable?

PETER JACK: The unforgivable is perhaps what concerns
us least of all.

HANS JOSEPH: There are demands of justice.

PETER JACK: Justice is not ours.

HANS JOSEPH: It is no one else's.

PETER JACK: I mean, let justice belong to God.

HANSJOSEPH: You don't believe in God.

PETERJACK: I think we should live as if there were God.

HANSJOSEPH: It's priests' talk all the same.

PETERJACK: The moment for justice has passed.

MARINA: I agree.

HANSJOSEPH: You be silent at least here! I saw you prettying up your hair with my son three days in his grave.

MARINA: That's not true! You've turned against me just because—

PETERJACK: Please!

HANSJOSEPH: What do you say, Maxim? By right this task is yours.

MAXIM: You speak to me of a task but you scream the place down if I poach his pheasants.

PETERJACK: Well?

MAXIM: I reject your old blind justice just as much as I reject his meaningless authority. The whole situation here makes me sick to my soul. As soon as the spring comes I'm going away for good.

PETERJACK: And meanwhile?

MAXIM: And meanwhile nothing.

PETERJACK: If you two are silent the others will be content. Especially after today. Let it be, Hans Joseph my dear. Enough of the past, let the past go. The old man is dead. Let it go at that.

MAXIM: Yes. The old man is dead. Perhaps we ought to have killed him. We didn't. He died in his bed. But now what does it all matter. And if you choose to kiss the hands of the son who will soon be as bad as the father, that's your affair. It's nothing to me either way. I hate the guts of this place. Everything here needs to be changed completely or better still blown to pieces.

PETERJACK: You're young, Maxim, and you want things to be perfect, but human beings aren't made for perfection. We have very little goodness in our hearts and yet we have to live with each other. It's better to do the simple things that can be done. We can make this place very much better.

MAXIM: I agree there are other kinds of boot-licking from the kind we've been used to.

MARINA: Maxim, do you promise—

HANS JOSEPH: It is not for you to ask him to promise anything.

MAXIM: Since you are all here, my grandfather, my mother and my step-father elect, let me tell you this. From now on until the spring I will live by myself. I reject everything here. I want no part in your allegiances and your servitudes, and any thoughts I may have about the past are my own private affair.

MARINA: You will not—offend him?

MAXIM: I shall keep out of his way. I shall shoot his birds and eat them. And when the snow melts I shall go away and never come back.

MARINA: My dear son—

MAXIM: No empty sentiment, please, mother dear. Get yourself married. [*To* PETER JACK] Marry her and make her obey you. And do it soon. She's as slippery as an eel.

MARINA: Maxim, don't talk in that horrible way.

MAXIM: Goodbye. And keep away from me, all of you. [*Exit.*]

MARINA: Maxim!

PETER JACK: Let him be. [*To* HANS JOSEPH] You agree now?

HANS JOSEPH: What will the others think?

PETER JACK: That the past is past.

HANS JOSEPH: The past is present. It is indelible. You cannot suffer as we have suffered and then declare a new day.

PETER JACK: We can make some things here more decent and more kind. That is all human beings can do anyway.

HANS JOSEPH: I am an old man, Peter, and I am deeply hopelessly unhappy with an unhappiness which will travel with me into my grave. I don't want to do anything really. But his honour will find this thing out and then something will happen—

PETER JACK: There is no reason why his honour should ever find out. No one will take this out of your hands.

HANS JOSEPH: All right.

PETER JACK: Thank you.

HANS JOSEPH: Maxim was right. Marry her. If you want her. Marry her soon. [*Exit.*]

[MARINA *and* PETER JACK. *Another atmosphere again. He moves to touch her but she eludes him.*]

PETER JACK: You won't let me touch you.

MARINA: I don't like being touched.

PETER JACK: I know all those awful years with *him*—

MARINA: Everyone blames me for everything.

PETER JACK: I don't blame you. Marina, we are betrothed, aren't we?

MARINA: [*dully*] Yes.

PETER JACK: We are going to be married, aren't we?

MARINA: [*dully*] Yes.

PETER JACK: Not if you don't want.

MARINA: It wasn't my fault.

PETER JACK: I know that. The old man did what he liked with us all. He wanted you. He took you. But now—

MARINA: His honour is such a lovely gentleman. [*Accusingly*] You told him about us pretty quick, didn't you!

PETER JACK: Wasn't that right?

MARINA: You did it on purpose so that I couldn't back out!

PETER JACK: But you have said yes, you have decided.

MARINA: I'm sorry, my nerves are broken. What has happened to me cannot be put right again ever. You can't help feeling that I ought to be grateful that you love me. Perhaps I ought to be. Perhaps I am. But oh, Peter the spirit has just gone out of me, the heart has gone out of me. I feel I've never really been free or been my own self at all.

PETER JACK: You may have to learn to touch and kiss again.

MARINA: It's not just that. I want to be courted and cherished, not possessed and owned.

PETER JACK: I wouldn't "own" you, Marina!

MARINA: Yes, you would. A married woman is a slave. Men are all the same. You are kind to me now. But once we were married you wouldn't value me any more. And you'd be violent in the end. All men are violent in the end.

PETER JACK: Marina, you *know* that you are talking nonsense. You know that I've always loved you, always, always, since childhood, right from the start. You know what I suffered when you got married and—later on. You know that I will always treasure you and worship you and love you. You know *me*, you can see right through my soul. Look at me now.

MARINA: Yes, I can see right through. And that's part of the trouble too. After it all, there's old familiar you. It ought to be reassuring. It isn't. There are things inside me that you can't deal with. I need something new, even something terrible. Oh if we could only go away! I've never been farther away than the river in my life. [*Pause*] I'm sorry, Peter, I'll marry you. It's fixed, isn't it? Especially now that you've told his honour.

PETER JACK: Once we're married you'll feel calm and happy and safe. You'll be a different woman.

MARINA: I don't want to be a different woman. I don't want to be safe. I want—oh— Listen. [*Distant sound*] It's Patrice playing his fiddle. It's the only music that I've ever heard, except the singing in church. And it's so different. It's not like anything in the world.

PETER JACK: I won't be anxious or—jealous—after we're married. All right I won't touch you! I sometimes wonder if you don't despise me for being so patient. I'm ready to wait for you to get used to me—as a man. But I want to do that waiting—after our marriage.

MARINA: When I'm safe inside the cage!

PETER JACK: I love you.

MARINA: I love you too, dear Peter, but in such a quiet sad
sort of way. I've never had any gaiety or fun—

PETER JACK: Love is more important than fun.

MARINA: Is it? Yes, I suppose it is.

[*The sound of* PATRICE'S *fiddle continues in the background.*]

[MAXIM *and* MIKEY *are sitting on the ground forward. The
cupboard, half closed, is visible behind them.* MIKEY *is learning
to read.*]

MAXIM: Go on, go on.

MIKEY: Ti-ger, ti-ger bur-ning bright,
In the—

MAXIM: You read that bit before. You know it by heart.

MIKEY: Ti-ger-ti-ger-bur-ning-bright
In-the-fo-rests-of-the-night.

MAXIM: You aren't *reading*. I can tell by your eyes. You're
just reciting by heart. Look, read this different other bit
here. READ!

MIKEY: I can't read that, it's all different-looking.

MAXIM: If you were *reading* it wouldn't be different, it'd be
the same.

MIKEY: But you *said* it was different.

MAXIM: You're stupid!

MIKEY: I don't understand. I don't know what reading is.

MAXIM: How do you think you'll ever get out of this place
if you don't learn to read?

[*A maddening sound comes from the cupboard of a violin bow
drawn slowly and squeakily across a string.* MAXIM *looks up
angrily but decides to ignore it.*]

Look, don't you recognise these letters? I've showed them
to you a hundred times.

MIKEY: Ti-ger-ti-ger-bur-ning-bright
In-the—

MAXIM: No, this bit here! Look at the *letters*. What's that?

MIKEY: D.

MAXIM: That's right. I. D. H. And there's our old friend E,

You remember, E for Elephant. Now what are those two words? *Did he.* Now go on.

MIKEY: S. M.

MAXIM: Read the words, you fool, not the letters!

MIKEY: But you asked me to read the letters.

MAXIM: Because I wanted you to read the words! The letters don't matter. It's the words that matter.

MIKEY: Then why did I have to spend all that time learning the letters?

[*Again the maddening sound from the cupboard.*]

MAXIM: Shut up! Come on. And *look*.
Did he smile his work to see,
Did he who made the lamb make thee.

MIKEY: Did he smile his work to see.

MAXIM: Did he who made the lamb make thee.

MIKEY: Did he who made the lamb make thee. That's silly.

[*Shrill squeal from the cupboard, followed by the sound of plucked strings.*]

MAXIM: Shut up, or I'll break your bloody fiddle over your head! Now again.

MIKEY: Did-he-smile-his-work-to-see.

MAXIM: *Read* it, don't recite it!

MIKEY: I can learn it just as well by listening to you.

MAXIM: You're learning to *read*, you're not just learning these sentences.

MIKEY: Anyway it's a kid's book, it's all nonsense. I want to read a proper book.

MAXIM: I know it's nonsense, but you have to start with something easy. Again!

MIKEY: I've forgotten it now.

MAXIM: If you've forgotten it you can't read it! There it is, *there*.

MIKEY: Those things aren't real words.

MAXIM: They are real words, they're *written* words!

[*Squeal from the cupboard.* MAXIM *leaps up.* PATRICE *hastily closes the doors and bolts himself in.* MAXIM *bangs on the panels.*]

I'll kill you, gipsy, if you aren't careful! You keep your dirty hands off what doesn't concern you. Do you understand me?

PATRICE: [*Inside: plunk, plunk!*]

MAXIM: Ach! [*He bangs again and returns to* MIKEY.] Now we'll try again.

MIKEY: [*breaking down*] I can't do it, I don't understand what I'm supposed to do.

MAXIM: You're a very stupid boy!

MIKEY: That lady hasn't sent for me. She said I was to come to her and be with her all the time and she'd dress me in nice clothes.

MAXIM: She's probably forgotten. These people treat their servants like toys. And if you let her make you into a pet monkey I'll box your ears. Now where's that book.

MIKEY: I can't do it, it makes my head miserable. I won't, I won't! It's all silly baby stuff.

[*He eludes* MAXIM *and dances about chanting.*]

Tiger tiger burning bright
In the forests of the night,
Did he smile his work to see,
Did he who made the lamb make thee.
Maxim is a dirty pig,
Maxim's nose is much too big,
Maxim put his nose to bed,
Maxim found his nose was dead.

MAXIM: Well, you are a baby. And you'll be a snotty little kitchen boy all your life. You'll be sorry when you've got a bald head and you're still cleaning saucepans! All right! I'm going!

[*As* MAXIM *strides off* MARINA *appears, hides quickly from her son, and then moves onto the scene. She looks after him.*]

MIKEY: Tiger tiger burning bright
In the forests of the night.

MARINA: Stop that noise. Mikey, come here. Mikey, did you say anything to Peter Jack about me and Patrice?

MIKEY: [*struggling as she holds him*] Tiger tiger burning bright. No, I didn't! You're hurting me. I'll tell the lady about you.

MARINA: I'm not hurting you, stop shouting. You're hurting yourself. Keep still! Don't you dare say anything to anybody about things you don't understand, *will you?*

MIKEY: No, no, I won't, I promise—

MARINA: All right, now go away, off with you.

MIKEY: I don't want to go away, I'm cold, I want to go in the cupboard.

MARINA: Be off!

[*She chases* MIKEY *off, then tiptoes to the cupboard. As she kneels outside it* PATRICE *begins to play his fiddle inside. After a phrase or two* MARINA *gives a special knock.* PATRICE *looks coyly out.*]

PATRICE: Who's there?

MARINA: Miauw!

PATRICE: It's my little pussy cat!

[*He seizes her, pulling her half inside the cupboard. They kiss,* MARINA *returning his caresses half playfully, half passionately.*]

MARINA: Patrice, I'm so afraid somebody will see us.

PATRICE: I'll put the doors so. Now we've got our own little housey. Come right inside, come on. It's so nice in my cupboard. It's quite warm really. I know you didn't dare to when the old devil was alive—

MARINA: [*resisting*] I feel so bad about this because of poor Peter.

PATRICE: Devil take poor Peter. When the spring comes you're coming away with me, you said you would.

MARINE: When the spring comes I shall be married to Peter. I can't put him off any longer.

PATRICE: You're all dreamy, Marina. Don't marry somebody you don't want in a dream. Wake up! We'll go away sooner. I can take you any time, through the snow, through the storm.

MARINA: Across the river?

PATRICE: Far across the river, to the great gipsy camps, where life is free, where every man sings and every woman dances!

MARINA: You make me want to laugh again. You take all the horrors away.

PATRICE: I take the heaviness out of your bones, I make you as light as a little bird, to fly away, with me! You'll like it with the gipsies. No more servitude, no more work.

MARINA: I think I'd be sort of anxious and bored if I had no work to do.

PATRICE: That's because you don't know how to live freely inside yourself, like an animal. Animals are never bored. They're content just to be. That's what the gipsy life is: joy in just being, in breathing, in seeing the sky, in feeling the wind. There are no masters and servants there, and women are the equals of men.

MARINA: I don't know whether I'd like that either.

PATRICE: If women are not men's equals they become men's destroyers. All gipsy marriages are happy.

MARINA: And we'd have a gipsy wedding like you said?

PATRICE: Jumping across the fire!

MARINA: Couldn't Father Ambrose marry us here before we went?

PATRICE: No, no. There are other gods, Marina, real gods. Father Ambrose's gods are dead.

MARINA: You mustn't say that! [*She crosses herself.*]

PATRICE: Don't do that, my darling. It's just a nervous habit and it makes me uneasy.

MARINA: Peter thinks I can't touch a man since—you know. Poor Peter, he seems so quiet and old. How old are you, Patrice?

PATRICE: A gipsy never tells.

MARINA: I love Peter too, but I love him in a sort of tired quiet way, while I love you in a mad wild way.

PATRICE: That means that you love me and you don't love

him. Why do you think that I come back here every
winter, Marina? We must go away together.

MARINA: If only I could know the future. You won't read
my hand?

PATRICE: I don't want to look. When a thing matters
absolutely it's better not to know.

MARINA: You looked at her hand. You kissed her hand. I
was watching through the door!

PATRICE: That was just policy.

MARINA: What was it that you saw there, in her hand?

PATRICE: [*after a moment*] Nothing. I was just pretending.
You will come away?

MARINA: I don't know.

PATRICE: You will, you will.

MARINA: I don't know, I don't know.

[*The White Drawing Room.* BASIL *is dressed in outdoor clothes
with riding boots and whip. He strides about excitedly while*
PETER JACK *sits at a table in the background studying papers.*
HANS JOSEPH *is in the foreground with* BASIL *and* FATHER
AMBROSE *is at the side trying vainly to attract attention. The
scene should go at a fast pace.*]

HANS JOSEPH: Your honour, if you let all the servants hunt
anything they want to—

BASIL: There's plenty of game. Yes, Father, in a minute.

HANS JOSEPH: I think you should keep the old rules.

BASIL: I hope you're doing your homework, Peter. [*To*
HANS JOSEPH *and* FATHER AMBROSE.] I've drawn up a
new plan for the whole estate. Did my wife speak to you
about the pepper? Yes, yes, Father.

HANS JOSEPH: We servants don't eat highly spiced food.

BASIL: Yes, but you must have some pepper somewhere.
What do you think Peter, does it look feasible?

AMBROSE: I wonder if I could talk to your honour?

BASIL: We're going to have a school, they'll be at their
lessons until they're fourteen.

HANS JOSEPH: [*disgusted*] Fourteen!

BASIL: You said the snow had broken through the church roof, Father, well, we shall rebuild the church—

AMBROSE: I doubt if that will be necessary, your honour.

BASIL: You have to take Mass in the Servants' Hall! We'll have a splendid church! You know I'm a humanist but I believe in freedom of worship and—What do you think of it, Peter?

PETER JACK: Very interesting, your honour.

BASIL: You see it all depends on two ideas. First we divide up all the original land of the Home Farm so that everyone has some land of his own.

HANS JOSEPH: We servants have never owned land.

BASIL: But you ought to, my friend. Property is good, it means responsibility and dignity and incentive. And the second idea is the assembly of servants. Elected representatives will meet every week and then everything that is being done on the estate can be explained to everybody and everybody will be consulted—

HANS JOSEPH: They won't understand.

BASIL: My friends, I have so much power it terrifies me.

PETER JACK: [softly] Yes.

BASIL: My great grandfather murdered people he didn't like and slept with all the local girls on their wedding night, my grandfather— I must get rid of this heritage of power. It's not that I want to use it differently. I don't want to have it. If I have to rule here I want to rule by love, and that won't really be ruling at all. Isn't that so, Father? Surely your religion advocates this. I want the whole estate to be a house of virtue.

AMBROSE: It seems to me, your honour, that virtue resides in these arrangements only in a rather negative sense.

BASIL: Come. Virtue is a positive, not a negative. Do I have to tell *you* that, Father?

HANS JOSEPH: There must *be* rule, Sir!

PETER JACK: [*to* FATHER AMBROSE] I know what you mean. [*To* BASIL] You can't hustle a lot of people into being good. All you can do is stop them from hurting each other, and let them do things for themselves which are fairly sort of harmless. When people are all together they aren't even decent unless they have to be.

[PETER *is desperately trying to express something important which he can only partly grasp.* BASIL *is authoritative, impressive, explaining gently.*]

BASIL: Peter. Unless we attempt far more than we can achieve we won't achieve anything. Morality is a matter of at least *aiming* at perfection.

PETER JACK: Well, yes, but the estate—it's different—it isn't quite like that just a matter of morality—

BASIL: What could be more a matter of morality than when we decide about the most general arrangements of our lives!

PETER JACK: No, I mean— When men try to be decent together it isn't like when a man tries to be good by himself.

BASIL: Why?

PETER JACK: Forcing oneself isn't like forcing other people.

BASIL: But nobody will be forced. That's the point.

HANS JOSEPH: There must be force, Sir.

PETER JACK: And if, just by yourself, you try too much and get in a muddle, that's your affair. But if we are all together trying for too much and we get in a muddle everybody will suffer and bad people will take advantage.

[FATHER AMBROSE *is nodding agreement.*]

HANS JOSEPH: That's what I say, Sir, you must keep them down, keep them down.

PETER JACK: I don't mean that either. Sorry, I can't put it. But—I think now we should just improve a few things— let people live a bit more conveniently and not be afraid and—

BASIL: We must aim at a high quality of human life—

[*Enter* ORIANE *and* GRUNDIG. *They wear outdoor clothes, snow-sprinkled.*]

ORIANE: What must we aim at, Basil dear?

BASIL: A high quality of human life.

ORIANE: Mr Grundig was just showing me round. Then it started to snow again like mad. Oh I am so tired of the snow.

[*She sits down and without embarrassment this time, or even noticing it, lets* HANS JOSEPH *pull her boots off.*]

There was no pepper again at luncheon today!

HANS JOSEPH: I'm sorry, your ladyship, I will look—

ORIANE: Well, mind you find some by dinner time.

BASIL: We've just been discussing my Plan, Oriane.

ORIANE: Your? Oh yes, your Plan. What do you think of the PLAN, Mr Grundig?

GRUNDIG: Naturally I think that many of these improvements will enhance the value of the estate.

BASIL: Never mind that!

GRUNDIG: But to be perfectly frank, Sir, I think that these ideas need to be very carefully considered.

ORIANE: So do I!

GRUNDIG: I would not advocate what you call the er assembly of servants. Perpetual explanation tends to undermine the habit of obedience.

BASIL: I don't want obedience!

GRUNDIG: Secrecy is a very important ingredient of power.

BASIL: I don't want power. I regard myself here not as an owner but as a trustee. I'm not a good enough person to rule all these men.

PETER JACK: I think that's irrelevant, your honour.

GRUNDIG: Never mind being good enough, Sir, concentrate on being strong enough. All rule rests ultimately upon force. Human beings are hopelessly frail. Is that not so, Father?

AMBROSE: Yes.

GRUNDIG: Almost everyone in the world, Sir, saving your presence, is a petty criminal by nature, and I think we would be wise to organise the estate upon that assumption.

48

ORIANE: And I think there are rats here. Hans Joseph, are there or are there not rats?

HANS JOSEPH: Occasionally, your ladyship—

ORIANE: Well, I want those rats poisoned.

BASIL: Oriane, I feel—

ORIANE: Basil, you aren't going to be sentimental about the rats! And I must have a lady's-maid. How about that girl Marina? She seemed rather simple but I expect I could train her.

BASIL: Marina is Peter Jack's fiancée, Oriane!

GRUNDIG: You probably know, Sir, excuse me, Peter Jack, but I feel that the facts ought to be known before any—

PETER JACK: Yes, yes.

GRUNDIG: The girl Marina was your father's mistress for many years during the lifetime of her husband.

BASIL: [*fascinated*] Really?

GRUNDIG: It's not that I'm unduly old fashioned, but I felt that in the circumstances her ladyship might prefer not to—

ORIANE: I don't mind about the girl's sexual morals so long as she's not a thief.

BASIL: Of course we don't mind! I would regard this girl rather as a victim to whom we should make some sort of restitution. Don't you agree, Father?

AMBROSE: There is much to redeem here.

ORIANE: Could somebody fetch the girl Marina, and that boy, the little boy, Mikey, oh and Frederic—

AMBROSE: Your honour, I'd like—

BASIL: Tomorrow, tomorrow. Thank you, dear friends.

[*Exeunt* FATHER AMBROSE, PETER JACK *and* HANS JOSEPH.]

Oh Oriane, it's all so exciting!

[*He tries to kiss her but she pushes him away.*]

ORIANE: Dear Basil, I'm sorry, I'm tired. It's so cold out. Did you talk to that priest?

BASIL: Not yet.

ORIANE: He gives me the creeps. I think you're confusing these people. You ought to bully them more.

BASIL: Darling, I wish you'd be a bit more polite to Peter and Hans Joseph.

ORIANE: Nonsense, they love it. Don't you see how sentimental they are, in spite of everything, about the old days with your father? It's odd, Basil. I think after all I shall fit into this scene better than you will!

BASIL: Oriane, all these people don't just exist for our benefit.

ORIANE: I think it would be better for everybody if we assumed that they did.

BASIL: They don't work just so that we can put on nice clothes and do nothing.

ORIANE: Yes, they do. We are their achievement. Our idleness and our luxury are the crown of their toil. Without us their lives would feel pointless.

BASIL: No!

ORIANE: And when my brother the General comes to stay I feel sure he will agree with me. You mustn't be always explaining and justifying everything to them and talking everything to bits. What they understand is orders. That's what they're used to and that's what they like. [BASIL *tries to interrupt*.] Oh, I know it's all a new toy to you. But be careful. Running a big place like this is like taming lions. When you lose your nerve the lions know.

BASIL: It's not like that! Can't you see the loyalty of these people?

ORIANE: You were talking of equality, but now suddenly it's loyalty!

BASIL: I should hope the two are compatible!

ORIANE: You want it both ways, my dear. You want to consult them yet you still want to think of them as your children. You don't really want to give up your power, but because you're a nice man you want to exercise it pleasantly. You're frightened of them really.

You think that for two pins they'd start despising you.

BASIL: Well, I don't think I'm God. Why should all these people obey me?

ORIANE: That question would never have occurred to your father.

BASIL: Then so much the worse for him!

ORIANE: You feared and hated your father, didn't you?

BASIL: Well—

ORIANE: Admit it, Basil.

BASIL: Yes. I feared and hated him.

ORIANE: And so you want to be as unlike him as possible. What you think is idealism is really just a private feud with papa.

BASIL: You are a materialist, Oriane! Perhaps all women are.

ORIANE: I'm a realist, Basil. We do much less harm than you do in the end.

[*Enter* MARINA *and* MIKEY. *They kneel in the background.*]

BASIL: Get up!

[*They rise and come forward.*]

Well, Marina, my dear, you're looking very bonny today. [*He pats her cheek.*] Won't she make a lovely bride, Oriane?

ORIANE: [*absorbed in* MIKEY] There's a pretty boy. I think I'll cut his hair so and so.

BASIL: Yes, but I think not just now.

ORIANE: Why not?

BASIL: I've just noticed that his head's covered with lice.

ORIANE: [*faint shriek*] Ooh! Take him away, please. Yes, I see. It makes me feel quite sick.

BASIL: Come on, Mikey, we'll see that you have a nice bath. Sois gentille avec la petite, Oriane.

[*Gesture of exasperated compliance from* ORIANE. *Exeunt* BASIL *and* MIKEY. *The two women eye each other.*]

ORIANE: Well, Marina, I'm not going to eat you. I hope your hair is quite clean. Let me look.

[MARINA *undoes her long hair which sweeps about her*.]
I didn't mean you to take it all down. It makes you look ridiculously— How old are you?

MARINA: Thirty-six, please.

ORIANE: Put it up again neatly, that's right. Aren't you older than that? That rather rude boy Maxim is your son.

MARINA: He's only eighteen, please. He is difficult, children are difficult, your ladyship is lucky not to have any.

ORIANE: [*not sure if she is being got at*] Er—yes. Would you like to be my maid?

MARINA: [*with genuine enthusiasm*] Yes, please!

ORIANE: Are you discreet?

MARINA: Oh yes!

ORIANE: What does "discreet" mean?

MARINA: Pretending not to notice things.

ORIANE: Good enough. I believe you lived on terms of intimacy with your late master. That's all right, I'm not making any moral judgments. I expect you were an important person here in those days. I hope you will adapt yourself to your new situation in a sensible way.

MARINA: I wasn't important, your ladyship, no one was, except *him* of course.

ORIANE: I trust you are not meaning to criticise your former master. I daresay you were pleased to be his favourite, weren't you?

MARINA: Well, I—

ORIANE: Come. You were pleased.

MARINA: He *was* the master.

ORIANE: Quite. And now you're going to marry Peter Jack.

MARINA: Perhaps— I—

ORIANE: Isn't it fixed?

MARINA: A wife has to do what her husband wants and not what she wants so I've been thinking that it might be nicer really to remain single.

ORIANE: The sooner you get married the better!

[*Enter* FREDERIC.]

Ah Frederic, there you are. This woman is going to be my lady's-maid. Now what can we do about dressing her properly. She can't serve me dressed in that, she must have some nice clothes.

MARINA: [*thrilled*] Ah!

FREDERIC: Madam may remember that Annabelle's box of clothes came with us by mistake. I think this lady and Annabelle are about the same size.

ORIANE: Good. You go with Frederic and get fitted out with some decent clothes. There now.

[MARINA *kneels and kisses the hand which* ORIANE *graciously offers.* ORIANE *meets* FREDERIC's *eyes above* MARINA's *bent head.*]

What is it, Frederic?

FREDERIC: Nothing, Madam.

[*Exeunt* FREDERIC *and* MARINA. ORIANE *lets down her hair and surveys herself thoughtfully in the looking glass.*]

[*As soon as* FREDERIC *and* MARINA *are alone together* FREDERIC *begins to go through antics for* MARINA's *benefit, grimaces, puts his thumbs in his ears and waggles his fingers and so on.*]

MARINA: You *are* a funny one!

FREDERIC: You're all so solemn here.

MARINA: You're like a monkey, I've never seen a monkey.

FREDERIC: You've seen one now.

MARINA: I expect you think we're very slow after the city and that.

FREDERIC: You're all so secretive. Why does everybody always stop talking whenever they see me coming? What's the big secret?

MARINA: Nothing.

FREDERIC: I'm not going to stay here, you know. When the spring comes I'm going into service with Madam's brother the General.

MARINA: What's he like?

FREDERIC: He's a real boss. When I've saved up enough

money I'm going into business. Then—bzzzz. [*He indi-cates his meteoric rise in the world.*] Here are Annabelle's clothes.

MARINA: Who's Annabelle?

FREDERIC: My wife, as was. She's run off with somebody else.

MARINA: I'm sorry.

FREDERIC: I'm not. I didn't want her here. I told her there'd be bears all the winter and snakes all the summer. I scared her proper.

MARINA: Why didn't you want her?

FREDERIC: I wanted to be free for you! I saw you in my dreams!

[*They are playing with the clothes.* MARINA *is delighted.* FREDERIC *flourishes underwear, puts on hats and minces around.*]

Well, try it on, dear.

MARINA: I can't, not with you here.

FREDERIC: Oh go on, I won't look!

[*He does look a bit all the same as* MARINA, *unable to wait, puts on a dress. It transforms her.*]

I say! Madame la Marquise, may I have the pleasure of the first waltz?

MARINA: I can't waltz.

FREDERIC: [*seizing her and singing*] You waltz—a like this, like this, like this, you waltz—a like this, like this, like this—

MARINA: [*breaking away*] Please. I want to show my dress to somebody, I must—

FREDERIC: There is another man, you are making me mad with jealousy!

[MARINA *laughing dodges him and runs off with* FREDERIC *in pursuit.*]

[*The cupboard with doors shut is dimly in view. Enter* MARINA *running laughing towards it, looking over her shoulder. She meets* MAXIM *in mid-stage. He grips her by the wrist and swings her round.*]

MAXIM: Well, mother?

[FREDERIC *runs on, sees* MAXIM *who gives him a withering glare. Exit* FREDERIC *with rueful mimed dismay.*]

Where are you going, mother?

MARINA: Nowhere special.

MAXIM: You were romping with that lackey. And you've got a ridiculous dress on. You were going to show that dress to the gipsy.

MARINA: No. It's a pretty dress.

MAXIM: You let them buy your servility with a silk dress. You were practically mistress here and now you are flattered because this female wants to make you her lady's-maid.

MARINA: It's very kind of her.

MAXIM: Don't you see that she's only taking you up in order to put you down. She sees you're someone important here. No woman can bear to have another woman as a serious rival. She intends to humiliate you. Were you going to see the gipsy?

MARINA: I wanted to show him my dress.

MAXIM: Mother, you're like a little child. But you're a child playing a very dangerous game. The gipsy is courting you, isn't he, he's telling you lies.

MARINA: He tells me about the life of the gipsies. He tells me women are the equals of men there.

MAXIM: Women are not the equals of men anywhere. With the gipsies, women are chattels.

MARINA: He says it's like being an animal and being happy simply to exist.

MAXIM: Animals are not happy. They live in perpetual hunger and perpetual terror.

MARINA: He says with the gipsies everyone is free.

MAXIM: He lies. The big gipsy camps are places of horror where every man's hand is against every other man and the strong rule the weak without mercy. Where there is lawlessness and total freedom all men are swine. What they call liberty is the war of everyone against everyone. Their lives are nasty, brutish and short. Don't go to the gipsy, dear mother. Go to Peter Jack. Show him your pretty dress if you must. It may not be very gay here and the arrangements may be stupid, but at least there are arrangements and there are rules and that's better than having none at all. If you marry Peter Jack you'll be faithful to him. If you run off with the gipsy you will become a drab. You are half one already. Oh if you knew how my shame for you has weakened me! All women weaken a man through shame. If it were not for you I might have been so much braver and stronger in the past. Well, it is past. Don't let that woman make a plaything out of you. There, don't cry. I didn't mean to be rough with you. Come now, and I'll take you to Peter Jack. Come, mother.

[*Exeunt.*]

[*More light upon the cupboard. The doors are open.* PATRICE *has raised a floor-board and is feeding a piece of cheese to his friend the rat.*]

PATRICE: No one is afraid of me. Not even the rats. Here, old friend. We're both thieves, aren't we. But I must be the cleverer thief of the two. Because you're always so hungry. Ooh, mind my fingers! You live in your house between the floor-boards and we live in ours above you, below you. You are the rats in our house. We are the rats in your house. We listen with anxiety to each other's little stirrings. You did us no harm, ratty. We could spare the little that you stole. But now they're going to poison you. You'll die, old friend, and you'll stink, and I shall pity you. And I shall pity myself. And I shall die too one day in a rat hole, poisoned by my life. She won't come, ratty. She said she'd come. She hasn't come. She won't come. She'll marry the other one. Why do I waste my life for a woman who is not wise, not good, not beautiful, not even young any more? Why does nothing else in the world

matter except one silly frail ageing animal? Old grey
muzzle, did you feel that when you were young and slim?
Here. Mind my fingers, old muncher, poor old muncher.
We are all born for failure and the dose of poison when
the journey ends. And there's a perpetual smile on the face
of Nature as she despatches us, one after the other.

[*Enter* FATHER AMBROSE *leading* MIKEY *by the hand.*
MIKEY *is dressed in his new page's rig and is crying.*]

AMBROSE: Don't cry, Mikey. Why are you crying?

MIKEY: She was kind to me, and now she's not kind any
more.

AMBROSE: She will be kind again.

MIKEY: I want a nice lady to be kind to me.

PATRICE: We all want that. Keep your distance, Rev.

AMBROSE: All right, all right. I just brought Mikey home.

PATRICE: Home. I say what a get-up!

MIKEY: I don't know who I am.

AMBROSE: God knows who you are.

MIKEY: Nobody loves me.

AMBROSE: God loves you.

PATRICE: Why do you tell the boy these lies? You know
your God doesn't exist. I can see that you know. I look
into your eyes, Rev, and what do I see? I see horrors in
your eyes.

AMBROSE: I look into your eyes, gipsy, and what do I see?

PATRICE: Sunlight, air, sky, the trackless passage of the
winds.

AMBROSE: Emptiness, nothingness.

PATRICE: That's better than lies. Don't trust them, Mikey.
Never trust anyone who makes rules. And don't expect
love. Nobody has a right to it.

AMBROSE: I didn't tell him to expect human love.

PATRICE: If you expect any other kind you are the friend
of tyrants. If you make humiliation holy you are the
friend of tyrants. Your big God is dead and your little
gods are dying. And you are mortally sad because you

57

have forgotten nothing and because you know that even though you willed all manner of good things and hoped all manner of good things you have still been all your life the friend of tyrants.

AMBROSE: Put the child to bed.

PATRICE: I will not bow down to a fake God, but I will bow down to you, because you are so sad and because there are horrors in your eyes. [*He bows.*]

MIKEY: Patrice—

AMBROSE: Goodnight.

[*Father* AMBROSE *moves away from the scene but is still faintly visible where he kneels and fingers his rosary.*]

MIKEY: Patrice—

PATRICE: Yes, my little duckling.

MIKEY: I don't know who I am. How do I know I won't wake up one morning and find I'm somebody else?

PATRICE: It wouldn't matter so long as you didn't know that you had. Perhaps we all wake up every morning and find we're somebody else. I've never had any identity and I've never missed it.

MIKEY: Patrice, you're the only person I'm not afraid of. I miss you so terribly when you go away in the summer. You will always come back, won't you.

[*During this talk* PATRICE *is preparing* MIKEY's *bed on the upper shelf of the cupboard.*]

PATRICE: It's bed-time, Mikey.

MIKEY: If you went away and didn't come back how would I find you?

PATRICE: You wouldn't find me. No one unguided can find the gipsy places.

MIKEY: Patrice—

PATRICE: You must take your fine jacket off. I'll hang it up. See.

MIKEY: Patrice, may I sleep with you tonight? It's so cold and lonely up there and I keep dreaming that you've gone away.

58

PATRICE: All right then. [*They begin to settle down together.*]

MIKEY: I only sleep up there because I'm afraid of the rats.

PATRICE: Soon there will be no rats. Come.

MIKEY: I won't be able to sleep, Patrice, I know I won't. Tell me a story. Tell me how it will be when we go away together to the gipsy land.

PATRICE: We'll pack up our things, just the two of us, and it will be twilight and a big moon will be rising and we'll go off down the road together and we'll go on and we'll come to a dark place and we'll go on and on and we'll come to another dark place and we'll go on and on and on and we'll come to another dark place and we'll go on and on and on and on . . .

[*As* MIKEY *goes to sleep in* PATRICE's *arms the light fades from the cupboard and comes up upon* FATHER AMBROSE *who is still kneeling on the other side of the stage. He is leaning against something and seems to be asleep. Enter* BASIL.]

BASIL: Why, Father, good morning. I'm so sorry, were you asleep? Why, you'd fallen asleep on your knees. Here, let me help you. Have you been on your knees all night?

AMBROSE: A lifetime on my knees would not atone for my sins.

BASIL: Nonsense. You have no sins. You priests are so masochistic. Not that it isn't a good thing in a way of course. Look. I want to show you the plans for the new church. [BASIL *produces plans.*]

AMBROSE: A new church will not be necessary, your honour. I shall have no successor here. When I die, which please God will be soon, these people will revert to a paganism which is very much more natural to them than the religion which I have preached and failed to practise.

BASIL: You are in a pessimistic mood! Of course we must have a church. Even if one regards religion, as I do, as something purely symbolic it can still play an important ethical role. It can add solemnity to human things. By the way, how soon could you marry Marina and Peter Jack?

AMBROSE: As soon as you will, my son. All things are in order for it.

BASIL: Would the day after tomorrow be too soon?

AMBROSE: No. It could be done then.

BASIL: I feel somehow that this marriage should take place at once, as a part of my arrival here. I shall give the bride away. I'm a tolerant man but I think a certain regularity of life is very important. I want this marriage to symbolise that. I want it to symbolise the disappearance of the past. The absolute end of—all those things.

AMBROSE: Look out of that window, my son.

BASIL: Peter tells me the weather is going to change. We may even have some sunshine. The roads will be open and Mr Grundig will be leaving us.

AMBROSE: What do you see?

BASIL: I see the courtyard, the stables, the barn, the spire of your ruined church. I see the forest and the snow.

AMBROSE: What else do you see?

BASIL: I see my father's tombstone. He had it carved during his lifetime. It's so big it climbs right up out of the snow.

AMBROSE: Have you visited your father's grave?

BASIL: No.

AMBROSE: You should go there.

BASIL: I have no father. You shall be my father. You shall be my *good* father.

AMBROSE: I am too loaded with sin, I am old with it and dying of it. And you are the last one to whom I can be a father. I am a pensioner in your house, you feed me, you clothe me—Your father relieved his conscience by confessing to me.

BASIL: [*understanding*] Yes. It must have been— Yes.

AMBROSE: Go to his grave, my son.

BASIL: No. Let him rot. I shock you.

AMBROSE: No. But the past does not disappear. Sometimes the past turns out to be—the future—after all.

BASIL: Let him rot!

[*The bedroom. The room is strewn with clothes.* ORIANE's *jewel box is open and jewellery trails about.* ORIANE, MARINA, MIKEY *and* HANS JOSEPH. MARINA *is pouring champagne.* HANS JOSEPH *is on his knees.*]

HANS JOSEPH: I've looked everywhere, your ladyship. I'm sure there was some pepper once, but it seems to have vanished into thin air.

ORIANE: Well, look again. I am most displeased. What a barborous place this is! All right, I don't want your excuses I want the pepper. I don't want to see you till you've found it.

[*She waves him off. Exit* HANS JOSEPH *protesting.*]

More!

[MARINA *refills her glass.*]

Where's that boy?

MIKEY *has a shawl round his shoulders.* ORIANE *and* MARINA *hilariously dress him up with a necklace, a hat.*]

Now you must walk like this with little steps and curtsey. So. Can't you act, have you never done any charades? Have you never pretended to be somebody else? The child doesn't know how to play!

[ORIANE *and* MARINA *laugh at* MIKEY, *who begins to cry.*]

There now. Good heavens, what have we done? It's only a game, Mikey. Well, all right, you sit down over there until you're good again. More!

[*During these goings on* MARINA *has been burrowing in* ORIANE's *jewel box, admiring this and that. She takes out a diamond ring and puts it on her finger. In what follows she forgets about it and leaves it there.*]

What's that?

[*A distant sound of a fiddle playing a gipsy air.*]

MARINA: That's Patrice, your ladyship. He's playing his fiddle. He plays so beautifully. He's gone out into the courtyard. That means the weather is going to change.

ORIANE: The gipsy. He's almost under my window. [*They*

look out.] You've never heard real music, have you, Marina. He plays well. Very well.

MARINA: He's wonderful.

ORIANE: He said he saw something in my hand but he didn't say what it was. I must ask him. I shall take him up. I might even send him to the conservatoire. He shall be my court musician and when my piano comes we shall play duets together. Yes, he really does play well. What a marvellous tone. I wonder if he knows how good he is. I must tell him. Go and fetch him to me now, would you. The lady and the gipsy. There's a song about that. He shall have a special uniform. He shall fall in love with me. [*Sings.*] "She's off with the raggle taggle gipsy O."

MARINA: His heart is not free, your ladyship.

ORIANE: What do you mean?

MARINA: Patrice is in love with me, your ladyship.

ORIANE: But you're going to marry Peter Jack.

[MARINA *is upset.* ORIANE *ironical, determinedly gay, a little tipsy, swaying as she continues to hum the gipsy song.*]

MARINA: I don't know about that, your ladyship.

ORIANE: But it's all settled.

[*Enter* BASIL.]

BASIL: Ah my dear, hello. Marina, I was just looking for you. I wanted to be the first to tell you the splendid news. You are going to be married to Peter Jack the day after tomorrow.

[MARINA *bursts into tears.*]

My dear child, what is it? My little Marina—

MARINA: I'm sorry—

ORIANE: Send her away please, Basil. All this weeping is getting on my nerves.

[*Marina runs off.*]

BASIL: What is all this?

ORIANE: I told her to fetch the gipsy up here to play to me.

BASIL: Oriane, really, you can't have the gipsy in your bedroom!

ORIANE: I think in some ways I'm more democratic than you are!

BASIL: But why was she crying?

ORIANE: She's in love with the gipsy.

BASIL: She can't be.

ORIANE: She's a man-chaser. She wants them all.

BASIL: She must have had a terrible time with my father.

ORIANE: She enjoyed every moment of it. She probably seduced him.

BASIL: No woman could have wanted to live with my father.

ORIANE: Why not? He was a very attractive man. He was rather frightening, but women like that. I found him attractive. He found me attractive too!

BASIL: Oriane! [*He notices* MIKEY.] Good heavens, what's that?

ORIANE: I'd forgotten the boy.

BASIL: Take those things off. You're a boy not a performing poodle. Off with you! [*Exit* MIKEY.] The boy heard what you said just now.

ORIANE: Oh never mind.

BASIL: You mustn't play with the servants. We must behave with some sort of dignity.

ORIANE: We have no dignity.

BASIL: You've been drinking champagne!

ORIANE: You spoil everything. You knew how much I didn't want to come here and you made me. I haven't any natural way of living here. In the city I understood myself. Here it's all just scrappy and awful. I've got so little left of my own and you spoil it and take it away from me and turn the servants against me. I'm cheated out of my whole life by you. [*Tears.*]

BASIL: Oriane, darling, I'm sorry, please—

ORIANE: Sorry, Basil, I will try to be brave and support you. I know I'm awful but my nerves are so on edge and I'm so frightened, there's something here which

63

deeply frightens me, something we don't know about yet.

BASIL: There's nothing to be frightened of. There. We must help each other mustn't we—

ORIANE: What's that noise? [*They listen.*]

BASIL: I think it must be wolves. They sometimes come at this time of year.

ORIANE: Wolves!

[*They listen to the strange distant howling.*]

[*The cupboard.* PATRICE *and* MARINA. MARINA *is crying incoherently.*]

PATRICE: My darling, if we are to go we must go now.

MARINA: You mean really now, now at once?

PATRICE: Yes.

MARINA: I can't.

PATRICE: We must. The moon's shining. It's a clear night. No one will know till the morning and then we'll be miles away. Tomorrow they wouldn't leave you alone for an instant. Marina, it's our only chance of freedom, it's our last chance of freedom. Oh be brave, my queen.

MARINA: I won't be that woman's slave. Maxim was right. She only took me up so as to humiliate me. I'd do anything for his honour, he's a great gentleman, I'd serve him. But not that woman.

PATRICE: Come, Marina, have your cry and then let's be going. You're very nearly in the trap. Don't let it close on you.

MARINA: I love poor Peter. I can't leave him. He's loved me ever since I was six.

PATRICE: You pity Peter. You love me. Marina, face the *truth* of it at last. Look at me. Isn't that so?

MARINA: Yes.

PATRICE: Now enough of crying. We must leave at once. We'll go through the forest by a special way I know. Marina, the moon shines. The air is clear. The roads are firm. It's a sign. You are coming away with me forever.

MARINA: I've never left this place, I've never been across the river.

PATRICE: Do you want to be a slave all your life? Do you want never to see me again?

MARINA: Patrice—

PATRICE: Do you imagine I'd come here if you were married to Peter Jack? I would leave this place for good on your wedding day.

MARINA: Someone will see us.

PATRICE: No, they won't. We'll go through the stables. I've filed through the catch on the last loose box. There are two horses waiting. I've got our clothes and everything ready. See.

[MARINA, *still doubtfully, begins to dress. She puts on boots, cloak.* PATRICE *is already attired to go.*]

MARINA: We'll be caught.

PATRICE: No, we won't.

MARINA: The wolves have come.

PATRICE: The wolves are my friends.

MARINA: Ooh!

PATRICE: What is it?

MARINA: I've got her ladyship's diamond ring on! Oh no! I put it on, just for a moment, when we were trying her jewellery and I forgot to take it off. Oh dear, whatever shall I do? Where shall I put it, Patrice? Her ladyship's diamond ring! Oh—

[*She has pulled the ring off and darts about with it, wanting somehow to get rid of it.*]

PATRICE: Let me look. Give it to me. Well, it's not the sort of thing I usually take—

MARINA: Patrice, you can't!

PATRICE: I can. It's your dowry.

MARINA: But it's stealing.

PATRICE: My darling, you are about to leave the domain of private property.

[*He tries to put the ring on her finger, but she resists.*]

All right, I'll wear it. It'll just go onto my little finger. And, Marina. One more thing. Take this off.

[*He takes the cross off her neck. Reluctantly she lets him.*]

MARINA: Don't hurt it.

PATRICE: No. It shall live here. Where I lived.

[*He hangs the cross inside the cupboard.*]

Let me kiss you, my gipsy queen. Here for the last time. Come.

[*They creep out.*]

[*The moonlit courtyard. The tomb and the church tower are outlined against the sky. Outdoor sounds, soft clinking, footsteps on snow.*]

PATRICE: [*whispering*] Follow me, hold onto my belt. No, I'll carry that. Put your feet quietly, don't slip.

MARINA: Patrice—

PATRICE: Yes.

MARINA: I can't ride without a saddle and bridle.

PATRICE: Sssh. It's all right, I've got a saddle for you hidden in the forest. Careful.

They move across the scene. Enter MAXIM *in front of them with a lantern, carrying his gun.*]

MAXIM: [*quite softly*] Stop, gipsy. Good evening, mother.

[MARINA *gives a smothered scream.* PATRICE *gathers her to him and is about to push past* MAXIM.]

I said stop, gipsy. If you try to run I'll shoot you and I'll kill you. Go back to the house, both of you. Quietly, please, mother.

PATRICE: How did you know?

MAXIM: I saw my mother's cross hanging in the cupboard.

PATRICE: She wants to go. Let us pass.

MAXIM: And let my mother deceive a decent man and ruin her life with a gipsy? Go on.

MARINA: Please don't tell Peter.

MAXIM: Oh mother—

[*Enter* BASIL *and* FATHER AMBROSE.]

BASIL: What's going on here. I heard someone scream.

MAXIM: My mother was running away with the gipsy.

BASIL: Is this true?

[MARINA *hangs her head and weeps*.]

Come inside, please, all of you. [*To* MAXIM] Fetch Peter Jack and Hans Joseph to the drawing room.

[*The White Drawing Room*. BASIL, MARINA, PATRICE, *and* FATHER AMBROSE.]

MARINA: [*incoherent*] I didn't really mean to go.

BASIL: All right, don't cry. If you want to go nobody shall stop you. You're not a prisoner!

MARINA: I want to stay here with you!

[*Enter* MAXIM, *now unarmed, with* PETER JACK *and* HANS JOSEPH.]

BASIL: I'm sorry, Peter.

PETER JACK: I'm sorry too, your honour. But I think if they want to go they should go.

MARINA: I don't want to go.

[*Enter* ORIANE.]

ORIANE: What is all this?

BASIL: Marina and the gipsy were running away together.

ORIANE: I see. And what do you think *you're* doing, Basil?

BASIL: I felt that everybody should have a chance for second thoughts.

ORIANE: My diamond ring! Look, he's wearing my diamond ring! I looked everywhere for it. That is my ring, isn't it?

PATRICE: Dear me, however did that get there!

[*He tugs at the ring, pulls it off and hands it to* MARINA *who drops it on the floor with a little scream.* PETER JACK *picks it up and gives it to* ORIANE.]

ORIANE: Yes. My engagement ring.

BASIL: The ring I gave you!

ORIANE: [*to* MARINA] You stole it!

MARINA: I didn't, I swear, I don't know anything about it!

BASIL: Oriane, did you let that gipsy come upstairs?

ORIANE: No! She stole the ring and gave it to the gipsy.

MARINA: I didn't, I didn't!

HANS JOSEPH: Let me thrash him now, Sir, we've caught him stealing at last!

BASIL: [to PATRICE] Well?

PATRICE: I admit it, your honour, I did steal the ring. I'm very sorry.

HANS JOSEPH: Let me have him, your honour. I'll—

BASIL: No. I propose to hand him over to the police.

HANS JOSEPH: That makes no sense, your honour. The police are miles and miles away—

PATRICE: [falling on his knees] Not the police, your honour, please, please! They'd just put me in prison and forget about me forever!

PETER JACK: That's true, your honour.

PATRICE: Don't send me to the police, please!

BASIL: Get up! Behave like a man!

[PATRICE gets up, but kneels again directly.]

I thought you only stole things you needed!

PATRICE: I know I shouldn't have—

ORIANE: He didn't steal it!

HANS JOSEPH: Let me deal with him!

ORIANE: Basil, are you out of your mind? He's protecting the girl. She stole it.

BASIL: He was wearing it.

HANS JOSEPH: We have to be our own judges and executioners. If your honour will permit me—

BASIL: He shall be made to work.

HANS JOSEPH: He wouldn't work.

PATRICE: I would! I would!

HANS JOSEPH: It's far simpler and better to beat him.

BASIL: [to PATRICE] Get up!

[He gets up, but kneels again.]

PATRICE: Please, your honour—

ORIANE: [to MARINA] You took it.

MARINA: I didn't steal it.

BASIL: He took it, he's admitted it, he's a professional thief and he must be punished. It'll do him good.

PATRICE: It won't!

BASIL: And it'll discourage others. Besides, it's just. Crimes demand punishments.

HANS JOSEPH: That's right, Sir.

ORIANE: But you didn't mind his taking things before.

BASIL: A diamond ring is different from a loaf of bread.

PATRICE: Indeed it is, your honour, and I shouldn't have, I see now—

ORIANE: I don't see why guilt should be in proportion to the value of what's stolen. Anyway, the ring is mine. If you forgive him for stealing your bread I don't see why I can't forgive him for stealing my ring, especially as I've got it back!

BASIL: You wanted me to be firm. I'm being firm. You wanted me to exercise my authority. I'm exercising my authority.

ORIANE: You let that boy Maxim steal your birds.

BASIL: That's different.

ORIANE: You victimise defenceless people and let the strong ones get away with it because you're afraid of them.

BASIL: Oriane. Not here!

ORIANE: Poor gipsy. Basil, let him go. I'll get the truth out of the girl.

MARINA: Don't let her hurt me!

ORIANE: Stop whining.

PATRICE: Your honour, please—

HANS JOSEPH: It's so much simpler, Sir, just to hand him over to me.

BASIL: All right then, take him away, beat him, do what you like, the whole thing sickens me.

ORIANE: Basil, how can you, after you said—

PATRICE: [following BASIL on his knees, as HANS JOSEPH tries to drag him off] Your honour, please listen to me. I know these people. They won't leave off till I'm dead. I don't deserve death, your honour, please save me!

BASIL: Hans Joseph, I hold you responsible. A life for a life. I want him hurt, not damaged.

PATRICE: They'll kill me, they'll kill me!

ORIANE: Stop, please—

BASIL: Father, you go with them and see that—

ORIANE: Stop!

BASIL: Oriane, don't question my orders. Out of the way!

[PATRICE *is dragged off lamenting by* HANS JOSEPH, *followed by* FATHER AMBROSE.]

ORIANE: [*to* MARINA] This is all your fault!

MARINA: Your honour, please, I did it, I took the ring.

ORIANE: There you are!

MARINA: But it was an accident. I tried it on my finger when her ladyship was showing us her jewels and then I forgot I'd put it on.

ORIANE: That's likely, isn't it! Basil, will you stop Hans Joseph?

BASIL: No, I won't. You would have put it back, wouldn't you, Marina, little Marina?

MARINA: Yes, your honour.

BASIL: Then the gipsy stole it. Let them beat him. Even if he doesn't deserve beating for this, he deserves it for something else. Now I'm going to bed.

ORIANE: All right. Leave the girl to me.

MARINA: No!

ORIANE: Give me those keys. House Keeper! Public Prostitute. And telling blatant lies to put the blame on the gipsy, and save yourself.

MARINA: I didn't!

BASIL: Oriane, don't torment the poor child.

ORIANE: Poor child! I'll deal with her.

MARINA: Oh no you won't! You won't touch me!

[*She hurls the keys on the floor.*]

BASIL: Marina, how dare you!

MARINA: You've destroyed my love for Patrice, both of you!

BASIL: Take her away, Peter Jack. I'm sorry—

[PETER JACK *advances.*]

MARINA: I'll tell you something. Something you don't know. You sit in judgment over us. But you don't know!

PETER JACK: Marina! No, no!

[*He tries to put his hand over her mouth.*]

MARINA: It's got to be told! They can't judge us after that. You can't keep silent about murder.

PETER JACK: Marina, stop! I'll take her away, she's hysterical.

BASIL: Let her speak! what was that you said, Marina? Let her go at once. Will you obey me, Peter? What did you say?

MARINA: Your father murdered my husband.

PETER JACK: Stop it, oh, stop it—

MARINA: He killed him, we heard him screaming—

[HANS JOSEPH *and* FATHER AMBROSE *are at the door.* PETER JACK, *distraught, tries to close the door against them.*]

BASIL: Let them in.

HANS JOSEPH: She has told.

PETER JACK: Yes.

BASIL: Father, is it true that my father murdered Francis James?

AMBROSE: Yes, your honour.

MARINA: He did it for me, because he was getting old and he was jealous, and he did it horribly— We were all driven mad, we are mad with it, mad— He killed him, my husband—

BASIL: Peter, is this true?

PETER JACK: Yes, your honour. But we must immediately forget it.

BASIL: Are you insane? Do you imagine that I would pursue the matter of a diamond ring, and not the matter of a murder—even if the murderer is my father? Especially if the murderer is my father!

HANS JOSEPH: What will be will be. It was inevitable that

71

somebody should speak of this. The horror of it has not left this house. We did not stop him.

AMBROSE: Your honour, I agree with Peter Jack. It may sound insane. But other courses are perhaps more so. You have learnt something terrible. Leave it there. Share it with us in silence.

MARINA: How can they! Is there no justice? He killed him! Aaaah! [*She screams.*]

PETER JACK: Be silent! There is nothing you can do. You cannot give life to the dead. Let this thing remain between us in this room.

HANS JOSEPH: That is already impossible. Everyone will know what this outcry means. It is an alarm signal for which many people have been waiting. Every servant in the house is now thinking of one thing. We cannot keep secret or forget what has come this night into consciousness.

BASIL: I am appalled—there must be a public enquiry into this—I will conduct an enquiry myself. This terrible thing must not be left as a secret horror in the house, how could you think this possible. I will have a—an inquest—with all the servants present—

PETER JACK: No. That we all share the guilt is a reason for silence. Do you want to punish us all?

BASIL: But silence is what would be mad here. This thing must be somehow—cleared up—cleared away—I cannot live with such a—I must take responsibility. I must make full restitution.

PETER JACK: *How*? [*Pause*] Do not make an issue of it.

BASIL: Do you expect me to shield my father?

PETER JACK: For all our sakes you must shield yourself. A public scene would not profit Francis James. It would merely put your honour's own life in danger.

BASIL: My life in danger?

HANS JOSEPH: Yes, Sir. As you yourself said just now: a life for a life.

BASIL: I don't understand. I have done nothing. Who would I be in danger from?

HANS JOSEPH: From us. From all of us. From any of us.

BASIL: Hans Joseph, old friend, what are you talking about?

PETER JACK: If only you had come here at once and stepped directly into your father's shoes. It was the six months interval, and everybody talking and thinking and remembering—

HANS JOSEPH: This is nothing personal against your honour. You said that you accepted responsibility. And blood guilt cries out for justice whether we would or no. I am Francis James's father, Maxim is his son—

BASIL: Maxim.

MAXIM: Don't worry about me. I am not as mindlessly simple as my grandfather. I ought to have killed the old man. I wish I had killed him. But you need have no fear of me. I regard you as nothing. [*Exit.*]

BASIL: Peter Jack, please help me to understand.

PETER JACK: A blood feud is not easily ended here, and you are your father's son. There are very deep compulsions, primitive ideas of justice which are still alive in this place, perhaps because of the long dark winter times, perhaps because of the snow.

HANS JOSEPH: An eye for an eye, a tooth for a tooth, it says in the book.

AMBROSE: It also says if a man strike you on one cheek offer him the other.

HANS JOSEPH: Blood calls for blood.

BASIL: Then why didn't you kill my father. Why didn't you all sentence him to death and execute him.

PETER JACK: We wanted to, But we could not.

HANS JOSEPH: It was unthinkable to exact retribution from your father. We could not touch him. He was like God in our lives. Even Maxim could not touch him.

BASIL: But you can touch me.

HANS JOSEPH: Yes, your honour.

[HANS JOSEPH *kneels on one knee, bowing his head. The sound of wolves howling is heard, nearer to the house.* BASIL *and* ORIANE *cling together.*]

Curtain

END OF ACT ONE

ACT TWO

The White Drawing Room. A big window, shuttered hitherto, reveals a sunny snow scene with a view of the courtyard, BASIL's father's tomb, the church, the forest. BASIL is again dressed for riding, with boots and whip. He sits with GRUNDIG at a table strewn with papers.

GRUNDIG: I believe you don't understand double entry book-keeping, Sir?

BASIL: [*preoccupied*] No, I'm afraid I don't.

GRUNDIG: Well, Peter Jack understands, so that's all right, he'll explain it all, don't you worry. You see, here we have last year's accounts, broken down according to the various sources of revenue. The home farm is kept separate here in this schedule. And the forestry account here. The rest is divided under, beef cattle—

BASIL: So you don't think it's serious?

GRUNDIG: I don't, Sir. These peasants are dishonest people and they're such fantastic people. Especially in the winter. I sometimes think they get a little bit mad. My wife and my little daughter say that when I've been over here for a while in the winter I get a little bit mad too. They say it just to tease me of course. Oh these peasants— I sometimes wonder if they are lying or if they really can't tell the difference between what's real and what they dream about.

BASIL: You think they just invented this story of the— murder?

GRUNDIG: I do, Sir. I think it's very likely. They're completely self-centred people, always on the make, always trying to draw attention to themselves. They want to get money out of you, that's what's behind it all.

BASIL: I can't believe that of Peter Jack and Hans Joseph and Father Ambrose.

GRUNDIG: The priest is the worst of the lot, Sir, they

always are. You'd be surprised. These little country priests that go around in rags and look so humble, you'll find in nine cases out of ten they're the local money-lender and a regular blood-sucker to their clients.

BASIL: I don't know what to think. This morning with the sun shining it all seems like a bad dream.

GRUNDIG: Don't you worry, Sir, it'll be all right, don't you worry then.

BASIL: I suppose you'll be leaving us, now that the weather's changed.

GRUNDIG: That's right, Sir, I'll be off this afternoon. It makes a lovely sleigh-ride when the sun is shining on the tree-tops, makes you feel good to be alive on a day like this. I shall wrap up well of course—

BASIL: I can't believe they were lying last night. Not Peter Jack and—no. I must investigate, I must get to the bottom of this business.

GRUNDIG: I should leave it alone if I were you, Sir, I should leave it absolutely alone. It doesn't do to over-excite these people.

BASIL: But suppose something awful did really happen—

GRUNDIG: Well, Sir, suppose it did. *We* can never find out from *them* what it was. There'll just be muddle on the top of muddle. They're so fantastical and they exaggerate so. And it's always wanting money that's behind it. You take my advice, Sir, and simply forget about it.

BASIL: I can't!

GRUNDIG: Leave well alone, is my motto. Let sleeping dogs lie.

BASIL: Besides now—after what I told you about—last night—they'll all know that I know and they'll expect me to do something.

GRUNDIG: It's just as likely, Sir, that they'll expect you to do nothing, and that's what I advise you to do. And if any of them has the impertinence to make any further reference to the matter just tell them that you don't know what they're talking about. They'll soon be quiet when they see they aren't going to get anything out of you.

[*Enter* ORIANE, *dressed for out-of-doors.*]

BASIL: Oriane, Mr Grundig thinks we shouldn't take this thing seriously. He thinks they may have invented it anyway.

GRUNDIG: Or exaggerated it out of some incident, who knows. They're so fantastical. Don't you worry then.

ORIANE: I had just come to exactly the same conclusion myself, Mr Grundig. I've been talking the matter over with Frederic this morning. Frederic is so calm and sensible, it's quite a relief to talk to him. I think we should ignore the whole thing.

BASIL: That's what Mr Grundig says.

GRUNDIG: That's right, Ma'am. It's just a sort of servants' impertinence.

ORIANE: I think you must try to keep these people at a distance, Basil. You've encouraged them too much. Then they take liberties. Don't you agree, Mr Grundig?

GRUNDIG: Exactly.

ORIANE: You ought to be much more remote. Why should they know what you're thinking or imagine they can converse with you as equals? No wonder their heads are turned.

GRUNDIG: I agree with her ladyship. A little secretiveness is always a good thing in a situation of this sort. Even a little mystification.

ORIANE: This is a real chance for you to assert yourself, Basil. Not in a sort of meaningless way, like having that poor gipsy beaten, but in a way that will make these people respect you. Show them that you're not upset by their antics and that you propose to go on as if nothing had happened, and just don't be so friendly with them from now on. Their conduct last night was most offensive.

BASIL: But supposing my father did murder Francis James?

ORIANE: I'm sure he didn't. And anyway it's no concern of ours.

GRUNDIG: Her ladyship is right.

BASIL: You are going out, Oriane?

ORIANE: Yes. I've decided it's such a lovely day I'll take a drive around. I haven't really stirred outside since we came. I've told them to bring the big sleigh round to the front door. There it is. [*Sound of sleigh bells.*]

GRUNDIG: I should take the road round by the mill and the lake, your ladyship. The driver will know. The lake is very beautiful frozen with the reeds all bright crimson and the water birds walking on the ice.

ORIANE: You are poetical today, Mr Grundig. It all looks so delightful this morning, I feel quite glad to be in the country! Aren't you glad that I'm glad, Basil?

BASIL: Yes, Oriane, my darling!

ORIANE: Well, I'm off. You pay attention to Mr Grundig, Basil. He understands this place better than you do. I'm sure he knows best. [*Exit.*]

BASIL: I wish I knew what to do.

GRUNDIG: Could I just show you this, Sir.

BASIL: Yes, yes. All the same, when we've finished the accounts I think I'll go round to the Servants' Hall.

GRUNDIG: Very unwise, Sir, if I may say so. Your father never went near the Servants' Hall.

BASIL: In that case I shall certainly go!

[*The Servants' Hall. Mass is in progress. A rather dim scene, incense, an impression of a lot of people kneeling. An impressive plain song chant, strong and very solemn.* FATHER AMBROSE *obscurely officiates. Enter* BASIL. *Sudden silence. Everything stops. The servants fade away, with the exception of* FATHER AMBROSE, PETER JACK *and* HANS JOSEPH.]

BASIL: I'm sorry. I didn't realise you were celebrating Mass. I wouldn't have dreamt of interrupting. And now everyone's—gone away. I'm terribly sorry—I didn't mean to butt in—

AMBROSE: That's all right, your honour.

BASIL: Peter Jack, could I speak to you. No, don't go. What we—talked about last night. Was it—serious?

PETER JACK: I don't understand.

BASIL: I mean, did that really happen, what you said happened? It wasn't just a fiction, something you'd all invented?

[PETER JACK *and* HANS JOSEPH *are silent, affronted.*]

AMBROSE: [*after a pause*] It really happened.

BASIL: You must forgive me, I— Obviously this thing must be—gone into. I thought at first that some sort of public enquiry—with all the servants present—would be what would be most—proper. But I've been thinking it over and I feel that—as you said, Peter—one can't undo what has been done and—it may be better to be discreet and prudent and—not stir things up too much. Something must be done by way of—dealing with the thing—but I think now that this had best be settled privately between me and the people most closely concerned, that is you and Hans Joseph and Maxim and Marina.

PETER JACK: What had you got in mind, your honour?

BASIL: Well the only kind of—compensation I can make, as far as I can see, is a material one. I mean a financial one. I know it's impossible to put a price on something of this sort—but money and land and material advantages such as I have it in my power to give are at least a token of a payment for what has happened.

[PETER JACK *shakes his head almost with disgust.*]

HANS JOSEPH: Your honour—it is not thinkable that I should accept money in return for the life of my only son.

PETER JACK: That's no use, Sir.

BASIL: Well, what is of use? Help me, friends, please. I want to do what's right. Also I don't want it all to get somehow —out of hand—I want to see clearly. Father, what do you think?

AMBROSE: That the past should be pardoned and let alone.

HANS JOSEPH: Pardoned, no. The past is too strong for us.

AMBROSE: If power must be met with power and strength with strength, consider that pardon is the greatest power of all. You are an old man. As you hope for mercy when you confront your maker let this thing go. What you do will influence the others.

HANS JOSEPH: I do not hope for mercy. I do not even hope for justice. The God I worshipped has grown old with me and died before me. When I lie in that churchyard all that there is of me will lie there. I heard my son cry out.

BASIL: Please. Let us, the four of us, form ourselves into a sort of—committee—to deal with this matter and keep it between ourselves.

HANS JOSEPH: Everyone knows what has happened. Everyone is waiting. There must be satisfaction.

BASIL: You mean—public satisfaction, of some kind. Is there nothing I can do—I would willingly—what do you think, Father—would some kind of public penance meet the case? Suppose I were to, I don't know, bind myself to act as a servant, to perform some sort of menial work here for a period of time. I know this sounds mad, but you speak of paying and I haven't anything to pay with.

PETER JACK: Except—

HANS JOSEPH: No, no, you are the master here, it would be most unbecoming. People would be shocked and upset and would think it was some kind of mockery.

BASIL: Well, what am I to do? Or since you won't accept any of my suggestions, why should I do anything? I am a completely innocent person. I wasn't even here at the time.

AMBROSE: Hans Joseph, you know that his honour's father was insane.

BASIL: That's right, he was insane! A mad person can't be guilty of anything.

HANS JOSEPH: That was not madness. Pain is pain and blood is blood.

AMBROSE: Then the guilt is ours. We were here.

HANS JOSEPH: His honour is our representative and our head.

BASIL: Then am I not to be obeyed, even in this?

HANS JOSEPH: Where the head is, there the prime guilt lies. There are laws to which even your honour is subject.

BASIL: Hans Joseph, what are you going to do? You dressed me as a child, you taught me to fish.

HANS JOSEPH: I don't know, your honour. You ask me questions and I answer them.

BASIL: This is all absurd and—nightmarish.

PETER JACK: It isn't just Hans Joseph, your honour, and it isn't only Francis James. There have been so many other things. Almost everyone here nurses some unforgettable indelible wound, and these wounds cry out inevitably for satisfaction. What happened to Francis James has become a symbol for everybody. There was not one of us who was not mortally afraid. We were divided against each other. We all consented to shameful things, to things that we detested. This is not forgiven either. We cannot forgive ourselves—or each other—or him—or you. Perhaps it would have been better if you had never known this at all, or if you had simply silenced us and taken no responsibility. Your concern about this thing looks like weakness and weakness looks like guilt. People who would have obeyed you without a thought if you had been more like your father are reflecting and brooding upon the past. I do not want to alarm your honour, but it could be that you have now become something like an outlaw among us.

BASIL: An outlaw in my own house!

PETER JACK: These are simple people, Sir, and the idea of blood guilt is very real to them. They can bow to you and obey you and even love you, but this might not stop one of them from—

BASIL: Killing me.

PETER JACK: Anyone who did so would be protected. But there are just—possibilities—

BASIL: What do you advise me to do?

PETER JACK: Mr Grundig is leaving here today. I would advise you to go with him.

[*The Bedroom, lit by bright snowy light.* FREDERIC *is helping* ORIANE *to take off her coat and boots.* HANS JOSEPH *is on his knees.* MIKEY *sits unobserved in a corner.*]

HANS JOSEPH: But your ladyship, I cannot make pepper out of nothing. There is no pepper.

ORIANE: You haven't looked properly, there must be. I'll look myself. [*She clanks the bunch of keys which lies on the table*]. And if I find any you'll be in trouble.

[*Exit* HANS JOSEPH, *bowing.*]

FREDERIC: Did Madam have a pleasant drive?

ORIANE: It was lovely! The lake was so beautiful in the sun. And all the trees were glittering.

FREDERIC: Just like fairyland, Madam.

ORIANE: Ouf, I feel quite tired after breathing all that cold air!

FREDERIC: Would Madam like to change her dress?

ORIANE: Yes, I think I will. You are becoming quite an efficient ladies' maid, Frederic.

[FREDERIC *helps her off with her dress, helps her on with another one, and buttons up the back.* MIKEY *peers over the bed.*] Ooh, what's that? It's the boy. Whatever are you doing here boy?

MIKEY: I thought you said I could come and be with you always.

ORIANE: I didn't say anything of the sort. You must wait until you're sent for. You are a servant, not a member of the family. Run along now.

[FREDERIC *sees* MIKEY *to the door.*]

FREDERIC: [*unheard by* ORIANE] Clear off. We don't want you hanging around here watching and listening. Go away and stay away. [*He kicks* MIKEY *out.*]

ORIANE: Poor child. I'm afraid he's not very bright. Thank you, Frederic. You know, you are a great support to me Frederic. It's like a bit of—home—you know.

FREDERIC: I am glad that Madam thinks so. I went down to the cellar where the trunks are and I got what Madam asked me to find.

ORIANE: Oh you found it? Give it to me.

[FREDERIC *gives* ORIANE *a pistol.*]

Good. I knew there was one. Is it loaded? Yes. Not a word to your master, Frederic. He would not approve.

FREDERIC: I hope Madam will feel safer now.

ORIANE: Yes, I will, much safer. Not that there's anything to worry about, of course. It was all a false alarm—some peasant fantasy. Mr Grundig said they'd probably invented it all.

FREDERIC: Just what I said to Madam.

ORIANE: If we ignore it and show we're not interested it'll all just—blow away. Ooh! What was that noise?

FREDERIC: Snow falling off the roof, Madam.

ORIANE: I'm nervy. Set out the table for cards, would you, Frederic.

[*He sets the table and they begin to play cards.*]

Are the Servants' Hall still cold-shouldering you?

FREDERIC: Yes, Madam.

ORIANE: You mustn't mind. You belong up here with me —with us. Did you see the gipsy?

FREDERIC: Yes, Madam.

ORIANE: What did he say?

FREDERIC: He groaned.

ORIANE: He was a fool to get himself into trouble. He's a weak man. I think I won't take him up after all.

FREDERIC: I'm glad to hear that, Madam.

ORIANE: Why are you glad to hear that, Frederic?

FREDERIC: [*after a moment's silence and a glance at* ORIANE] Madam has won again.

ORIANE: Are you missing Annabelle, Frederic?

FREDERIC: No, Madam. I am very glad that Annabelle is not here.

ORIANE: Are you? Why are you glad that Annabelle is not here, Frederic?

[*As* ORIANE *reaches across the table to pick up the cards* FREDERIC, *with deliberation, lays his hand down on top of her hand.*]

You have put your hand on top of my hand. What does that mean, I wonder?

FREDERIC: Madam knows what it means.

ORIANE: Take it away.

FREDERIC: Madam knows why I came here to this terrible place.

ORIANE: Yes. Frederic, please take your hand away.

[*He slowly lifts* ORIANE's *unprotesting hand, kisses it, and relinquishes it. They regard each other. Just too late to see any of this, enter* BASIL.]

BASIL: Oh, Oriane, I wondered if you were back from your drive. I must talk to you. Frederic, please.

[*Exit* FREDERIC.]

I've been talking to them in the Servants' Hall.

ORIANE: You mustn't *talk* to them, Basil!

BASIL: I had to. I couldn't just leave it. I'm afraid it's much more serious than we thought. And yet it's so nebulous— I just don't understand.

ORIANE: Serious? You mean—?

BASIL: This is no joke, Oriane. It did happen, what they said. It seems mad—but these people are dangerous.

ORIANE: You ought never to have listened to them. Oh Basil, I wish we hadn't come here, I *begged* you not to come here! They could easily murder us and no one would ever know. I think they're all mad in this awful place with the darkness and the snow and—Basil, I think we ought to go away at once.

BASIL: That's what Peter Jack said.

ORIANE: Then we must.

BASIL: It's unthinkable, Oriane.

ORIANE: I'll pack straightaway, just a few things. Mr Grundig is going and we could go with him.

BASIL: No. Oriane, if I ran away from this I could never hold up my head again.

ORIANE: Don't let us die for your dignity, Basil.

BASIL: It's more than dignity. All my life I've felt that some sort of test was coming to me. I've spoken to you about this before. Well, this is it.

ORIANE: Basil, consider me even if you don't consider yourself. Oh, if only my brother the General were here! At least let Mr Grundig inform the police when he gets to the town.

BASIL: I can't invoke the police against my own servants! If I'm ever to belong here properly I've got to go right through with this thing. It's a test. I think in a curious way *they* see it as a test too. I can master this situation, Oriane.

ORIANE: I think we should go, Basil. If we don't go now the blizzards will start and the roads will be closed and we shall be trapped.

[*Enter, after knocking*, GRUNDIG.]

Oh Mr Grundig, I'm so frightened. Do persuade my husband that we ought to go away.

BASIL: I'm afraid it's a serious matter, Mr Grundig, and not quite like what you thought.

GRUNDIG: Don't you worry then—

BASIL: Oh I'm going to manage all right—

GRUNDIG: They're like children, these people. They get excited about something and then they forget it again directly.

ORIANE: I do wish you were staying here, Mr Grundig. You're so normal—and ordinary—and real.

GRUNDIG: I just came in to say goodbye. My sleigh is waiting at the door. I must be getting back to my wife and my little daughter. They'll say I stayed on here because of the good food. "Daddy's getting fat," they say. They do tease me so!

ORIANE: Do you or don't you think that we should leave?

GRUNDIG: I really can't advise your ladyship, it's not for me—

ORIANE: All right, you won't commit yourself. But I notice *you*'re pretty anxious to get away!

BASIL: Oriane, don't be silly. Mr Grundig is just going home to his family. Look, if you feel nervous and want to go I think you should leave now with Mr Grundig. I'm sure he'd wait half an hour while you packed up some things. I must stay here but there's no reason why you should.

ORIANE: [*pause*] No. I can't go away and leave you. If you stay, I stay.

BASIL: Thank you. My darling. Well, goodbye, Mr Grundig. I hope you have a pleasant journey. Please give our regards to your wife and daughter.

GRUNDIG: [*bowing*] Goodbye, don't you worry, goodbye, goodbye.

[*Exit* GRUNDIG. *After a moment his sleigh bells are heard diminishing into the distance.* BASIL *tries to embrace* ORIANE *but she eludes him. They listen to the fading sound of the bells.*]

[*The cupboard.* PATRICE, *defeated, lies prostrate. He groans softly. Enter* MIKEY *with a letter.* PATRICE *looks up eagerly.*]

MIKEY: No, it's not from her. It's just your own letter back again. She wouldn't take it.

PATRICE: Was she with *him*?

MIKEY: Yes.

PATRICE: [*groan*].

MIKEY: Are you all right, Patrice?

PATRICE: If it were not that a gipsy never wishes himself dead I would be wishing myself dead. Yes, I'm all right, Mikey. I'm fine.

MIKEY: Patrice—

PATRICE: Yes.

86

MIKEY: It's got all dark.

PATRICE: Yes.

MIKEY: The sky's all dark yellow. It's like the end of the world.

PATRICE: There's going to be a snowstorm.

MIKEY: Patrice—

PATRICE: Yes.

MIKEY: What's that nasty smell.

PATRICE: A dead rat under the floor-boards.

MIKEY: It's so cold.

PATRICE: Yes.

MIKEY: Patrice, I'm frightened.

[*Enter* MAXIM.]

MAXIM: Well, gipsy, how is it with you? [PATRICE *does not reply.*] You feel it now, don't you. You know what it's like now. You thought you could stay outside and watch. See us under the yoke, and not feel it in your own flesh. How is it now, clever gipsy? You can't be neutral with something like this, you know. If you don't want it to destroy you, you've got to fight it or else clear out. [*Pause*] She won't come back to you, you know. Not after what's happened to you. Women are like that.

PATRICE: Shut up.

MAXIM: You were a splendid sight, crawling along on your knees, "Oh please, your honour, please, your honour—"

PATRICE: Go away.

MAXIM: I'm sorry for you. I didn't come here to mock you. Really. I've just come to give Mikey his reading lesson.

MIKEY: I'm not going to learn to read. Ever, ever, ever!

MAXIM: None of that, Mikey, now, Come here. Where's your book? Here it is. Now we'll look at this bit.

[MIKEY *pushes the book away.*]

Don't you want to read more about the tiger?

[MIKEY *tears the book up.* MAXIM *cuffs him, and* MIKEY *bursts into tears.*]

All right. Stay stupid.

[*The wind is heard howling.*]

It's snowing again. This is your freedom, gipsy. Stupidity, ignorance, hunger, cold, servitude— Goodnight.

[*The Servants' Hall.* MARINA *and* PETER JACK.]

PETER JACK: You really didn't want to read his letter?

MARINA: No.

PETER JACK: Marina, are you sure—?

MARINA: Do stop! I've finished with him. Oh how I wish I had a real man in my life!

PETER JACK: I'm sorry—

MARINA: Don't be *sorry*!

PETER JACK: You don't want to go away with the gipsy any more?

MARINA: I don't want anything any more.

PETER JACK: You're sure—?

MARINA: I've become bad. Perhaps it was the old man. He was so wicked—and I—because he cared for me I—so many awful things happened.

PETER JACK: We were all in that. When you marry me we'll live quietly and make everything ordinary and good. Won't we? Darling?

MARINA: Things can never be ordinary and good for me. Ever since I was ten no man has passed me by without pawing me.

PETER JACK: Marina—

MARINA: Listen to the wind. I feel so frightened and sort of shuddering in my heart. Peter, you know that I didn't have anything to do with my husband's death.

PETER JACK: Of course I know.

MARINA: Some people here think—God knows what they think. Hans Joseph is so terrible to me sometimes, when he looks at me he reminds me of the old man.

PETER JACK: The old man made other people become like him.

MARINA: You haven't become like him.

PETER JACK: Dear—

MARINA: It's snowing so dreadfully. I've never seen such snow. It'll bury the world.

PETER JACK: We'll get married, won't we?

MARINA: I'd always want to run away.

PETER JACK: Marina, we'll get married—

MARINA: I'd run away in the end. I care for you. I've always lived here. And I love his honour, I love him. But —Oh Peter, I'm so terribly frightened for his honour.

PETER JACK: So am I.

MARINA: Surely nobody would hurt him?

PETER JACK: I don't know.

MARINA: Can't you protect him somehow?

PETER JACK: I don't see how I can.

MARINA: Oh how I wish I had a real man in my life!

PETER JACK: Marina—

MARINA: I'd run away! I'd run away!

[*The White Drawing Room.* BASIL *and* PETER JACK. BASIL *is in riding kit with boots and whip.*]

BASIL: I don't understand.

PETER JACK: Let me explain again.

BASIL: It's an impossible idea!

PETER JACK: It is an assertion of authority, an act of power. Everybody would recognise it. After it you would be accepted, you would become as your father was— untouchable.

BASIL: So then I would become my father. No. This is too much like magic.

PETER JACK: Magic is what is needed. Magic is what everyone will understand. We live in a magical world.

BASIL: Anyway it's immoral! Marina would view this idea with repugnance.

PETER JACK: I don't think so, your honour. You see, it is a tradition and what is traditional is accepted. Nothing new is ever quite so real here as what is old. You are new, Sir, and this is one reason why you are in danger. Your father maintained the tradition of your forefathers. Whenever

any girl upon the estate got married it was with your
father that she spent the wedding night.

BASIL: I had heard this said of my great grandfather. I
didn't dream my father still—did it. *Droit de Seigneur.
Ius primae noctis.* It was certainly customary in the past
in various parts of the world for the master to deflower
every man's bride. But here and in this age! Why ever
was it tolerated?

PETER JACK: It may seem strange to you, but your father
was admired even though he was feared, and loved even
though he was hated. People prize what is big.

BASIL: Yes. God help them. But, Peter, let me get this clear.
You are suggesting that when you marry Marina—she
should spend—the wedding night—with me.

PETER JACK: Yes, your honour.

BASIL: And this would be generally known?

PETER JACK: Everything in this house is known. And if you
would be good enough to give the bride away, as your
father always did, it would be assumed—

BASIL: [*laughing madly*] God! But would *you* endure this?
Why?

PETER JACK: I suggested that you should go away. I knew
that you would not go.

BASIL: Thank you.

PETER JACK: In remaining here you remain, for the time
at least, in danger. Everyone here suffered at the hands
of your father and everyone has a motive for a revenge
which could not be taken against him and which is for
that reason more bitter. When human beings are deeply
hurt, these hurts do not go away, they bide their time. In
acknowledging your father's guilt you have been weakened in the eyes of the household. Wolves will pursue if
they scent blood. This weakness is the scent of blood.
Your father had no such frailty. It is your virtues which
have put you into danger.

BASIL: And are my vices to pull me out again? I can't

regard this as just a custom. If I sleep with Marina on your wedding night I am an adulterer.

PETER JACK: It is the key, your honour. Because of her relations with your father Marina holds a very special place here, she is a person of great significance and power. She could confer that power upon you. Because of her position she has been regarded with resentment of course, but also with respect, even with awe. A great prostitute is a great symbolic force. She has been like a goddess among us.

BASIL: And if I were to, as it were, marry her, I would become—a god.

PETER JACK: Exactly.

BASIL: But would people accept this, would Hans Joseph accept it?

PETER JACK: Yes. He would accept it as a sign that you were not to be touched. You would become a sacred object.

BASIL: You think there is real danger?

PETER JACK: Certainly until the spring. When the snows melt there is less madness in the soul. Now I fear for you every moment. We have had six months of sitting in judgment upon your father. And such a terrible judgment demands its victim.

BASIL: I don't want to die for my father. But that *you* should suggest this—

PETER JACK: Marina loves you.

BASIL: Only because I'm— Doesn't that make it worse? I confess I find her very attractive. How can you—offer her to me? I suppose it would have to be a—real night together, wouldn't it?

PETER JACK: Oh yes. You see. It's like this. I've loved Marina all my life. She has always caused me the most terrible pain. She always will cause me pain even as my wife. I know that. People don't change. I can face suffering, I've never really known anything else. What I can't face is the prospect of—death.

BASIL: You mean—

PETER JACK: If Marina went away from here, if I lost her, if I didn't know where she was any more. She very nearly went away with the gipsy. Even if she were married to me she might still run away, with him, with anybody. There's enough wildness in her soul, poor child. I can't hold her, I can't keep her, by myself.

BASIL: You want my help. You want me to—anchor her here.

PETER JACK: Yes. If you would only do this thing she would stay—with us—forever.

BASIL: No. Peter. You couldn't bear to be beholden to me in this way.

PETER JACK: Why not? She is not the only being whom I have loved ever since I was a child. You are a guiltless man and you are the master here. You and only you can transform this action into something else. There is a power of redemption in you which once it is released will be universally recognised.

BASIL: An odd way to redeem.

PETER JACK: I could not hate *you* for this.

BASIL: I wonder if you can be certain. You might kill me for it all the same.

PETER JACK: It will be an act of reconciling. Marina was Francis James's wife. You will put yourself in her power. A woman kills a man in love, so they say.

BASIL: Have you ever made love to a woman?

PETER JACK: No.

BASIL: Magic. I fear it. It's a step backward. It's dangerous.

PETER JACK: Who can rule without it? And sometimes, by some people, magical power can be transformed into spiritual power.

BASIL: Hmmm. I wonder what my wife will think about all this?

[*The Bedroom*. ORIANE *and* FREDERIC *are playing cards*.]

ORIANE: That's yours.

FREDERIC: You will let me talk to you.

ORIANE: I don't see how I can stop you.

FREDERIC: I love you.

ORIANE: My deal, I think.

FREDERIC: In this place we are a man and a woman together.

ORIANE: You are not attending to the game.

FREDERIC: This is no game. We are a man and a woman together, struggling, fighting.

ORIANE: Dear me, why fighting?

FREDERIC: Because any real encounter of human beings is a fight. The fight of one human soul for recognition by another. Human beings hardly ever really meet at all. They turn away, they close their eyes, they will do anything rather than endure another person face to face. But in love, and perhaps only in love, people meet. And when they meet they fight. As we are fighting now.

ORIANE: You are very romantic, Frederic.

FREDERIC: Look at me.

ORIANE: [*still busy with the cards, not looking at him*] It's probably all those novels you read.

FREDERIC: Romantic! I was born in a city slum among horrors which you would faint even to hear of. Only my cleverness prevented me from becoming a criminal or going insane. I am a hard real person. I am probably the hardest and realest person that you have ever met. The people in your world are soft, they're all hazy with luxury and idleness and vague useless thoughts. Even when they think themselves serious they are being stupidly frivolous. I may not be a very nice man but I am a real man.

ORIANE: You are an interesting person, Frederic. I have always felt this. Far too bright to be a valet.

[*As they talk they contrive to play cards,* FREDERIC *looking at* ORIANE *and* ORIANE *looking at the cards.*]

FREDERIC: You never felt anything of the sort. You never saw me at all. All you saw was a valet. But I am not a valet. I pretend to be a valet just as some people pretend to be masters. We produce the gestures which other people expect. It's a charade. But between us two now let there be no more play-acting. Please. Oriane.

ORIANE: You mustn't call me like that.

[*She looks at him at last and the cards are laid down.*]

FREDERIC: What's in a name? It thrills you, it brings the colour into your cheeks. So, I can make you blush. Yes. Be your real self with me. As perhaps you have never been.

ORIANE: Perhaps—

FREDERIC: Oriane— Oriane—

ORIANE: You mustn't—

FREDERIC: Why not? Who makes rules for us two? Be present to me. Give me your hand. You let me hold it once. You didn't resist.

[*He takes her hand.*]

ORIANE: I ought to have—

FREDERIC: You couldn't. I felt in your hand that you cared for me.

ORIANE: Then my hand knew more than I did.

FREDERIC: Let me kiss it for that knowledge. Oriane, we belong together here. This place rejects us both.

ORIANE: [*spellbound*] Yes—

FREDERIC: Stop thinking that you are holding the hand of your valet. You are not. Look. Really look.

[*He leads her to a settee. They stare at each other now without touching.*]

ORIANE: This is mad.

FREDERIC: It is real. That's why it seems so strange. Stop dreaming, Oriane. You grew up in a dream, you got married in a dream. You've lived inside conventions all your life. They've taken the edge off everything. You've never faced the really unexpected, have you. Even here you had to run away, you had to retire into your little dreamy corner. You ran away, up here, into this room. And what do you find here? Me.

ORIANE: Frederic, please—

FREDERIC: You're frightened. Let the unexpected take you by surprise and make you real. Taste reality at last, Oriane. Taste it. Here.

[*He kisses her gently.*]

ORIANE: Frederic, you—startle me so.

FREDERIC: I startle you into existing. It's painful.

ORIANE: Yes.

FREDERIC: It's beautiful.

ORIANE: Yes.

FREDERIC: Come.

[*He draws her to him and they begin to kiss passionately. Enter* BASIL, *dressed as in the last scene, holding* MIKEY *by the shoulder.* FREDERIC *and* ORIANE *spring apart.* BASIL *hurls* MIKEY *from him.* BASIL *is stunned, puts his hand to his head, then springs upon* FREDERIC, *throws him to the ground, and strikes him with the whip.* FREDERIC *does not resist.*]

BASIL: [*thick with emotion*] Get—out—get—out.

[FREDERIC *crawls, then runs away.*]

I didn't believe the boy, I couldn't believe—

ORIANE: You mean Mikey told you? That was nice of him. Whatever did he tell you?

BASIL: He said he saw Frederic taking your dress off.

ORIANE: He was just helping me.

BASIL: And now, I suppose!

ORIANE: Well, well, I surprise you, Basil. The unexpected.

BASIL: Oh Oriane, Oriane, don't speak in that tone—

ORIANE: Don't take on so.

BASIL: What do you expect me to do when I come in and find you kissing one of the servants?

ORIANE: He's not a servant. He's Frederic.

BASIL: I'll dismiss him, I'll—

ORIANE: You're just as primitive as those peasants! You humiliate me utterly and I won't forgive you.

BASIL: What do you mean?

ORIANE: I won't forgive you. You brought me to this horrible place against my will.

BASIL: You keep saying that, but it has nothing to do with this!

ORIANE: It has, it has. Oh get out, you humiliate me!

BASIL: I should have thought that you'd humiliated yourself! There was something important I wanted to tell you. But perhaps it had better wait. Oh dear! Oriane, I'm sorry.

ORIANE: I loathe and despise you and your "I'm sorry".

BASIL: Oriane—

ORIANE: Go away. *Please.*

[*Exit* BASIL. MIKEY, *who has been crouching by the bed makes a dash for the door but is caught by* ORIANE.]

Why did you do this? Why did you make up this story about me?

MIKEY: [*struggling*] It wasn't a story.

ORIANE: Why did you do it?

MIKEY: You said you'd love me and you didn't—

[MIKEY *escapes.* ORIANE *dissolves into tears.*]

[*The White Drawing Room.* BASIL *is dressed in his best clothes. He adjusts his cravat. Enter* PETER JACK *leading* MARINA.]

PETER JACK: Here she is, your honour.

BASIL: Peter, you will stay and—?

PETER JACK: No, no, it's better that you should talk to each other alone. [*To* MARINA] Don't be shy.

[*Exit* PETER JACK. BASIL *and* MARINA *are both very embarrassed.*]

BASIL: Marina, I expect that Peter Jack has told you of his rather unusual—idea—concerning you and me.

MARINA: Yes, your honour.

BASIL: I cannot sufficiently emphasise—Marina—that this—plan—is entirely dependent upon your free consent and approval. And if, as you may well, you feel any reluctance or any misgivings—

MARINA: Oh I don't, your honour!

BASIL: You—don't—

MARINA: No, I'm very pleased—I mean—I'm very anxious to do whatever you expect of me, your honour.

BASIL: This is rather—special—Marina—and far beyond what a master could reasonably expect of his servant.

MARINA: I am—yours.

BASIL: I think we must be very serious-minded about this, Marina. I mean—we are not just two people—a man and a woman—who are—er—envisaging—what we are envisaging—for—er—any mere reasons of private preference. You understand me.

MARINA: [*faintly*] Yes.

BASIL: It is rather a matter of sacrificing—er offering—ourselves for the benefit of the whole community.

MARINA: [*wide-eyed*] Yes, your honour.

BASIL: Peter believes—and after careful reflection I agree with him—that this rather strange device—my spending—we must be clear and frank with each other—your wedding night with you—with all that that implies—

MARINA: Yes, your honour.

BASIL: That this will resolve the crisis in my authority which has arisen out of the actions of my father.

MARINA: Yes, your honour.

BASIL: What we will be performing, Marina, will not be, really, a carnal action.

MARINA: No, your honour.

BASIL: It will be a—magical action—and yet also something—more than that. Sometimes, by some people, magical power can be transformed into spiritual power. It will be an action of reconciliation and healing of which we must both of us attempt to be worthy.

MARINA: Yes, your honour.

BASIL: It may seem strange to regard such a thing as a duty, but it must be so regarded by both of us.

MARINA: Yes.

BASIL: Otherwise we are—

MARINA: Yes.

BASIL: Well, that was what I wanted to say to you.

MARINA: Thank you, your honour. [*Pause*] I wonder if perhaps we could meet again just—before—you know—

BASIL: Yes, I'm sure we should have another—little chat—we're a bit shy and constrained with each other, aren't we? But after all we have been—friends a long time.

[*He makes as if to take her hand and then draws back awkwardly.*] Yes, we must meet again, Marina. Yes, well, that will be all for now. I'm glad you er— Thank you, thank you.

[*Exit* MARINA. BASIL *touches his temples gently, confused.*]

[*The Bedroom.* BASIL *and* ORIANE.]

ORIANE: I've never heard of anything more extraordinary in my life!

BASIL: The whole situation is extraordinary.

ORIANE: Marina and Peter Jack are going to get married tomorrow and you are proposing to spend tomorrow night with Marina.

BASIL: It's an old custom—

ORIANE: Oh I've heard of such things. But, Basil, either you're being very naive or else you've gone mad or—

BASIL: Oriane, I've *explained*. The danger we are in is a real danger. I've never been properly accepted here. And people who hated my father could very well take their revenge upon me. If I don't do something to assert myself —to, as Peter Jack put it, make myself untouchable—

ORIANE: You seem to be planning to make yourself rather touchable tomorrow night.

BASIL: Oriane, I hope you don't think—

ORIANE: That you're doing it out of vulgar inclination? Oh I'm sure you imagine you're doing it from lofty rational motives.

BASIL: You are a very intelligent woman, Oriane. Not every wife could be asked to understand something like this.

ORIANE: No, indeed! I wonder what my brother the General will think of these antics?

BASIL: There is no reason why he should know.

ORIANE: Oh I shall certainly tell him.

BASIL: I'm glad you're taking it so calmly.

ORIANE: We both of us seem to have a penchant for the Servants' Hall.

BASIL: Oriane, I've told you—

ORIANE: Better dead than dishonoured is evidently a slogan which doesn't appeal to you. I agree. It doesn't appeal to me either.

BASIL: Oriane—

ORIANE: Marina is one of those plump semi-conscious charmers whom for no very clear reason all men seem to want. You can't make this into a spiritual action, Basil. Do be honest. I see that it's a highly significant action and may well impress your simple peasantry in just the way that that cunning fellow Peter Jack anticipates. But something like this has many meanings and you can't just isolate it as a piece of magic. What it comes to is that Peter Jack thinks that half a wife is better than no woman.

BASIL: He did admit to me that he hoped that this would help to keep Marina here.

ORIANE: Exactly. And is he happy to envisage a permanent relationship of this sort between you and his wife?

BASIL: Of course not! No such thing is in question!

ORIANE: Isn't it? It might come to that, Basil.

BASIL: No! I—

ORIANE: Perhaps Peter Jack can't manage on his own.

BASIL: Oriane!

ORIANE: You've always wanted a prostitute.

BASIL: Really—I—

ORIANE: We've tried equality, Basil, and it hasn't worked. You're better off with a servant. A fat domestic damsel with easy morals and no mind. You expected some sort of happiness out of marriage which you haven't had.

BASIL: So did you. I haven't made you happy, Oriane. You never really wanted me.

ORIANE: Yes. Our trouble has been very deep. And now. I'm not really important. You're taking your final revenge upon your father. That's what it's all about. He's dead and you've got his girl. He's lying cold in his grave and you're just going to get into bed with Marina. What a moment of triumph.

BASIL: Oriane, that is *not* what it's about!

ORIANE: Oh how I wish I'd married a real man, with real power in him. Someone like my brother—or your father—

BASIL: [*after a pause*] Oriane, I'm sorry. We've had our difficulties. But you are my wife and I love you. And you could have gone away with Grundig and you didn't. And—

ORIANE: Ach. I was a fool. Once you start with this girl you won't stop.

BASIL: I promise you—

ORIANE: Go, Basil, please. I'm perfectly calm, as you see. I accept your plan. I don't like it but I see its point. I'm a very rational very exceptional woman. Now go and— make your wedding plans.

BASIL: Oriane, you do understand—

ORIANE: Yes.

BASIL: It is all right, isn't it—?

ORIANE: Yes, yes, of course.

[*Exit* BASIL. *It is now clear that* ORIANE *is very upset indeed. After a moment, enter* FREDERIC.]

FREDERIC: I was listening.

ORIANE: How dare you.

FREDERIC: Well, really, what an idea. He's got some nerve, hasn't he? If I was you—

ORIANE: Do not address me in that familiar way.

FREDERIC: Oriane—

ORIANE: I'm sorry. I am a very foolish woman. But the spell, such as it was, is broken. It amused me to flirt with you, because you are a valet. It amused me to hear you use my Christian name, because you are a valet. It is sometimes exciting to break a taboo. But there was nothing more. There was no encounter of human beings such as you dreamt of. You and I cannot meet. We are mistress and servant to each other until the end of the world.

FREDERIC: Listen to me—

ORIANE: You spoke of being beyond the conventions, but when my husband appeared you crumpled up. You were ashamed. You let him beat you and you crawled away like a guilty thing. You could not defend either yourself or me. The conventions defeated you utterly. I cannot forgive you for that defeat. You have been the instrument of my humiliation. Something that never was before. Because of you I cannot prevent this nightmarish thing that is going to happen to me.

FREDERIC: Listen, Oriane. I am not really clever or successful or even lucky. Perhaps what I did was stupid. But I did speak to you from my own heart and for me it wasn't just something amusing. Do you think it's pleasant to wear a servant's mask all the time with somebody you care for? Can't you see me now as a man who's taken off his mask? Can't you see the difference between play-acting and truth? All right I was defeated. I'm not a hero, how could I not be defeated. But I took all those risks for your sake. Forgive me and don't reject me now. I have nothing else in this house but you.

ORIANE: Then you have nothing in this house. You don't understand what you've done. You've been destructive to me and I hate the sight of you. Go away.

FREDERIC: Please—

ORIANE: Go away and don't come near me again ever.
[*Exit* FREDERIC. *After a pause* ORIANE *brings out the pistol. She checks that it is loaded. She lifts it to her brow, puts it down, lifts it again. Enter* FATHER AMBROSE. *He takes the pistol from her.*]

AMBROSE: No.

ORIANE: Why did you come here?

AMBROSE: I was looking for Mikey.

ORIANE: He isn't here. I suppose now you'll say that God sent you to me at exactly this moment.

AMBROSE: No.

ORIANE: Why not?

AMBROSE: God does not exist, my child. Chance brought me here. Why were you thinking of doing this?

ORIANE: Humiliation. Despair. My husband is going to—with that woman.

AMBROSE: I know.

ORIANE: He found me kissing the valet.

AMBROSE: I know.

ORIANE: I feel too ashamed and—defeated—to live.

AMBROSE: I know these feelings.

ORIANE: I've got to do something violent.

AMBROSE: Yes. Humiliation can make one mad with the desire to pass on what one has suffered.

ORIANE: What do you know about this?

AMBROSE: We all carry secret burdens. But let it be a burden of suffering, my child, and not a burden of sin. It is always better to undergo a humiliation than to inflict it, even upon oneself.

ORIANE: Am I not free to do what I please with *this*? [*She indicates her own body.*]

AMBROSE: Through yourself you take aim at others. Keep the suffering and the shame quietly inside you. Do not try to pass them on. That is how the world is redeemed. That is what *he* means.
[*He points at the crucifix.*]

ORIANE: I thought you didn't believe in him.

AMBROSE: I believe in *him*.

ORIANE: So I must suffer what my husband proposes?

AMBROSE: Yes, my child.

ORIANE: Well, I won't. Worldly conspiring priest. Go, and take that thing with you. Go on.

[AMBROSE *takes down the crucifix and carries it away. A large blank cross-shaped mark is left on the wall where it has hung. Oriane looks after the departing priest. She picks up the pistol which still lies upon the table. Then she suddenly notices the cross and stares at it.*]

[*The White Drawing Room.* BASIL *and* MARINA *are embracing each other passionately.*]

BASIL: I'm sorry. It's never been like this. I feel as if I were in a dream and yet everything's huge and far more real than ever before. I've known you such a terribly long time. I can't remember a world without you. You belong to the roots of everything. It's so strange. Your face is somehow tied in memory to my dear mother's face. You were a child like myself then. And she died so young. But it's as if you've somehow carried on all her sweetness and her protectiveness.

MARINA: I couldn't protect you, then or later.

BASIL: I know.

MARINA: I've loved you always, from the very start.

BASIL: And I've loved you. I feel so free with you, so absolutely at home with you. It's all so—direct.

MARINA: Yes. I can hardly believe I'm really holding you like this, I've wanted to so often, I've imagined—I never dreamt this could be.

BASIL: You make me feel—oh— You've got all my happiness hidden somewhere about you.

MARINA: Then you've got it. Because you've got me. Basil, this is a real thing, isn't it? It's not just like for—playing a trick—

BASIL: It's real.

MARINA: We must keep it, mustn't we? I couldn't bear it if this was just a single moment.

BASIL: It's not of the nature of a single moment. We've discovered each other. It's odd how talking to you I feel that I'm hearing my own voice for the first time.

MARINA: But—your wife—what does she think?

BASIL: She accepts it all. She knows it's necessary. She isn't hostile. She is a very remarkable woman.

MARINA: A woman can pretend, even out of anger. She must hate me.

BASIL: Of course not.

MARINA: And what is necessary—is not *this*.

BASIL: She accepts it. Nothing will interfere with anything else. No one will be hurt. There will be reconciliation and healing at last. Marina.

MARINA: I am so happy to be your servant.

BASIL: You are not my servant. We don't have to play at masters and servants any more.

MARINA: Oh if only it were all different—I mean—we will keep this, won't we?

BASIL: Yes.

MARINA: We will meet often, won't we, and we'll be together like this—?

BASIL: Yes.

MARINA: After—tomorrow night?

BASIL: Yes.

MARINA: I'll be a good wife to Peter Jack and I'll make him happy, but I'll love you until the end of the world.

BASIL: Yes.

MARINA: We will be together, won't we?

BASIL: Yes, yes, yes.

MARINA: We'll be happy somehow.

BASIL: We'll be happy, Marina.

MARINA: I think, after tomorrow night, just to be in the same house with you and see you sometimes will be heavenly happiness forever.

BASIL: Don't be afraid. Out of the far past into the far future we belong to each other. I'll make it up to you for all those awful years.

MARINA: Yes. It was terrible, and yet—for me—it was—I did love him.

BASIL: You loved my father?

MARINA: Yes. Does that hurt you?

BASIL: It's so strange.

MARINA: I wish you'd come to visit his tomb. You haven't been there yet, have you? No one has put any flowers or leaves there since the funeral, and I couldn't by myself.

BASIL: I'll go there sometime.

MARINA: Come now, Basil. Come with me. We'll go together. Somehow I wish that you'd forgive him. That would be reconciliation and healing, wouldn't it?

BASIL: I can't forgive him.

MARINA: Come with me to his tomb, please.

BASIL: No. I'll go there with you later, after we're married. I mean after you're married. Oh Marina, what a nightmare it all is!

[*The cupboard.* FREDERIC, *dressed in fur cloak, hat and boots strides across the stage.* PATRICE *emerges and catches him by the sleeve.*]

PATRICE: Where do you think you're off to, valet?

FREDERIC: I'm going.

PATRICE: Where?

FREDERIC: Away, right away. Let go of me.

PATRICE: Going, he says. Away, he says. Listen to that.

[*Sound of blizzard, ferocious whistling wind.*]

FREDERIC: Let go of me!

PATRICE: All right. You're going out of that door. Where do you imagine you're going next?

FREDERIC: I'm going to walk to the village. There's a perfectly good road. I've got money. When I get to the village I shall hire a horse.

PATRICE: The village is miles and miles away. The road is invisible. There are snowdrifts across it ten feet high. You would be lost in five minutes. Do you know what it's like to die in the snow?

FREDERIC: Let me go, gipsy!

PATRICE: The wind blows the snow into your mouth, you

can't breathe, your face freezes, your feet are like lead, each step feels like lifting the world, you fall on your knees, the snow is on your back like an animal, you're lying down, you're inside a snow cave, the wind is far away, you snuggle down, you cover your face, you feel sleepy, you feel warmer, you have such strange thoughts and then, and then, there are no more thoughts and no more sound of the wind blowing and they find you stiff and rigid and hard as a rock—

FREDERIC: Stop it!

PATRICE: A frozen man weighs three times his usual weight. The blood freezes in your veins—

FREDERIC: I can't stay here.

PATRICE: I know, I know. It's the same with you as with me, isn't it? Women never forgive a man for being humiliated by another man. They feel it as an affront to themselves. They won't help you up off the ground. They despise the defeated. Women are strange. And probably not worth our tears. All power rests on magic really. A little victory can make it. A little defeat can undo it.

[*During this speech* PATRICE *makes* FREDERIC *sit down and begins to pull his boots off.* FREDERIC *starts to cry.*]

There now. Have a good cry. A heroic role doesn't suit you, you know. It's out of character. Much better just look after number one in a quiet way. Isn't that so?

FREDERIC: [*weeping*] I wish I'd never come to this horrible place.

[PATRICE *kicks off his shoes and is putting on* FREDERIC's *boots.*]

What are you doing?

PATRICE: Could I have the cloak as well please? And the hat?

[FREDERIC *hands them over.*]

FREDERIC: What are you going to do?

PATRICE: I am going.

FREDERIC: But—the snow—

PATRICE: I can go through the snow. You couldn't. I can. My feet will melt it like the feet of the saint in the story.

FREDERIC: You're going away for good?

PATRICE: Yes. For good. Forever. She is getting married tomorrow. I would have left sooner only I hadn't any boots. Thank you. A gipsy's blessing. It may bring you luck one day.

[*He makes a circular sign over* FREDERIC.]

FREDERIC: What am I to do? Nobody wants me.

PATRICE: Stay here until the spring. You can live in this cupboard. I bequeath it to you. It isn't very comfortable but it never actually freezes, and it's quite quiet now that all the rats are dead.

FREDERIC: Yes. When the spring comes I shall go away, to the south, beside the sea.

PATRICE: That's right. You do that. Well, brother, good-bye.

[*They shake hands. Exit* PATRICE. *A door opens. The sound of the blizzard becomes suddenly louder. The door bangs again and muffles it.* FREDERIC *inspects the cupboard and begins to crawl in. Enter* MIKEY.]

MIKEY: Where's Patrice?

FREDERIC: He's gone.

MIKEY: Gone where?

FREDERIC: Gone away. Just now. Gone away for good.

[FREDERIC *points.* MIKEY *rushes out. The door opens, the blizzard howls, the door shuts again. As the cupboard scene, with* FREDERIC *still settling in, grows dark, we hear* MIKEY'S *voice.*]

MIKEY: Patrice, wait for me, wait for me.

[*Now visible, dimly outlined, are the tomb, the church, the trees.* MIKEY'*s voice sounds louder, then faintly dies away as the blizzard howls more and more ferociously.*]

Patrice, wait for me. Don't leave me behind. Take me with you. Patrice, Patrice, wait for me.

[*The White Drawing Room.* MARINA, *in a wedding crown, looks like a princess. She clings to* BASIL's *arm. Also present are* FATHER AMBROSE, ORIANE, PETER JACK *and* HANS JOSEPH.]

AMBROSE: Wilt thou have this man to thy wedded husband, to live together after God's ordinance in the holy state of matrimony? Wilt thou obey him and serve him, love honour and keep him in sickness and in health, and forsaking all other keep thee only unto him, so long as you both shall live?

MARINA: I will.

AMBROSE: Who giveth this woman to be married to this man?

BASIL: I do.

AMBROSE: Repeat after me. I Peter take thee Marina.

PETER JACK: I Peter take thee Marina.

AMBROSE: To my wedded wife.

PETER JACK: To my wedded wife.

AMBROSE: To have and to hold.

PETER JACK: To have and to hold.

AMBROSE: From this day forward.

PETER JACK: From this day forward.

AMBROSE: For better for worse.

PETER JACK: For better for worse.

AMBROSE: For richer for poorer.

PETER JACK: For richer for poorer.

AMBROSE: In sickness and in health.

PETER JACK: In sickness and in health.

AMBROSE: To love and to cherish.

PETER JACK: To love and to cherish.

AMBROSE: Till death do us part.

[*Enter* MAXIM *carrying a shotgun. He is followed by servants carrying* MIKEY's *body upon a stretcher.*]

MAXIM: [*incoherent with grief*] He's dead, Mikey is dead. He ran after Patrice. He ran away into the snow. He's frozen. He's dead.

BASIL: This is—terrible—but we must deal with it later. Please. A wedding is in progress.

MAXIM: Yes. You are getting married to my mother!

BASIL: Your mother is marrying Peter Jack. Please respect this occasion. I know this is dreadful but—later. I'm sorry Father. Can we now resume. I trust this makes no difference.

MAXIM: Doesn't a death make a difference? I know it's only a little boy, a little kitchen boy, a very unimportant person. [*To* ORIANE] Your little page you used to call him. Haven't you any tears for him now that he's dead?

BASIL: This is a tragic accident, but—

MAXIM: It wasn't an accident. Nobody in this house really cared for that child. Except the gipsy, and he didn't care.

MARINA: Has Patrice gone?

MAXIM: Yes. He's gone into the storm and I hope he freezes too. Anxious about him, are you, mother? You seem to have two husbands here, do you want a third?

AMBROSE: Go please, my son. I will speak to you later.

MAXIM: Even you, priest. You gave up truth-telling years ago. You want to hide everything and forget everything. But the time for hiding is past. [*To* BASIL] I accuse you of this boy's death.

BASIL: It was not my fault.

PETERJACK: We are all responsible. We all neglected him.

MAXIM: Yes, we all neglected him. I'm guilty too. I loved that child. But not enough to save his life, not even enough to learn how to teach him to read. Nobody cared for him, nobody looked after him, nobody really knew him at all. You and your wife took him up like a toy and then dropped him. Of course we are all responsible. But while there are masters and servants joint responsibility means nothing. I accuse you. You are pleased to be our figure-head and our sovereign. Keep your sovereignty then and keep its consequences as well. You can die for us all.

BASIL: I reject what you say. You can't put this thing entirely onto me. It's completely unjust.

MAXIM: Keep back. You imagined you could make everything new and wonderful here. But you weren't prepared to give up your power, oh no. And if you keep your power you can't undo the past and your responsibility for what happened then and for what happens now. And you're taking over my mother. Very suitable! For this death I condemn you. Because one little one has been utterly lost I condemn you. And for the past I condemn you too. You are your father all over again. You killed my father. You killed Francis James. We shall not endure you here a second time.

[MAXIM *raises the gun.* MARINA *screams.* FATHER AMBROSE *steps forward.*]

AMBROSE: Stop! The child's death was an accident.

MAXIM: There are no accidents here. Since there is no God *he* is responsible for the death of children.

AMBROSE: No one here is guilty of this. We are guilty, yes, but not guilty of causing this death. Be just. You cannot take a life for this.

MAXIM: All right then, for Francis James.

AMBROSE: No! That debt is already paid. A life has already been taken in payment for the life of Francis James.

MAXIM: What do you mean?

AMBROSE: I killed him. I killed the old man. [*To* BASIL] I killed your father.

BASIL: You killed my father?

AMBROSE: Yes. I murdered him. I stifled him with a pillow. There were—intolerable things—we all know. I ought to have confessed this before, but I was afraid. I confess it now. Let my life be given here and then let all rest.

MAXIM: If you killed him I'm glad. I wish I'd killed him myself. But it makes no difference to this.

AMBROSE: Let this thing end. Let it end in me.

MAXIM: Out of the way, I don't want your life.

MARINA: [*clinging to* BASIL] Maxim, don't hurt him, please, I love him!

MAXIM: Do you imagine that that moves me, mother? All through my childhood you lay in luxury with that other one, that devil. Now there is a new devil, young and strong and clever but just as wicked. And this blasphemous priest is marrying you to him. No, no. Mikey is dead. There will be no more deceptions. There will be no more masters here. [*To* BASIL] I condemn you to death and I appoint myself your executioner.

PETER JACK: Maxim, don't—
[*Cries of "No!"* MAXIM *shoots.* PETER JACK *intervenes and receives the bullet. He falls.* MAXIM *turns away, covering his eyes.*]

HANS JOSEPH: [*kneeling beside* PETER] He is dead.
[*Marina is in* BASIL'S *arms.*]

AMBROSE: No more, no more.

HANS JOSEPH: One man can die for another. A life has been given. So be it.

MARINA: You mustn't be hurt, you shan't be hurt—

BASIL: My darling, my own darling— It's all right now— Don't be frightened. It's all—over.

MARINA: Oh hold me—

HANS JOSEPH: Take the gun from him. All is satisfied now. Let it be—Let it be.

ORIANE: No, all is not satisfied. I am not satisfied. Look at them. They are the real murderers. No, no, no!
[*She produces her pistol and fires.* BASIL *falls.*]

MARINA: She's killed him! She's killed him! He's dead!
[*Enter* GENERAL KLEIN.]

ORIANE: My brother! My brother!
[*The military man takes in the situation at a glance.*]

HANS JOSEPH: They are both dead, your honour.
[*The General takes the pistol from* ORIANE'S *hand, sniffs it and puts it in his pocket. He points to* MAXIM *who is still holding the shotgun.*]

KLEIN: Bind that lunatic! Put him under a strong guard!
Take Madam away, she's fainting. All women back to
the kitchen quarters at once. No one is to leave the house.
Take all this religious stuff away. I'll get to the bottom of
this. Kneel when you address me, you swine . . .
[*As everyone runs to obey the General, the central stage darkens.
We now see the cupboard with* FREDERIC *ensconced in it. He has
been reading a romance. He reaches the end and closes the book.
Then he quietly pulls the cupboard doors and shuts himself in.
The stage darkens. Soft military music, which is gradually
drowned by the whistling of the wind.*]

FINAL CURTAIN

THE THREE ARROWS

A play in two acts

The scene is set in mediaeval Japan

THE IMPERIAL PALACE

Characters in order of their appearance

PRINCE HIRAKAWA ⎱ members of the Imperial house-
PRINCE TENJIKU ⎰ hold.

PRINCE YORIMITSU, a political prisoner.

TAIHITO, the Emperor.

GENERAL MUSASHI, the Shogun, the real ruler of the country.

LADY ROKUNI, mother of the Shogun. A nun.

KEIKO, the Crown Princess, sister of the Emperor.

KURITSUBO, wife of Prince Hirakawa, lady-in-waiting to the princess.

AYAME, lady-in-waiting to the princess.

FATHER AKITA, an old Zen teacher.

OKANO ⎱ Samurai, vassals of Prince Yorimitsu.
NORIKURA ⎰

TOKUZAN, the ex-emperor, now a monk, uncle of the Emperor and leader of the Imperial interest.

ACT ONE
SCENE ONE

*The curtain rises to reveal the prisoner's cell. An afternoon in
January. A barred window with yellowish winter light outside. A
low table and a brazier. A vase with three evergreen branches in it.
A painted scroll upon the wall.* YORIMITSU'S *sword in its scab-
bard also hangs on the wall.* PRINCE HIRAKAWA *is alone, kneeling beside a chess board. He studies the board, hesitates over a move.
Enter* PRINCE TENJIKU.

TENJIKU: Where's Yorimitsu?

HIRAKAWA: [*still intent on chess*] He hasn't grown wings.
He's out in the yard exercising.

TENJIKU: Mmmm. Chilly in here. [*Beginning to study the
board too.*] Who's winning?

HIRAKAWA: Who do you think.

TENJIKU: Whose move is it?

HIRAKAWA: Mine.

TENJIKU: What are you going to do?

HIRAKAWA: Shut up.

[HIRAKAWA *moves a piece.* TENJIKU *moves another.*]

TENJIKU: Check.

HIRAKAWA: Damn! You put me off.

TENJIKU: Well, move it back, at least you've learnt something.

[*He puts the pieces back as they were. Enter* YORIMITSU *from
the yard. A soldier, his guard, enters with him and proceeds to the
other door. The soldier and the prisoner bow to each other solemnly
and the soldier goes out.* HIRAKAWA *and* TENJIKU *are wearing court dress.* YORIMITSU, *under a fur cloak which he has just
taken off, is wearing black trousers and white shirt, standard
issue, Imperial prisoners for the use of.*]

YORIMITSU: Hello, Tenji. Gosh, it's cold out there!

TENJIKU: It's cold in *here*, dear! [*Arm-slapping movements to
restore circulation.*]

117

YORIMITSU: Well, it's bloody colder outside.

TENJIKU: Don't talk to me, I haven't been outside for a month.

[YORIMITSU's *gesture expresses scorn for this effete behaviour.*]

YORIMITSU: What's new in the palace?

TENJIKU: Lechery. Intrigue. Boredom.

HIRAKAWA: That's not new.

[*He moves a piece.* YORIMITSU *looks briefly at the board and moves another.*]

YORIMITSU: Check.

TENJIKU: And if I mistake not, mate.

HIRAKAWA: Oh hell!

YORIMITSU: If politics was like chess I wouldn't have been here for five years.

HIRAKAWA: Things will change.

YORIMITSU: You mean time will pass.

TENJIKU: I'm afraid there's another of those rumours going around.

YORIMITSU: You mean—? [*He draws his hand expressively across his neck.*]

TENJIKU: Yes.

HIRAKAWA: There's no need to tell him!

YORIMITSU: The relation of this to this could certainly change, any day.

HIRAKAWA: Those rumours don't mean anything. They send them round on purpose.

YORIMITSU: I know. I sometimes wish they would decapitate me. It's waiting for it that gets on one's nerves. And being nothing but a bloody pawn in somebody else's game. [*He is about to sweep the chessmen off onto the floor, but* HIRAKAWA *catches his hand. They smile at each other.* YORIMITSU *retires to the window.*]

Oh I do wish it would snow. At least I can see the snow—falling.

[*A sound of armed men in the corridor.* YORIMITSU *turns and listens until it has passed his door.*]

TENJIKU: By the way, old man, I forgot to say, the Emperor is coming to call on you.

YORIMITSU: The Emperor. I wonder what that means?

HIRAKAWA: Nothing. It's just a social call, isn't it, Tenji? When's he coming?

TENJIKU: Oh any moment now. I ran on ahead and then it went completely out of my mind. Of course it's just a social call, don't be so jumpy.

YORIMITSU: I keep looking for signs and clues and omens. Sorry, I'm just a bit mad today.

[*Muted gong. Enter a page with a letter. He kneels and hands the letter to* TENJIKU, *then waits until* TENJIKU *dismisses him with a wave of the hand. The routine of letter-delivery should be elaborate and always the same, gong, bow, dismissal, etc. The letters are large vari-coloured scrolls, rolled up and tied with ribbons. Official letters bear the seal either of the Emperor or of the Shogun. These seals should be large and easily recognised. Love letters and other personal missives have flowers or sprigs of evergreen tied to them.*]

YORIMITSU: A love letter!

[TENJIKU *unrolls the scroll. Beautifully painted characters are visible upon it.*]

HIRAKAWA: Rather nice writing.

TENJIKU: But an abysmally bad poem. Women are so terribly uncultivated these days!

HIRAKAWA: How is it they always know where one is?

YORIMITSU: They?

HIRAKAWA: I don't mean the girls. I mean—*them.* [*He makes conspiratorial signs and points all about him.*]

YORIMITSU: Yes. Both sides. Efficient lot, aren't they?

HIRAKAWA: You go to visit somebody for half an hour and a page arrives with your mail. Interesting!

YORIMITSU: It's a delicate hint.

HIRAKAWA: Yes. Nothing one does in this place is unobserved. Aren't you going to answer it?

[TENJIKU *has crumpled up the letter.*]

TENJIKU: Nah!

[YORIMITSU *has been fingering and smelling a pine twig which was attached to the letter.*]

YORIMITSU: I haven't seen a tree for five years.

TENJIKU: [*sympathetically*] You haven't seen a woman for five years!

YORIMITSU: I haven't seen a dog or a horse for five years.

HIRAKAWA: You seem more upset about the dogs and the horses!

YORIMITSU: I am. A horse—riding north—

HIRAKAWA: Don't, don't!

TENJIKU: My dear fellow, we hardly ever see any girls either, not as you might say *see*. It's the very devil catching a glimpse of a girl in the palace these days. In my grandfather's time there used to be special holes one looked through [*gesture*] it was quite a conventional thing, or else screens would fall over at convenient moments. On a windy day you could see all sorts of things. Now if you get past a screen there's a curtain and if you get past the curtain there's another curtain— Yet the place swarms with girls. You can hear their voices sometimes, hear them laughing. Maddening! But you can't even manage to get a peep at a girl's hair.

YORIMITSU: Peasant girls have hair. You can look at their hair.

TENJIKU: I don't count them. One is so hopelessly refined!

HIRAKAWA: Besides, when do *we* ever see a peasant?

YORIMITSU: I thought love affairs were going on the whole time in the palace. [*He looks at* HIRAKAWA *who looks away.*] I imagined pages were continually running to and fro with next-morning letters!

TENJIKU: Oh those next-morning letters! The next morning is just the time when you *don't* feel like composing a poem!

HIRAKAWA: Hear, hear!

TENJIKU: Of course it's sometimes possible to arrange

something if you're prepared to spend weeks planning it, bribing the servants or hanging round outside windows disguised as the gardener. But you have to be frightfully careful, you simply *must* avoid a scandal. And even then— you meet in some dark corner behind a screen some time after midnight, trying not to step on the house-maid—You can feel the girl's hair and hear her whispering and— But you hardly ever manage to *see* anything, and you have to leave before dawn!

HIRAKAWA: [*sighing*] Yes!

TENJIKU: It's all right for you, Hirakawa, you're married.

HIRAKAWA: Ha bloody ha.

TENJIKU: As for these letters, I get dozens. Often I can't make out who they're from. Bored idle women. It's probably quite impossible to arrange a meeting and they know it. I reply if I feel like it, if it sounds amusing or I like the writing. We correspond for a while, exchange a few insipid poems . . .

HIRAKAWA: Most of the women here are bored and idle.

TENJIKU: And boring!

YORIMITSU: They're corrupted by this rotten society.

TENJIKU: Oh don't be so horribly high-minded and bolshy, Yorimitsu!

HIRAKAWA: Women are corrupt by nature.

YORIMITSU: You've got some intelligence, Hirakawa, why don't you use it instead of talking mindless rubbish?

TENJIKU: Oh come! You're romantic about women because you haven't seen any lately. Surely you remember what they're like?

YORIMITSU: Trivial-minded, yes. But that wasn't their fault. Of course in the north women are much more free.

TENJIKU: Oh you in the wild north!

YORIMITSU: Well, it's all pretty academic as far as I'm concerned. But you make me feel I'm not missing much.

TENJIKU: You aren't even allowed to receive love letters, are you, Yorimitsu?

YORIMITSU: No.

TENJIKU: I expect you'd get plenty if you were. You're a bit of a romantic legend in the palace. You know, if you had anyone particular in mind, I might be able to arrange something. I know it's difficult, but— [*He rubs his fingers together and points at the door. The guard could be bribed.*] There's the most enchanting little creature who's just put on the skirt, one of the younger sisters of Prince Tekuan. I was rather interested myself, but I'd love you to have her. Why not? Think, Yorimitsu, a girl, in here!

HIRAKAWA: Don't be silly, Tenji. You're just romancing. You could never get a girl into this part of the palace.

YORIMITSU: It's impossible. And anyway it's far too risky. Any prisoner found with a woman is immediately beheaded. I don't want to make it that easy for them to get rid of me. I don't propose to die for a woman.

HIRAKAWA: Listen.

[*Sound of marching feet and clang of arms far off in the palace.*] That should be His Majesty.

TENJIKU: Yes, that sounds like the august approach of the Imperial presence.

[HIRAKAWA *and* TENJIKU, *who have been sitting on the floor, rise. All three adjust their clothes. The sounds come closer. Clangour as the Imperial Guard halt and present arms. The door is thrown open. Enter the* EMPEROR. YORIMITSU, HIRAKAWA *and* TENJIKU *begin to kowtow.*]

EMPEROR: Oh don't do that for heaven's sake!

[*He turns to attendants who are trying to bring in cushions etc.*] Go away, go away!

[*He shoos the attendants out and the door closes.*] Do scrub that, my dear fellows. I've had the most ghastly day. [*He flops down full length.*] I've been at that frightful interminable New Year Jamboree. Endless sutras. We must have had the Lotus Sutra at least six times over. You chaps got anything to drink?

YORIMITSU: There's some sake. [*He begins to get it out and serve it.*]

EMPEROR: I'm agonisingly sober. Uncle always smells my breath now before any sort of ceremony, ever since that rather regrettable incident at the Kamo festival. Thanks, my dear creature, you're saving my life, what a day! And then there was the horrible perfume competition, and I haven't even got a sense of smell. Sorry, do I absolutely reek? [*He sniffs his hand.*]

TENJIKU: You do rather pong, my dear.

EMPEROR: Why weren't you there, Hirakawa?

HIRAKAWA: I've got a pollution.

EMPEROR: I notice you always have a pollution when something particularly boring is on the programme! I say, it's cold in here. Remind me to send you another brazier, my dear fellow. I see you're playing that horribly intellectual Chinese game. Gosh, it's nice to be with human beings for a change.

[*He begins to pull off some of his ceremonial gear. Muted gong. Enter a page with a love letter for* HIRAKAWA. *A chrysanthemum is attached to the letter.* YORIMITSU *stares at* HIRAKAWA *who seems embarrassed. The* EMPEROR *stares at the page.*]

EMPEROR: Goings on, my dear Hirakawa, goings on, eh?

TENJIKU: I've just been telling Yorimitsu about the impossible obstacles in the way of getting hold of girls. No wonder we have to make do with each other.

EMPEROR: What do you mean, dear boy, "make do"? Not a bad-looking page, eh? Prince Natuka has got the most stunning Mongolian page, have you seen him? I wonder if he'd swop him for a couple of horses? Who's the letter from, Hirakawa? Of course I mustn't ask, must I? I wonder where she got that chrysanthemum from. The frost's had all mine. [*He has started to re-arrange the branches in* YORIMITSU's *vase.*] You don't mind, do you, old man? I just have got a natural talent. Have you got everything you want?

YORIMITSU: Don't be an ass! Your Majesty!

EMPEROR: Sorry, I'm so tactless. I mean fruit and things. You must see that you get enough vitamins.

TENJIKU: Enough what?

EMPEROR: Vitamins. They're something the Chinese have discovered.

YORIMITSU: Oh, I'm all right.

[*Armed men pass in the corridor,* YORIMITSU *listens.*]

EMPEROR: [*admiring the vase*] I'm so good at flowers and nature and all that. I ought to have been a painter.

TENJIKU: But your Majesty is a most distinguished painter.

EMPEROR: [*pleased*] Oh do you think so? [*Dashed*] The trouble with being Emperor is you will never find out whether you're a distinguished painter or not. Whenever I show people my paintings they say they're marvellous and then go straight off into one of those endless boring arguments about whether spring is better than autumn or—

HIRAKAWA: Autumn for me. Wild and sad.

TENJIKU: Spring for me. I adore the budding grove.

YORIMITSU: I'll have winter. Cold, clear, hard.

EMPEROR: [*peevishly*] That leaves me with summer—I *always* get left with summer. Well, there we go again, it's a sort of national disease. Do give me another drink, will you? I can't stay, I've got to go and see my uncle. I know he's going to be cross with me and I hate it when people are cross with me. He's so polite in public but he *reviles* me in private. Last week he called me a buffoon and boxed my ears. Probably caused brain damage.

TENJIKU: What damage?

EMPEROR: All right, I'm not the brightest member of the Imperial family. That's why I'm where I am, I suppose. Nobody asked me. I succeeded to the Throne at the age of two. I expect even then they could see I was a feeble character. I wear the clothes and Uncle Tokuzan rules the country.

HIRAKAWA: Or tries to.

YORIMITSU: Our friend the General really rules the country.

EMPEROR: I even have to ask my uncle's permission if I want to leave the palace.

TENJIKU: Tokuzan can hold his own against the General.

EMPEROR: He hardly ever gives it, of course.

YORIMITSU: Do you think so?

[*He has been a little apart from the conversation. Through most of the scene he has been standing by the window while the others recline. A certain prison awkwardness hangs on him perhaps.*]

EMPEROR: I'm really a blooming prisoner too!

HIRAKAWA: No, no. The General is the boss.

TENJIKU: But he needs the Imperial family.

EMPEROR: Not that I particularly want to leave the palace actually. Where is there to go to?

HIRAKAWA: He needs the Imperial tradition. But he *uses* it. He even lives in the palace.

YORIMITSU: And while those two fight each other the country perishes.

EMPEROR: I just can't wait to be old enough to retire. I wonder if I could retire when I'm twenty-three?

TENJIKU: What will you do when you retire, your Majesty? Go into a monastery?

[*Laughter.*]

EMPEROR: I don't know. I've heard of a monastery at Akashi where the most *extraordinary* things go on. I must arrange to go there on a pilgrimage.

HIRAKAWA: I'm afraid our monasteries are not what they used to be.

YORIMITSU: I'm told that monks carry arms now and employ mercenaries. Is it true?

TENJIKU: Yes. Some of them are quite bloodthirsty.

YORIMITSU: I detest the idea of a monk being either violent or political.

EMPEROR: Don't talk to me about political monks. My uncle is the absolute queen bee of political monks. *And* violent. [*He rubs his ear.*]

HIRAKAWA: You're so old fashioned about religion, Yorimitsu. You still take it seriously.

TENJIKU: It's his northern upbringing.

EMPEROR: I don't suppose my uncle would let me retire anyway. He'd have to find someone else as dumb as I am, and I appreciate it's not easy!

[*Muted gong. Enter a page with an official letter for* YORIMITSU. *The Imperial seal is prominent.*]

Love letter? Oh of course you're not allowed to get them, are you. Who's it from?

YORIMITSU: As a matter of fact, it's from you.

EMPEROR: My dear, I don't write the letters. I don't even read them. I just sign them. What do I say?

YORIMITSU: You say that as from the first of February next Imperial prisoners will receive their bamboo shoot ration every third week instead of, as hitherto, every second week.

EMPEROR: The things I think of!

YORIMITSU: The number of meaningless time-wasting letters—

EMPEROR: All that bumph going the rounds. I know.

YORIMITSU: Officially of course I'm your prisoner. "Detained indefinitely at the Emperor's pleasure."

EMPEROR: My dear, don't blame me! I didn't have anything to do with it!

YORIMITSU: [*smiling*] I know, I know.

[*The* EMPEROR *begins to make a paper dart out of the official letter.*]

HIRAKAWA: If you had a bit more power, Tai, you could help your friends. Don't you ever dream of a moment of glory?

EMPEROR: Please don't make me feel guilty. I hate it. Of course I have a sort of power in public, after all I am the emperor. I've sometimes thought of ordering all the priests to undress or something. But behind the scenes— Well I suppose I must go. Uncle says I've got to get married. Buddha!

TENJIKU: Married?

EMPEROR: Yes. To a woman. I suppose. Apparently there's a shortage of Imperial toddlers. He wants my sister to get married too.

TENJIKU: Your sister's getting quite old now, isn't she?

EMPEROR: Yes, she is. She's a year younger than me. She's eighteen.

HIRAKAWA: Is it true that your sister knows Chinese?

EMPEROR: Yes. She keeps it secret of course, it's so unfeminine. I haven't seen her for years of course, not since she put on the skirt, but we talk through curtains. Lovely voice. I hope they don't marry her off to some ghastly repressive old codger like Prince Mitachi.

YORIMITSU: They won't force her to marry, will they?

HIRAKAWA: In the end, yes.

EMPEROR: She's turned down all the eligibles.

YORIMITSU: Does she meet men then?

HIRAKAWA: ⎫ What a—!
TENJIKU: ⎬ [*general horror*] Really, my dear—
EMPEROR: ⎭ Of course not!

EMPEROR: She glimpses them out of windows occasionally. And she doesn't like the look of them.

TENJIKU: Perhaps she takes after you.

EMPEROR: [*not understanding*] But I adore male company.

HIRAKAWA: Tenji!

TENJIKU: There's some funny business about the marriage of the Crown Princess, isn't there? Some sort of traditional ordeal or something?

EMPEROR: Yes. The suitor has to choose between three

arrows. And if he chooses wrong he has to commit seppuku.

TENJIKU: Seppuku! [*He enacts it.*]

EMPEROR: Don't, dear boy, I shall faint!

YORIMITSU: It is an honourable death.

HIRAKAWA: But surely this doesn't happen nowadays, now that we're civilised.

EMPEROR: Oh now it's all fixed up beforehand and you're not allowed to enter at all unless you're Mr Right, and then they tell you exactly what to do.

TENJIKU: No suitor has actually been condemned in your reign, have they? Oh yes, there was that Korean prince.

EMPEROR: Yes, the Korean prince! Oh *dear*! This prince absolutely *insisted* on facing the ordeal and as he was a perfectly impossible person we just had to make him do himself in. It was most embarrassing.

YORIMITSU: Your sister must have been very upset.

EMPEROR: Oh no one told her. She was only six at the time.

YORIMITSU: What's the difference between the arrows?

EMPEROR: One is feathered with hawk's feathers, one with swan's feathers and the third with dove's feathers.

TENJIKU: I'd choose the dove. In a marriage situation it would be rather tactless and ungallant not to. Dove for love.

HIRAKAWA: I don't know. One might be expected to choose the swan—symbol of holiness or purity or something—the spiritual life.

TENJIKU: In marriage? My dear, be realistic.

YORIMITSU: I'd choose the hawk, and if my wife didn't like it, the sooner she knew the better.

TENJIKU: Our man of action!

HIRAKAWA: How do you know you've chosen the right arrow?

EMPEROR: You have to shoot it into a target, with one of those immense bows, you know, the kind I can't even bend. In the old days I suppose it was a marksmanship

test. In these blessedly effete days they put the target
about ten feet away. And if you've chosen right the target
turns green, and if you've chosen wrong it turns red or
something. I've never seen it, I was in my nursery when
the Korean prince got his. It's all rigged of course, it's a
sort of priests' spectacular.

TENJIKU: I think I'd be a trifle nervous even if they'd
assured me that I really was Mr Right. You have to kill
yourself immediately, don't you?

EMPEROR: Yes, and they wed you immediately too.

HIRAKAWA: So you're instantly either disembowelled or a
husband!

TENJIKU: Phew!

EMPEROR: Well, I must fly, my dears, I must go and be
admonished.

TENJIKU: I'll come with you.

YORIMITSU: Thank you for coming.

EMPEROR: Forgive me, my dear fellow. You understand.
You know how it is. I'll send some fruit and another
brazier and some more sake and some spring flowers when
there are any. Now I must *rush*. Goodbye, goodbye.

TENJIKU: Wait for me, Tai.

[*Exeunt the* EMPEROR *and* PRINCE TENJIKU. YORIMITSU
and HIRAKAWA *laugh and relax.*]

YORIMITSU: I can't chat any more, you know, or make
small talk. It's—this. [*He indicates the cell.*] The chatty part
of one dies quite early on.

HIRAKAWA: I know.

YORIMITSU: And *you* become different when they're there.
[*He puts his hands on* HIRAKAWA'S *shoulders. Faint sense of a
love scene.*]

HIRAKAWA: I'm sorry—

YORIMITSU: All the same, I must say that His Imperial
Majesty usually cheers me up.

HIRAKAWA: Yes. He's a guileless being. He's an awful ass,
but he's somehow uncorrupted by this bloody place.

YORIMITSU: I suppose so. I suspect everyone who visits me now. Except you. After a while it's like having hallucinations. Everything gets distorted. And one can't test the truth of anything.

HIRAKAWA: You don't suspect Okano and Norikura?

YORIMITSU: My own Samurai? No, of course not. I don't think so. No, no. But why are they allowed to visit me? Nothing here happens by accident. Why are you allowed to visit me, if it comes to that? Sorry, Hirakawa. One gets a bit crazed by this atmosphere of lies and spying.

HIRAKAWA: Obviously your Samurai are watched, followed, listened to.

YORIMITSU: Yes. I suppose *they* hope to learn something. You know, I'm afraid for my two men. They come here armed. One day they'll be provoked. One day I'll be provoked. That's why they've left me my sword. They think I'll go berserk and then they'll be able to cut me down without breaking the rules.

HIRAKAWA: You are getting nervy. The rules aren't saving you. It's the deadlock between Tokuzan and the General that's saving you.

YORIMITSU: The balance of power. Yes. If either side got strong enough to neglect the other my head would come off.

HIRAKAWA: They know you want the General's seat.

YORIMITSU: I could get it too. Even now. Oh yes, both Tokuzan and the General want me dead, but neither wants to have the odium of killing me.

HIRAKAWA: Because your friends would join the other side.

YORIMITSU: Long enough for revenge. It's a rather funny situation really!

HIRAKAWA: I think both sides fondly imagine they'll be able to use you against the other somehow.

YORIMITSU: When my nerve has broken. Oh, I'm a very valuable property! I have all sorts of possibilities.

HIRAKAWA: Is there any news—?

[YORIMITSU *cuts him off, waggles his fingers beside his ears and points to the walls, floor, roof, and makes a helpless gesture. He moves to the front of the stage and* HIRAKAWA *follows. They speak in low voices.*]

I was just wondering if you'd had any news of—anything?

YORIMITSU: No. There've been so many different plans— well, you know. But they all come to nothing. I think even Okano is beginning to give up hope. He's grown old in these five years. There's a military force, but it couldn't storm this place. Okano has made a plan of the palace. They've watched him doing it. They don't care. It's absolutely impossible to rescue me. I've dreamt of rescue, dreamt I heard those northern bugles blowing, coming nearer—I hear them in my sleep. But it's impossible.

HIRAKAWA: Has the Shogun been to see you lately?

YORIMITSU: The General? No.

HIRAKAWA: No more interrogations?

YORIMITSU: No. There's no point in interrogating some- one who's got nothing to tell. I have no plans for my im- mediate future unfortunately! Tokuzan hasn't been to see me either. Perhaps I'm really being—forgotten—at last.

HIRAKAWA: Don't worry, you're still the bogyman. How's your treatise on government?

YORIMITSU: [*cheering up*] My great book, yes. I've written a lot more of it. Let me show you. [*He digs out lengthy scrolls.*] Chapter on land reform. Chapter on agrarian reform. Abolition of the manorial system. Abolition of serfdom. Study of alternative systems of land tenure. That's the stuff on Chinese methods of rice growing, you remember. Rice cultivation in small fields best left to in- dividual enterprise. Chinese economic theory. Do you realise, Hirakawa, that there isn't a single economist in the palace?

HIRAKAWA: We seem to get on all right without them.

YORIMITSU: Of course the science of economics is in its infancy.

HIRAKAWA: From what I've seen of economists I suspect it will always be in its infancy.

YORIMITSU: [*digging out more stuff and flicking it through*] Decentralisation of the civil service. Constitutional monarchy. Taxation reform.

HIRAKAWA: [*looking*] What's this here? In-come tax?

YORIMITSU: Oh that's an idea I've just had. Everyone would give up a proportion of his income to the government.

HIRAKAWA: My dear chap, don't be mad. Nobody would stand for that.

YORIMITSU: No, I suppose they wouldn't. Do you think I'm getting a bit out of touch? I know I'm a military leader. I still haven't proved I'm a statesman. Oh it isn't just power I want, Hirakawa. That wasn't what it was about five years ago. This country could be a wonderful human place—happy, free. The General isn't a complete fool, but he has no sort of vision and he just isn't strong enough to do anything except pussyfoot around after Tokuzan. Neither Tokuzan nor the General really rules. The palace rules. But all this endless paper work, these theories and programmes and official letters, in a way they don't matter either, they're a kind of front. And behind it there's a cunning system of power—intrigue, bullying, fear. Always fear. The palace doesn't govern the country, it devours it.

HIRAKAWA: My dear, things have always been like that here. Few things are stronger than national tradition in politics. The labels change and the same old arrangements go on.

YORIMITSU: No! I love this country and I believe in it. We are a great people, Hirakawa. When that revolt began in the north I *knew* that things could be changed, made different and better. But this hideous deadening bureaucracy has got to go. If I were Shogun I'd employ a Chinese engineer to blow up the palace.

HIRAKAWA: What about the Imperial family?

YORIMITSU: Let them be religious symbols if they want to. If they don't, let them go and watch horse races.

HIRAKAWA: No wonder they keep you in a cage.

YORIMITSU: I'm lucky to be alive. People have rights, Hirakawa, nothing is more fundamental than people and their rights, that's what politics ought to be about. But if it's all wrapped up in suspicion and intrigue and lies and everyone is afraid to tell the truth, how can we expect to make any decent sensible arrangements? People who are spied on can't think. Lies and fear poison the heart and ruin the mind. Meanwhile out in the countryside, where the bureaucrats never go, men are ignorant and starving and struggling stupidly against each other. It isn't necessary. Intelligence and good will could change it. But intelligence and good will must be free.

HIRAKAWA: We need the palace. It's all we've got. You'd need it if you were out of here.

YORIMITSU: Cynicism. Bloody cynicism. There's another foul poison.

[*Muted gong. Enter a page with a love letter for* HIRAKAWA.]

You'd better go and get on with your wonderful love life.

HIRAKAWA: Don't be angry with me, Yorimitsu.

YORIMITSU: All right, and I have puritanical northern ideas about marriage. If I married a woman I wouldn't want to make her unhappy. I wouldn't want to see her trailing round the house like a wounded bird. I wouldn't want to think she was waiting for me while I was amusing myself—

[*Raised voices.*]

HIRAKAWA: Kuritsubo isn't waiting for me. She's with her current lover, whoever he may be. I prefer not to know. She bears no resemblance whatever to a wounded bird. She is not unhappy.

YORIMITSU: [*shouting*] You lie to yourself. She must be unhappy.

HIRAKAWA: Well—all right, but—It's like politics—Some things just can't be improved or mended. You're an idealist, Yorimitsu. But the facts are just grim. My wife hates me. Yes, I've been unfaithful, but I'm no worse than the others, perhaps I'm better than most. But she just hates me. I think she'd do almost anything to hurt me. It's another of those deadlocks. Most marriages are like that.

YORIMITSU: Then heaven preserve me from marriage. Sorry, Hirakawa.

HIRAKAWA: I'm sorry.

YORIMITSU: Look, it's snowing.

[HIRAKAWA *joins* YORIMITSU *at the window and they stand with hands on each other's shoulders.*]

How I would love to see Fujiyama with this snow falling. How beautiful he would look. Oh to see *mountains* again. To see the sea again. I'm in a stupid rotten frame of mind. Some days I endure it, I'm quiet. Other days I just want to pull my chain till the blood runs. Perhaps you're right, I'm becoming a bit mad.

HIRAKAWA: I didn't mean—

YORIMITSU: [*turning to him*] You don't do yourself any good by coming to see me, Hirakawa.

HIRAKAWA: My family are powerful. I can do as I please.

YORIMITSU: No one around here does as he pleases, not even the General. They're all slaves of the machine. In a bureaucracy like this there's a sort of super will that rules everybody. I can feel it touching me. It isn't even a human will any more. It's the will of the palace. Remember that you have political ambitions too.

HIRAKAWA: As soon as you make that sort of compromise for your political ambitions you begin to rot and stink. I'm not as cynical as all that, my dear.

YORIMITSU: [*moment of affection and relief*] All right. Oh I strut about and fluff up my feathers in here and lift up my crest, but I can't fly. I'm just a deferred victim. At any moment of any day the situation might have changed, someone might have panicked, the balance of power might have tilted, and the guard would come and lead me out—whenever I hear armed men in the corridor I think they're coming for me. I re-enact this every day, every hour. Especially at night. At four in the morning. That would be the time. There'd be nothing dramatic. Just bored tough soldiers doing their job. I wouldn't resist. I'd go quietly with my last little remnant of dignity. Nobody'd care. They'd probably behead me casually out there in the yard and send in a report in triplicate. But it isn't just that. I live well here, I have light and air and enough to eat. The Emperor sends me flowers! I have visitors, I can read and write. But the possession of these things can be—agonising—if they too can be taken away at any moment of any day.

HIRAKAWA: You've thought about that too?

YORIMITSU: Of course. The possibility of torment is never absent from my mind. They could make me solitary, forbid my books, starve me, make this room darker, make it smaller. How would I stand up to that? They could make me harmless without killing me.

HIRAKAWA: [*softly*] I know.

YORIMITSU: This is weakness, Hirakawa, deep weakness, cowardice. The place where I'm not a hero.

HIRAKAWA: Every human being has that place.

YORIMITSU: But it isn't even just that. It's not knowing the *future*, not knowing what one's life will have been, how meaningless, how defeated. If I knew there was a definite moment of release, even if it were years away, it would be different. I'm thirty-two years old. I've been in this room for five years. It's winter now. Spring. Summer. A year, another year, another—How long can a man of action sit in one room and play chess and read Chinese poetry and still remain a man of action? Now I'm a leader. If I were free I'd be a great general, a powerful politician. But the magic of one's name doesn't last indefinitely. Later, I'll be a story, a legend. People will feel sorry for me. Later still, I'll be growing old. My men won't remember me forever, won't wait for me forever. Why should they? Some younger man will come forward and take the place which has been kept empty for me. My moment of destiny is now, *now* when I'm caged in this room, in this courtyard, inside this fortress, inside this labyrinth, inside this palace. [*Gestures*] Spring. Summer. A year. Another year. I could grow old. I could die of old age in captivity, Hirakawa. I don't want to die here old with my heart broken. If only I *knew* that was how it would be I would take that sword and try to fight my way out and let them kill me somewhere at the end of that corridor, or the next, or the next.

HIRAKAWA: Yes. But it's part of our fate that we don't know the future and have to go on hoping.

YORIMITSU: I know. These are very base thoughts, Hirakawa, but they obsess me. [*He strikes his fist against the wall.*] I was talking about being a great statesman. But I'm a petty envious coward in my mind. I'm *tormented* by ambition. I'm tormented by the idea that some other man could come and take my place and do what I might have done. I live by ambition, but I know that ambition is eating me, it's killing me.

HIRAKAWA: Is there no way of laying aside ambition?

YORIMITSU: No.

[*Armed men pass outside. They both listen.*]

Well, yes, there is.

HIRAKAWA: You mean—

YORIMITSU: Yes. We've talked about this before. My dear father was a great leader. He really was a great man. But he died a monk, in a little mountain temple miles from anywhere. May his soul rest in Amida's paradise. [*Gesture of blessing*] Sometimes I know that worldly life, even what passes as a decent worldly life, is utterly corrupt and blind. It *is* all vanity. And I know this when I look into my soul and it's like watching a swarm of maggots; and when I think of what years and years of those rotten thoughts and cravings will do to me. I use big noble words but my desires are petty. Petty and mean and selfish and horribly strong. The only real freedom of the spirit is in the life of religion. I know this. And it tempts me. How mad. To speak of being tempted by a supreme good.

[*Silence. Snow. Gathering dark. Soft feet padding by outside.*]

The palace never sleeps. Always soldiers, messengers, officials, spies. People going to make plots, people going to make love. Surreptitious secret feet. I hear them passing in the corridors all night.

But you see it's no good. I couldn't do it here.

HIRAKAWA: Do what?

YORIMITSU: Become a monk. I'd have to be outside, somewhere in the mountains, in the light and the air. In here it would somehow make no sense. It would be poisoned. Like everything else.

HIRAKAWA: You're sentimental about religion. You're a hawk, not a swan, Yorimitsu. I can't see you embracing the life of contemplation. Any more than your father would have done at your age.

YORIMITSU: Ah— At my age my father was ruling half Japan. No, it's a dream, it's a dream. Like all the rest probably, just a prisoner's dream. You must go, my dear. [*He puts his hands on* HIRAKAWA's *shoulders.*] A host who is always home should have the privilege of dismissing his guests. If you stay I shall become emotional. You know. And somebody is waiting for you, I'm sure. I'm sorry I was rough with you. I'm probably just—jealous! Go then, go.

HIRAKAWA: Don't stop hoping.

THE THREE ARROWS

YORIMITSU: Ach!

[*He motions* HIRAKAWA *to go away.* HIRAKAWA *goes.*
YORIMITSU *kneels beside the brazier and puts his hands over
his face, as the stage slowly darkens.*]

ACT ONE

Scene Two

The office of the SHOGUN. *Night. The* SHOGUN *is seated cross-legged on a low throne. His age is indeterminate but youngish. He might be thirty-five or forty. His mother,* LADY ROKUNI, *stands before him, Her head is shaven and she wears the habit of a nun. Low tables carry in-trays and out-trays. Documents with official seals— both the* SHOGUN'S *seal and the Imperial seal—are prominent.*

ROKUNI: He must die. [*Pause*] He must die, he must die, he must die.

SHOGUN: It's not so simple, my dear mother.

ROKUNI: I'm not saying it's simple, I'm saying it's necessary.

SHOGUN: It has been necessary for five years. It has also been impossible.

ROKUNI: You are the Shogun. You are the master of this country.

SHOGUN: He is not my prisoner.

ROKUNI: You should never have let him be classified as an Imperial prisoner. You should never have let him live. You ought to have killed Yorimitsu at once, when that peasants' revolt he got hold of went wrong. After that battle when you captured him. You should have despatched him immediately, that night in your tent.

SHOGUN: [*gloomily*] We started arguing about Confucius.

ROKUNI: The country was in chaos. No one could have accused you of anything.

SHOGUN: I was a good deal less powerful then than I am now. And he is a great name.

ROKUNI: Name, name! What is your power worth now if you cannot get at that man's life. He sits in his cage and laughs at you and waits. You might at least have put out his eyes when you had the chance.

SHOGUN: I agree with you, mother, that I ought to have killed Yorimitsu. But now—it matters very little whose prisoner he is. Once he was known to be captured he was a pawn in the game. Don't you think that Tokuzan wants him dead? Of course he does. From Tokuzan's point of view Yorimitsu is an even more dangerous man than I am. But he daren't kill him for the same reason that I daren't.

ROKUNI: You are an opportunist, my son. An adventurer, a bandit, a man without theories or principles of any kind. If you want to survive you must have the virtues of the bandit: ferocity, courage, will. You are not as clever as Tokuzan. You must make up the deficit by being more ruthless. Tokuzan ought to fear you, he ought to fear you in every inch of his mortal flesh, he ought to shudder at every day's darkness because of you. You must be dangerous, my son. You will never beat Tokuzan at his game. [*She indicates the paper work.*] You must make him play your game. Make a new start by killing Yorimitsu. Now. Send your men to his cell. Just like that. No warning, no talk, no formality. Just slaughter him in a corner. And let Tokuzan mop up the blood. And let Tokuzan reflect and be afraid.

SHOGUN: [*faint smile*] Suppose the Imperial Guard will not allow my men to pass?

ROKUNI: [*gesture of exasperation*] What are Samurai for?

SHOGUN: [*getting up and walking about*] I live here now. I *need* the Imperial family. Without them I couldn't rule. I have to play Tokuzan's game. If his men and my men began to fight in the corridors of the palace this would create an entirely unpredictable situation, which at the moment I simply cannot afford.

ROKUNI: Nothing would happen except a little bloodshed. And a man in your position needs blood like a plant needs water. You must make yourself universally feared. You could get away with that murder, easily.

SHOGUN: I don't think so. If I kill Yorimitsu his friends will love Tokuzan long enough to have my head. In fact the Imperial Guard would probably not oppose my men. Tokuzan would be delighted if I killed his prisoner. Yorimitsu is greatly loved. Names *are* powerful and to be trembled at. This man is a great symbol. To revenge him would be a sacred duty for which men would die joyfully. It would not be difficult to assassinate me. If it hasn't happened already it may even be because of Yorimitsu. If I were out of the way Tokuzan would be powerful enough to kill him. Yorimitsu is a hostage. And hostages are only valuable with their heads on.

ROKUNI: [*nodding*] If there were only some way of forcing the Imperial party to kill him, or tricking them into killing him, or making it seem that they had killed him. I won't sleep at night until that man is dead. I wonder if we could poison him. I must consult my doctor.

SHOGUN: Tokuzan fears the north as much as I do. I want that fear to stay with him. We've kept Yorimitsu quite successfully caged for five years.

ROKUNI: You've kept him safe and well for five years, you and the old fox between you. You'll regret it. He is a man of ferocious ambition. He is a thorn in your side. He will become a dagger. While he lives the north will never be at peace.

SHOGUN: When was the north ever at peace. He *can't* be rescued. His friends know that by now.

ROKUNI: You are too confident. The country groans in its sleep. The stupid peasantry believe that Yorimitsu is their friend. You fear an unpredictable situation in the palace, but there is an unpredictable situation out there! [*Pointing.*]

[*Muted gong. A page arrives with official letters and removes others from the out-tray.*]

Here in the palace you spend your time trying to deceive each other, but you are really deceiving yourselves. You imagine that all this paper work is ruling the country. You write a memorandum and think this settles something. You were not like this once. Tokuzan has bewitched you into thinking that all this is important. It suits him all right if you waste your time in here. But one day you'll wake up to find that the fate of the country has been settled somewhere quite else, somewhere far away from here, by men who have not lost the touch of reality. While you sit and exchange witty minutes with Tokuzan.

SHOGUN: His are wittier than mine. No, no, mother, I assure you. Yorimitsu's followers are rational men. They *see* there's nothing to be done. Yorimitsu is important as a hostage. But as a national force—no—he's nothing—he's a museum piece.

ROKUNI: Yorimitsu's followers are not rational men because no men are rational men. You have no sense of history, no sense of how and why things happen. Yorimitsu's followers know with half of their mind that he can't be rescued. With the other half they are forever scheming, planning, hoping. He is an inspiration. So long as he is alive his people will be restless, dangerous, in the mood for revolution. There could be another peasants' revolt, anything could happen to sweep these men into action, even against their own will and judgment. History does not work through the reason of mankind. That is why it is so insanely dangerous to leave that man alive. Kill him, my child, kill him. He is the head of all your troubles. The limbs might beat about but they would not survive for long.

SHOGUN: Maybe. But I might not survive for long either! Let Yorimitsu's followers dream. It keeps them occupied.

ROKUNI: And Yorimitsu waits for his hour.

SHOGUN: His hour has passed. He has already waited too long. Action is a habit. He will lose even that in the end. Time will dispose of him, mother. It will break his heart.

ROKUNI: No. He has the heart of a tiger.

SHOGUN: Any man can be broken by torment.

ROKUNI: By real torment, yes. Not by this shilly shallying. What do you mean?

SHOGUN: There are things which are more to be feared than death.

ROKUNI: That's my good boy! You've got a plan?

SHOGUN: I am going to visit the monastery at Midera.

ROKUNI: Midera. Why?

SHOGUN: I am going to see Father Akita.

ROKUNI: He's still alive, is he? He taught Yorimitsu's father.

SHOGUN: I am going to ask him to see the prisoner.

ROKUNI: You are mad, my child, if that's what you're thinking. Yorimitsu could never be persuaded to give up the world. And if he did, what would it profit you if he were to command his troops from a monastery?

SHOGUN: Of course he would have to act of his own free will and let that be known. But I understand his mind this much. If he became a monk he would be a true contemplative. He would not be a political monk. And I happen to know that he really does think about giving up the world.

ROKUNI: You mean that man seriously considers the religious life?

SHOGUN: Yes.

ROKUNI: If his followers knew that he was really not in play any more— But no, he would never consent.

SHOGUN: It's worth trying. And one might add—other inducements.

ROKUNI: That's what you meant—I see.

SHOGUN: One might stiffen the alternative.

ROKUNI: There are fears which can move even the bravest of men, yes. If he thought that the conditions of his imprisonment were going to change— [*She brings her hands together expressively.*] But *you* can't change them.

SHOGUN: He isn't to know that. Besides, if Tokuzan thought it possible that Yorimitsu might give up the world—

ROKUNI: He might cooperate.

SHOGUN: It might be the one point at which Tokuzan and I could trust each other.

[*Muted gong. Enter page with official letters. The Imperial Seal is visible.*]

So you see my paper work has not been entirely valueless, my dear mother.

ROKUNI: Well, try it then. It might work. But I'd be very much happier seeing his head on the end of a spear.

ACT ONE

SCENE THREE

The apartments of the princess. Afternoon. A latticed-window makes the room curiously reminiscent of YORIMITSU'S *cell. Rocks, stones, dwarf trees, sand, etc., ingredients for making a miniature garden, in the foreground. The princess is at the window.* KURITSUBO *reposes.* AYAME *kneels. The princess is eighteen,* KURITSUBO *is twenty-two,* AYAME *fourteen. The girls all have very long hair.* KEIKO *and* KURITSUBO *have elaborate coiffures.* AYAME *has a long plait. As the stage lightens* AYAME *is playing the zithern. The music stops. Silence. Atmosphere of female ennui.*

KEIKO: [*sighing*] Oh dear, I feel so sad.

KURITSUBO: Bored, dear, bored. Not sad. Call things by their right names.

KEIKO: [*annoyed*] No, not bored. Sad. It's quite different. [*She yawns. Silence*] I do wish it would snow. At least I can see the snow—falling.

KURITSUBO: It has snowed. It will snow.

[*She yawns. Silence.* AYAME *plays a few more notes on the zithern.*]

KEIKO: Please, Ayame. It makes me so sad. [*Sighs.*]

AYAME: I'm sorry, I'm afraid I don't play very well.

KURITSUBO: It is true that your playing is entirely without expression.

KEIKO: It's because you're so young. You haven't suffered yet. [*Sighs.*]

KURITSUBO: You think you've suffered? You wait till you're married.

KEIKO: I wish you wouldn't be so cynical, Kuritsubo.

KURITSUBO: You're in a silly frame of mind, Keiko. What you call suffering is just yearning. You're in love with the idea of being in love. I can remember being like that at your age.

K

KEIKO: You're only four years older than me.

KURITSUBO: Four very educational years, my child! Anyway, I've always seen far more of the world than you have.

KEIKO: I've seen nothing. It's *wretched* being the Crown Princess. You two can walk about. Of course you have to stay in the women's quarters [KURITSUBO *smiles*] but you can walk down corridors. Walk down corridors! If I ever go anywhere in the palace, which I hardly ever do, I'm carried in a litter with two sets of curtains. I can't even peep out.

AYAME: I'd rather go in a litter. I don't like walking. It hurts my feet.

KEIKO: Well, all right I *am* in a silly frame of mind. Shall we do something, shall we make a garden?

[*They begin to play about with the stones, dwarf trees etc., arranging them in a large shallow tray. They pour water over some of the stones and admire them.*]

How lovely the stones look when they're wet, it makes them such bright colours. Then they get all dry and dull again.

KURITSUBO: Fortunately we have a rainy climate.

KEIKO: Not inside the palace. I was born here in the palace. I've never been outside it. I've spent all my life here. I don't know what the world outside is like. I don't even know if there is a world outside. I've never been farther than this garden. [*Gesture*] And the walls are so high you can't see out. Perhaps I'll live through my whole life here inside the palace. Perhaps I'll die here.

KURITSUBO: Well, it doesn't matter if you do. Women have to stay in the same place mostly. It may as well be a nice place. You should have seen the dump we lived in when my father was provincial governor of Mutsu. At least here there's plenty of space and it's not draughty.

AYAME: It's awfully crowded over where we are. The maids all have to sleep in a sort of heap. Mama says that's why they all have colds all the time.

KEIKO: I've never seen real rocks, I mean rocks in nature, like in pictures. I've never seen a real mountain, a real river. Kuritsubo, have you ever seen a mountain?

KURITSUBO: Yes, I've seen Mount Fuji.

KEIKO: Great Fujiyama. How much I would love to see him. I've only seen him in pictures. Is he wonderful?

KURITSUBO: I love the way you call it him! Yes, he's wonderful.

KEIKO: And big?

KURITSUBO: Very big. Huge! [*She lifts her arm.*]

KEIKO: I've never seen anything really big in my life. I've only seen—miniature things. Like this. [*She indicates the miniature garden.*]

KURITSUBO: We are women. They make our lives miniature.

KEIKO: They— You mean men?

KURITSUBO: Yes.

KEIKO: You always speak as if men were our enemies.

KURITSUBO: They are.

AYAME: The palace is awfully big, isn't it?

KEIKO: Yes, but we're inside it, we can't see it. And we're just stuck away in one corner of it. I don't even know what the rest of the palace is like. I know there are other courtyards, other gardens, many, many, many of them, but— Oh if only one could get *out*.

AYAME: I heard of a girl, and she wasn't even married, who disguised herself as a maid and just left her rooms!

KURITSUBO: [*ironical*] Dear me!

KEIKO: [*shocked*] Left her rooms? How dreadful!

AYAME: They found her and made her go into a nunnery.

KEIKO: Oh poor thing!

KURITSUBO: An unmarried girl—whatever else could they do? Anything might have happened to her and probably did!

KEIKO: How awful to be forced to become a nun!

KURITSUBO: [*suddenly virtuous*] It's quite right. *Before*

marriage a girl just can't be too careful. The least breath of scandal and they shave your head straightaway. There's just no alternative.

KEIKO: Ouf! How horrid! [*Shudders, touching her hair.*] Oh dear, I feel so stupid today. Let's do something else, let's play a game.

KURITSUBO: Let's have a poetry competition.

KEIKO: You're so good at poems, Kuritsubo, I wish I was.

AYAME: Please, I can't write poems— You two write— I can't.

KURITSUBO: Don't be silly, Ayame, you've got to try. You've got to learn. When you have suitors however will you answer their letters if you can't write poems?

AYAME: I've got a suitor.

KURITSUBO:⎫ [*laughing*] She's got a suitor, she's got a
KEIKO: ⎭ suitor!

KEIKO: What's his name?

AYAME: Prince— Oh dear, I can't remember. I think it begins with R.

KURITSUBO: But how *do* you answer his letters if you can't write poems?

AYAME: My nanny writes the answers.

KEIKO: You two are lucky. I'm not even allowed to receive love letters.

KURITSUBO: That's being strictly brought up, dear. It's supposed to be a great advantage!

KEIKO: Well, let's have a poem competition and Ayame shall do the best she can and you'll win because you always do!

[*The girls settle down to write their poems. They write with brushes in large conspicuous characters upon long rolls of prettily coloured paper. Much todo over this.*]

KURITSUBO: I've finished mine!

KEIKO: Sssh! There. All right. Shall we read them out? I'll read mine first, shall I?

KURITSUBO: Yes, go on.

KEIKO: "High in the cedar tree the dove
    Moans because spring has come,
    But not love."

KURITSUBO: Your poems are all so soppy, Keiko. And you're rhyming "dove" and "love" again, it's so hackneyed.

AYAME: I think it's lovely.

KURITSUBO: Here's mine.

"At a man's faithlessness my sleeve is wet,
But hard the glitter of my eyes:
Diamond, agate."

[*She mops her eyes with her sleeve.*]

KEIKO: That's awfully clever. But it's a bit sort of—sinister, isn't it? Now let's hear yours.

AYAME: "Beside the river the frog."

KEIKO: Well, go on. "Beside the river the frog."

AYAME: That's all.

KEIKO: That's not a poem. You have to have three things for a poem.

KURITSUBO: You must make your frog *do* something.

KEIKO: He must jump in the river.

KURITSUBO: Or catch flies.

AYAME: He can't catch flies. That's not poetry.

KURITSUBO: Anything's poetry if you know how. Anyway it doesn't scan and you'll never find a decent rhyme for frog. Nothing rhymes with "frog" except "log" or "bog" —or "dog".

KEIKO: Or "sog" or "tog"—

KURITSUBO: You'll have to change it round.

"The frog beside the river"—

[*She alters* AYAME's *characters.*]

KEIKO: Or "mog", or "pog", or "shog"—

KURITSUBO: Shut up, Keiko. Look, let us both finish he poem for her.

KEIKO: Yes, good, quickly, the first thing that comes—

[KURITSUBO *draws a line down the rest of the scroll. She and*
KEIKO *rapidly paint in their conclusions to the poem, one on each
side.*]

KURITSUBO: "The frog beside the river eats
　　　　　　The gilded flies—
　　　　　　May they be bitter sweetmeats."

KEIKO: Ouf! Here's mine.
"The frog beside the river
Waits for her froglove—
Must she wait forever?"

KURITSUBO: I know half-rhymes are supposed to be *in* this
year, but that really won't do, Keiko. And you can't have
"froglove". "Froglove!"

KEIKO: Well, "froggylove" then.

KURITSUBO: [*gesture of despair*] And you seem to have but
a single thought.

KEIKO: Well, so do you! I prefer my thought! And you've
won, as usual.

AYAME: You're both so clever. I can never think of anything for a poem. Do you think it matters if I can't write
poems?

KURITSUBO: [*bored again*] No. Poetry isn't very important.
Nothing is very important, really.
[*She settles back on the cushions, pulls out a scroll and begins idly
to peruse it.*]

KEIKO: Is that a love letter?

KURITSUBO: Yes. I get lots [*yawns*] and lots.

KEIKO: Whatever must it be like to see a man close to?

KURITSUBO: They smell—and prickle.

AYAME: I sometimes see my father. And I'm allowed to see
my younger brother.

KURITSUBO: Really, our society is becoming quite permis-
sive!

KEIKO: I can't remember my father. Oh I've *seen* them, of
course, out of windows, a few times, in the distance, you
know, at the archery contest or the cherry festival or the

races—But they all look alike. When my uncle speaks to me of one or another I pretend I know who he means but I don't really. How can I choose when I don't know?

KURITSUBO: You won't choose, dear. I didn't choose. And they don't just look alike, they are alike.

AYAME: I know my mother will choose for me. She says it's just a matter of looking at the book of pedigrees.

KEIKO: Oh Kuritsubo, I want love, I want love, I want love.

KURITSUBO: Please, Keiko you're making me feel slightly sick!

KEIKO: Is it really true that men go away from their wives to other women?

KURITSUBO: Yes.

KEIKO: And women go away from their husbands to other men?

KURITSUBO: Yes. In other parts of the palace, my pet, things go on which you just couldn't dream of. Boredom is our lot—and when we are bored we have to—play games.

KEIKO: When I am married will my husband go secretly to other women?

KURITSUBO: Of course he will.

KEIKO: And will I go secretly to other men?

KURITSUBO: You'll want to, dear, but being the Crown Princess you probably won't be allowed to!

KEIKO: No, Kuritsubo, no, no, no. I will not have lies and deception in my life!

KURITSUBO: My poor girl, your husband will introduce lies and deception into your life six weeks after your marriage, probably sooner.

[*For a little while now* AYAME *has been playing with the miniature garden.*]

AYAME: They're going to behead that man.

KEIKO: [*not very interested*] What man?

KURITSUBO: [*ditto*] Oh good. There hasn't been an execution in the palace for ages. It does cheer one up so. [*Yawns.*]

AYAME: That man, I forget his name.

KURITSUBO: [*watching* AYAME's *efforts*] Really, Ayame, you're hopeless. You mustn't put that rock right up against the tree like that. They want to be able to look at each other.

[KURITSUBO *begins to rearrange the garden.* KEIKO *joins in.*]

AYAME: What *is* his name?

KEIKO: I think that should go there.

AYAME: [*triumphantly*] Yorimitsu!

KURITSUBO: [*rising*] Yorimitsu?

KEIKO: Who's he? Oh yes, I do vaguely remember.

[*She and* AYAME *go on playing with the garden. Neither has noticed* KURITSUBO's *distress.*]

AYAME: He's been a prisoner for, oh, years and years.

KURITSUBO: [*softly*] Five years.

KEIKO: Poor chap. There. That's better. Now some sand. What's the matter, Kuritsubo?

KURITSUBO: Yorimitsu. They're going to behead him, are they?

KEIKO: Well, why not? You seem quite upset.

KURITSUBO: I saw him once.

[*The other two are now most interested.*]

AYAME: How exciting. Where?

KEIKO: You saw him? Wasn't he the man who led the revolution or whatever it was?

KURITSUBO: Yes. A revolt of peasants. About land or something. It was five years ago. He very nearly became the Shogun. His army had complete control of the north.

KEIKO: And where did you see him?

KURITSUBO: His men stopped our coach. It was when we were coming back to the capital from Mutsu. I was seventeen. My father had gone ahead and there was just my mother and me in the coach and a few servants riding with us. Suddenly we were surrounded by soldiers. [AYAME *squeaks*.] We had to stop. Then when Yorimitsu found it was only women in the coach he let us go on.

KEIKO: How did he know there were only women in the coach?

KURITSUBO: He pulled back the curtain.

AYAME: Ooh!

KURITSUBO: [*spellbound by her own narration*] He looked in. He looked straight into my eyes.

AYAME: Did you scream?

KURITSUBO: Then he smiled at me. And we went on.

KEIKO: How terribly romantic.

KURITSUBO: I watched out of the window. He galloped away. I could see him marshalling his troops on the hillside. Then a few weeks later he was a prisoner.

KEIKO: What did he look like?

KURITSUBO: [*making a gesture*] Like a real man. Not like the ones we have here.

KEIKO: How strange to think that he's been in the palace ever since.

KURITSUBO: Yes. I know exactly where his cell is. It's at the corner of the seventeenth courtyard. Here. [*She draws a map in the sand.*] I've felt [*she sighs*]—oh so—odd—about him. [*Hand on heart.*]

AYAME: [*keen on her little bit of news*] Well, they're going to behead him now, I heard my mama say so.

KURITSUBO: I wonder. [*Sighs.*]

KEIKO: The palace is always full of false rumours.

KURITSUBO: Yes. I've heard that one before, actually.

KEIKO: What did your husband think about your romantic meeting with Prince Yorimitsu?

KURITSUBO: I never told him. [*Pause*] Yorimitsu is a friend of my husband. A close friend. Perhaps a par-tic-u-larly close and special friend!

KEIKO: What do you mean?

KURITSUBO: Oh, you're too young to understand, my dear.

[KURITSUBO *goes to the window. She takes up the pose which was* KEIKO's *at the beginning of the scene. She sighs.*]

KEIKO: [*reflecting*] How strange. How very strange.

KURITSUBO: It's snowing.

[*The other two join her to look out. The yellow winter light, the snow, the three girls at the lattice, make a pretty picture.*]

ACT ONE

Scene Four

A mountain temple. A large window has a view of snowy slopes, snow-laden bamboos, etc., and Fujiyama in the farther background. The sun is shining. The effect of light and air after the claustrophobic atmosphere of the palace is staggering. The scene is extremely beautiful. The audience ought to gasp. A sense of extreme cold. Within the room, altar, images of the Buddha, etc.

The ROSHI, FATHER AKITA, *and some of his monks. The latter all speak with Irish accents. They are examining some sort of beastie in a basket.*

MONK A: Look at the little black nose on him!

MONK B: He's some sort of bear, isn't he, Father?

AKITA: I think so.

MONK A: He was so white with snow I thought he was a stone. And then I thought he was dead.

MONK B: Sure he's as cold as the devil's forehead.

AKITA: He's certainly not dead. He's just asleep. He's hibernating. We mustn't wake him up.

[*He restrains the monks who want to poke the beastie.*]

MONK C: Shall we keep him, Father, and make a pet of him? Sure I think he's just a young one.

AKITA: We might try. We had a bear once, you remember.

MONK B: We did that—until some bloody bastard shot him. Sorry, Father.

MONK A: He was so white with snow I thought he was a stone.

MONK C: All curled up he is. Look at the cut of him!

MONK B: Where'll we put him then, until he wakes up again?

AKITA: He mustn't stay in here—it would wake him up too soon. Put him somewhere where he'll be cold but not frozen. Let me think—

MONK C: What about the old shed, the rotten old shed that's after falling down half of it.

AKITA: That would do—

MONK A: [*at window*] Father, there's a whole mob of fellows coming up the mountain.

[*They all lean out.*]

MONK C: Soldiers they are. I don't like that.

MONK B: Shall I go and fetch the pikes, Father?

AKITA: No, don't fetch the pikes. I don't know where they are, anyway. I feel sure these men are coming in peace. If they aren't there's nothing we can do about it. You've got good eyesight. Can you see the device on their shields?

MONK B: I cannot, Father.

AKITA: Well, if they stop here I will receive their captain. Go and put the little creature in the shed, put something over him, sacks or something—but [*shouting after* MONK A *departing*] see that he can breathe all right. You go to the gate [*this to* MONKS B *and* C] and receive these people politely. With dignity. And [*shouting after* MONKS B *and* C *departing*] don't look so nervous. And [*further shout*] oh Patushi, hide the golden Buddha in the usual place.

[*Exeunt* MONKS *severally.* FATHER AKITA *sits down and begins to meditate. A silence seems to surround him, although in the background there are sounds of the arrival of the soldiers. Words of command, clash of arms, perhaps the neighing of a horse. If possible these sounds should give a sense of huge space, distance, mountain air. They should retain the interest of the audience. After an interval a* MONK *enters and whispers something to* FATHER AKITA. *As* AKITA *rises, enter the* SHOGUN. *A moment of hesitation. Then the* SHOGUN *kowtows and the* ROSHI *merely bows. Old teachers are very important people in mediaeval Japan. (An exchange of salutations can be battle of nerves, like a gun duel.)*]

SHOGUN: Do you remember—who I am, Father?

AKITA: Perfectly, your excellency.

SHOGUN: It is many years since we met.

AKITA: [*smiling slightly*] I remember the occasion.

SHOGUN: Yes, well, I er— I was rather young then and a soldier, you know. I'm afraid—

AKITA: Don't apologise, my son. You were just in rather a hurry. One should never be in a hurry. Please be seated. Won't you take your coat off?

[*The* SHOGUN *is heavily muffled in snow-besprinkled furs. The* ROSHI *is barefoot. Throughout the interview the* SHOGUN *displays the characteristic nervousness of the layman in an unfamiliar religious setting.*]

SHOGUN: I don't think I will, if you don't mind. It's so damnably—terribly—cold here. I can't think how you don't all get frostbite.

AKITA: We are used to it.

SHOGUN: I hope I'm not interrupting your—er—whatever you do up here.

AKITA: No, not a bit, not a bit. All the time in the world. We have nothing to do.

[*They have sat down. A* MONK *brings the paraphernalia of the tea ceremony. With maddening slowness* AKITA *begins to make the tea.*]

SHOGUN: [*nailbiting nervousness*] Lovely place you've got up here. Marvellous air. Fine view of Mount Fuji.

AKITA: Yes, Fujiyama is a wonderful companion. He is so serene. And the light changes all the time about his head.

[*The light in fact does change during the scene. This should be marvellous.*]

SHOGUN: Ages since I've been in the mountains. Did plenty of climbing as a boy, of course.

AKITA: You come from the province of Satsuma, I believe?

SHOGUN: Yes, marvellous scenery, mountains, sea. Haven't been down there for ages. I've been rather tied to my desk lately. Yes, lovely view. I expect you get some jolly good hunting around here, don't you, bears, wild boar—?

AKITA: We are vegetarians, my child. And we do not kill animals for sport.

SHOGUN: Oh—er—yes, I forgot. I'm—er—sorry to drop in on your like this. If there'd been more time I would have sent a messenger first, but—

AKITA: We are delighted to see you. You should drop in more often. We love visitors. A visit from outside is quite a treat for us.

[*The* ROSHI *should be tremendously calm but not withdrawn. He has a marked physical grace. In his presence the* GENERAL *seems clumsy, doesn't quite know how to sit, etc.*]

SHOGUN: That's very kind of you—

AKITA: I'm sure you should get out more into the country-side.

SHOGUN: I have to work fifteen hours a day keeping the country on its feet.

AKITA: If you were to relax a little I expect the country would remain upright. Won't you have one of these little cakes, they are made by the nuns of the Datoki Convent in the next valley. They are quite excellent.

[*Cracked bell in the distance. Perhaps at the Datoki Convent.*]

SHOGUN: Thank you, thank you. Father, I want your help with something rather important.

AKITA: This tea will warm you a little after your journey. I hope you don't find that this sort of tea keeps you awake at night?

SHOGUN: No, no, not a bit.

AKITA: Some people say it tends to keep them awake. I can't say I've ever noticed it myself.

[*During these exchanges the* ROSHI *is slowly, rhythmically, busy with the tea arrangements.*]

SHOGUN: It's about Prince Yorimitsu.

[*Enter* MONK *with a brazier.*]

AKITA: Ah here comes a brazier. You shall have it. [*To* MONK] No, there, there. [*The brazier is put beside the* SHOGUN, *who clutches at it, To departing* MONK] See that the soldiers get some tea, won't you. Yes, of course there's enough!

[*Exit* MONK.]

I'm sure you should take your coat off. Then you'll feel the benefit when you put it on again, as they say.

SHOGUN: [*taking his coat off*] I'm sorry, I'm afraid the melting snow is making an awful mess of your floor.

AKITA: Don't worry. The snow lives in here with us too.

SHOGUN: [*feelingly*] Yes! Father, it's about Prince Yorimitsu.

AKITA: Yes.

SHOGUN: You taught his father, I believe, at the end of his life.

AKITA: Yes. Do have another, take pity on that one. [*Offering cakes.*]

SHOGUN: And you know Prince Yorimitsu.

AKITA: Yes.

SHOGUN: Father, Prince Yorimitsu is thinking of entering a monastery.

AKITA: You mean that it would be very convenient for you if he were to enter a monastery.

SHOGUN: No, he really has been thinking of it, really. I assure you. I know this. [*Pause*] Of course it would also be convenient for me.

AKITA: And for the Imperial family. More tea?

SHOGUN: And for the Imperial family. And for Prince Yorimitsu himself.

AKITA: The religious life is not "convenient". It is many things but not convenient.

SHOGUN: I mean that this—move—might save his life.

AKITA: Who endangers his life? You? Your excellency.

SHOGUN: He is not my prisoner.

[*The* ROSHI *looks as if he imagines that the* SHOGUN *could doubtless dispense with formalities if he cared to. Gesture perhaps.*]

Yorimitsu is a very dangerous man. He is the darling of the north. There are many voices, both among my own people and in the Imperial household, crying out for his head. This is only a matter of time. Somebody's nerve will break. Somebody will hire somebody to put a sword through him or poison his food. His continued existence makes too many powerful people sleepless.

AKITA: You live in a world of fear, my child, a world of sleeplessness. Why don't you set him free? Oh I know he isn't officially your prisoner, but I have no doubt that you could find means to set him free just as you could find means to kill him. A gesture of mercy, an act of compassion, can change situations and people very deeply, often much more deeply than can possibly be foreseen beforehand. If you were to release Yorimitsu you would create a new and very much better scene in this country.

SHOGUN: This is not anything which I've ever thought of.

AKITA: Think of it now, my son. Mercy is infectious.

SHOGUN: Release him—and rely on his generosity?

AKITA: Yes. He is a magnanimous person.

SHOGUN: [*hardening after a moment of hesitation*] A man as ambitious as that has no generosity. And the forces which he represents probably cannot be controlled even by him. If he were free— [*Gesture.*]

AKITA: Would it not be possible to talk instead of fighting?

SHOGUN: I don't like talking with a sword at my throat.

AKITA: [*after a pause. He sees he cannot persuade the* GENERAL] What are Yorimitsu's chances of being rescued from the palace?

SHOGUN: None whatsoever. Even he sees that now.

AKITA: [*considering*] I wonder how seriously he really has considered the religious life?

SHOGUN: You must ask him that.

AKITA: All right. Bring him up here.

SHOGUN: No. He would be rescued on the way. His friends have a way of finding things out. At least four different horsemen followed me up the mountain. You must come down to the capital.

AKITA: I would be very reluctant to do so, my son. It is

many many years since I left this place. And my life is
near its end.

SHOGUN: [*firm*] I'm sorry.

AKITA: And many years since I thought about your politics.

SHOGUN: You live remote from the real world, Father.

AKITA: *You* live remote from the real world, my son.

[*A sound of sutras being chanted nearby. First loud then falling
softer. The* SHOGUN *jumps.*]

If Prince Yorimitsu became a monk would he be allowed
to leave the Imperial palace and live where he pleased?

SHOGUN: Yes, er, in, er, due course.

AKITA: Hmm. There is no question of forcing him? It would
be a genuine choice?

SHOGUN: There would be no point in forcing him. For this
move to be of any value to *us* he would have to let his
followers know that he had given up his political ambitions of his own free will.

AKITA: You request me to come? Are you not in fact ordering me to come, your excellency?

SHOGUN: [*bowing*] A sleigh is waiting at the door.

AKITA: I do not want to enter your world, or think of your
things. I will talk to the prisoner. But a persuasion hand
in hand with a threat is not likely to appeal to a brave
man.

[*They both rise.*]

SHOGUN: I am extremely grateful to you, Father. If you can
succeed you will have performed a most important service to the state.

[*The sutras fall silent. Bell nearby inside monastery.*]

AKITA: The state? I often wonder what that word means.
Look out of the window. You see those huts over there,
half buried in the snow? And a path where a man walks,
followed by his dog, past the bamboos, carrying logs on
his back. People live there. In this valley and the next
valley and the next. In huts which they have built with
their own hands. They grow rice and eat it. They collect

wood and burn it. They are composed of needs which cry out to heaven to be satisfied. What has the state ever done for these people?

SHOGUN: I'm afraid you just don't understand politics, Father, why should you. Come now, please.

AKITA: Always in a hurry, my child.

[*They go out. Mount Fuji reddens and darkens.*]

ACT ONE

SCENE FIVE

The prisoner's cell. A clash of swords as the scene lightens.
YORIMITSU *is fencing with* NORIKURA. OKANO *watches with*
professional interest. They stop breathless, laughing.

YORIMITSU: Well, Okano, how did that look to you?

NORIKURA: You did splendidly, my lord. I am quite out of
breath!

YORIMITSU: I did splendidly, except that I would have
been dead three times.

NORIKURA: Possibly four!

OKANO: You do well, my lord, except that your thoughts
are still here. [*He touches the point of the sword.*]

YORIMITSU: I know. I can feel them running down my
sword arm.

OKANO: Watch Norikura for a moment as he fights with me.
[OKANO *and* NORIKURA *exchange a few passes.*]
You see there is a difference.

YORIMITSU: Yes. Years and years and years of difference.

OKANO: Of course I have been teaching Norikura ever
since he was a child. An idle disobedient boy, but I believe
he has learnt a little!
[*It should become apparent during the scene that* OKANO *and*
NORIKURA *are lovers.* OKANO *is about thirty-five,* NORI-
KURA *about twenty-one.*]
Don't be discouraged, my lord. You defend yourself well.
But one must strive to be—not efficient but—beautiful.

YORIMITSU: And when one is beautiful one will be—
deadly. Yes. I try not to think about the sword, but the
harder I try not to think about it the harder I think about it.

NORIKURA: I can remember that stage.

OKANO: Not only that. You are constantly watching your
opponent.

163

YORIMITSU: Yes! Yes! [*He has been told all this many times before.*]

OKANO: You must not. You must not watch, you must know. You must not even know, you must move. Without watching, without thinking. You must be quiet and purposeless. Out of an absolute absence of thought and purpose the flower of pure action will unfold. Evasion must be instinct and attack instinct too. Until there is no *you* that evades or attacks. There will simply be evasion, attack. It evades, it attacks.

YORIMITSU: The master always speaks in riddles! Sometimes when I watch your eyes or Norikura's eyes when you are fighting I feel that I understand. Yet when I fight myself I know that I have understood nothing.

OKANO: [*bowing*] If you think that you are well on the way to learn.

YORIMITSU: But here—without daily practice—

NORIKURA: Don't be cast down, my lord. It *will* come—suddenly.

YORIMITSU: I hope so!

OKANO: I am hard on you because I know you will love nothing but perfection. You are a very fine swordsman.

YORIMITSU: So I would have thought myself if I had never known you. [*Bows.*]

[OKANO *bows back. They lay aside the swords.*]

OKANO: You are in hard condition. [*He feels* YORIMITSU's *arm.*] You don't forget your exercises?

YORIMITSU: Of course not.

[NORIKURA *suddenly springs on* YORIMITSU *from behind. They wrestle.* YORIMITSU *doesn't do too badly. They laugh.*]

Thank you, Norikura, I really wasn't expecting that one! What a mountain cat you have here, Okano!

OKANO: A wild mountain cat. I sometimes wonder if I have really tamed it.

[*He grips* NORIKURA's *arm. Trial of strength.* OKANO *wins.* NORIKURA *rubs his arm ruefully.*]

NORIKURA: You are a natural wrestler, my lord. I had very little advantage over you.

YORIMITSU: Oh I'm fit enough inside my cage. But at any moment they could break my legs.

[*Armed men pass in the corridor.* YORIMITSU *listens.*]

Let's have the news session. Norikura.

[*He gestures.* NORIKURA *goes to the window and looks out. Then he seats himself beside the door and begins to hum a monotonous tuneless ditty so that the guard outside cannot overhear the talk.* YORIMITSU *and* OKANO *move to the front of the stage and speak in lowered voices.*]

OKANO: The General went to the Midera temple yesterday. Kokushi and Minoku followed him. He took about fifty soldiers, but Minoku said he could have got him with an arrow on at least two occasions.

YORIMITSU: Yes. It wouldn't be impossible to assassinate the General. But as soon as the General was dead Tokuzan would kill me! What was he doing at Midera?

OKANO: He took a priest away with him.

YORIMITSU: I can't see the General installing a spiritual adviser. Anything else on that?

OKANO: No, but we'll find out.

YORIMITSU: What's the general situation?

OKANO: Well, my dear lord, unchanged. I still think—

YORIMITSU: It's no good, Okano.

OKANO: Tokujo has five thousand disciplined troops. We can't keep them together indefinitely.

YORIMITSU: I know. Perhaps the palace is not unassailable, but so long as I am in this part of it, I am unrescuable. I don't want any useless blood shed on my behalf. Anyway, as soon as the alarm was given I'd be slaughtered. It's a completely mad situation. We're all paralysed by it, the General, Tokuzan and me.

[*Muted gong. Enter page with official letter for* YORIMITSU. NORIKURA *stops humming.* YORIMITSU *opens the letter.*]

Well, well. The ex-emperor Tokuzan is graciously

coming to visit me. This morning. Now. What does that mean? Oh I'm always wondering what things mean. What does it mean that I've still got my sword? What does it mean that you two are allowed to visit me?

NORIKURA: They are stupid. They think they can find out something by following us. But as soon as we are outside we lose them. Outside a man is free.

OKANO: They think nothing is really planned yet.

YORIMITSU: I know. And if it were— You put yourselves in danger by coming here. One day they'll provoke you and— Perhaps you ought to come unarmed.

NORIKURA: Unarmed! My sword is my hand.

YORIMITSU: [*half to himself*] Everything in here means something, only you never know what it is. They steal the natural meaning out of everything and give it their horrible meaning. How do I know that you two aren't just a part of their plan? I don't know whether what you tell me is true. Perhaps you're working for them. Perhaps I'm just being entangled in something which will make it easier for them to kill me.

[*Silence.* YORIMITSU *realises he has said something terrible.*]

I am sorry, my dear friends, I didn't mean that.

[*This is not good enough.*]

Okano, Norikura, please forgive me, I'm just poisoned by this place. I've been corrupted by imprisonment and breathing this foul air. They've infected my mind. Please.

[*Still not good enough.*]

Norikura, bring me my sword. Here. I swear on this sword that I trust you both with all my heart and soul.

OKANO: [*still rather grim*] All right, my lord.

YORIMITSU: You believe me?

[*The Samurai look at each other.*]

OKANO: Yes. But it was a very bad thing to say.

YORIMITSU: I'm deeply sorry. I trust you and I love you, my dear comrades. You must pardon these moments of insanity, it's like an illness. It's—this place. Listen. There is something I must say to you. Come here, both of you. This is hard to say. I've been in here five years. As far as we can see I can't be rescued. I can't be got out alive. And if either Tokuzan or the General dies the other will probably kill me. I haven't got a future. Would it not be better if you all—forgot me?

NORIKURA: How can we forget you, my dear lord? We think of you day and night, we think only of you.

YORIMITSU: But I'm useless. Oh we've lived on hopes and schemes. But this is something which I've tried just in these last months to understand and face. There is a force, there is a cause, there are brave men and good men and all sorts of people ready to follow. I might have been the leader. I thought this was my destiny. But it's—impossible. And all this waiting and dreaming about rescue wastes time and power and good will. It wastes the strength of the north. Because of me the whole operation is paralysed. As you said yourself, Okano, disciplined troops can't be held together indefinitely without a purpose. Forget me. Act without me. Choose another leader. Tokujo perhaps. Or some younger person. Someone I've never heard of. I may be in here forever.

NORIKURA: [*passionately*] Then we will wait forever. We are your Samurai. We do nothing without you.

OKANO: I have thought of this too.

[*This causes* YORIMITSU *pain.*]

I am sorry, my dear lord. I have lived with the impossibility of this situation too during these five years, and one's thoughts may change though one's heart does not. But really, there is no one else but you who would be followed.

[YORIMITSU *is relieved. It was indeed hard for him to say what he said.*]

Tokujo is old and has no kind of status. The younger men are followers not leaders. There is only you. You are a great prince and a tried general and a natural leader.

This is known. You are still waited for. You are essential.
You are the one.

YORIMITSU: [*sighing*] Thank you, Okano.

OKANO: You haven't given up hope, have you, my lord?

YORIMITSU: It's a tormentor, Okano.

OKANO: [*with passionate emphasis*] Keep hope with you.
Your hope is the life blood of the north.

YORIMITSU: Yes, yes. I still hear those bugles blowing in
my dreams.

[*Distant sounds in the corridor.*]

That will be Tokuzan. You must go, my children. And—
oh, be careful. However much they provoke you, don't
draw. You believe what I said?

OKANO: Yes. You believe what I said?

YORIMITSU: Yes. Goodbye, Norikura. Goodbye, my dear
master. Buddha go with you. And my thanks.

[*They begin to kneel but he embraces them. Exeunt Samurai.*
YORIMITSU *covers his face. The brouhaha arrives at the door.
Enter the ex-emperor* TOKUZAN *with attendants. They arrange
a low throne, cushions, etc., for him while he stands by, fussing
slightly at their arrangements. He has the shaven head and robes
of a Buddhist monk. When the attendants have finished he motions
them out and turns to the prisoner. The prisoner at once kowtows.*
TOKUZAN *bows and then sits cross-legged. The prisoner kneels.*
TOKUZAN *has a rather civil servicy manner, but is clearly a monk
of iron.*]

TOKUZAN: Those two men going away. Samurai of yours,
aren't they?

YORIMITSU: Yes, your Majesty.

TOKUZAN: Shouldn't trust them if I were you.

YORIMITSU: I do trust them.

TOKUZAN: Everyone's bought these days. A man in your
position can't afford to trust anybody.

YORIMITSU: [*not able entirely to conceal the emotion he still feels
from the last scene*] I've got to trust somebody in order to
stay alive.

TOKUZAN: Why? I don't trust anyone. You're getting soft, Yorimitsu, soft and sentimental and womanish. It's the prison air. Any complaints?

YORIMITSU: [*still emotional*] Yes. I can't walk out of that door.

TOKUZAN: I mean any serious complaints.

YORIMITSU: [*calmer*] I should have thought that was serious enough.

TOKUZAN: I did not come here to indulge in frivolous badinage.

YORIMITSU: Why did you come here then? Whenever you visit me I assume you are going to announce my forthcoming execution. Are you?

TOKUZAN: As far as I know there are no plans for your death just at the moment.

[*Muted gong. A page delivers official letters to* TOKUZAN. *He glances at them. The* SHOGUN's *seal is prominent. He ticks one or two documents, which the page removes.*]

YORIMITSU: I suppose these pages are all spies too.

TOKUZAN: Useless lot. Most of them are double agents.

YORIMITSU: What a scene. What a government, for a country reeling with poverty and misery and disorder.

TOKUZAN: Which you fondly imagine you could mend?

YORIMITSU: Yes! I do!

TOKUZAN: You are young, Yorimitsu, and you are perforce [*he indicates the cell*] very inexperienced. History is a great machine and we travel inside it. We have to. Political power is the product of history. It is also a sort of miracle. After all, why should anybody obey anybody?

YORIMITSU: Well, I think it's a good question!

TOKUZAN: Yes, but the answer is not a study in moral ideas. It is a study in historical necessity. You speak as if this country were a sort of jungle—

YORIMITSU: It is a sort of jungle, where the government goes on looting expeditions.

TOKUZAN: [*ignoring the interruption*] But in fact it is a complex and highly determined system, a system of loyalties and customs—

YORIMITSU: Aren't you talking about the palace, not the country? The palace is a highly determined system all right. A system which automatically creates more system, more complications, more paper, more suspicion, more espionage, more fear—What is the strange smell one breathes in all the time in this place? Fear.

TOKUZAN: Perhaps it is your own fear you are smelling, my friend.

YORIMITSU: As soon as people start being frightened and suspicious, thought stops, art stops, love stops and the country perishes.

TOKUZAN: I'm afraid your sort of idealism is purely destructive. [*He is glancing at a letter.*]

YORIMITSU: I don't believe that history is a great machine. That's a rotten palace idea. It stops you from thinking. All right, circumstances change. But people don't change and what they need doesn't change. They need food and shelter. And they need truth and justice and freedom, and talk and art which isn't just propaganda. And however untidy and unsystematic and, all right, destructive it may be one must keep on coming back to these big simple needs people have. And they aren't just needs, they're rights, and one must never forget their names and one must go on and on and on shouting out their names.

TOKUZAN: All right, but don't shout at me now please.

YORIMITSU: Governing a country isn't such a mystery. Ordinary people outside this place aren't morons. In my part of the country there's order and government. All right, it's military rule at the moment, but that's because, although you like to deny it, the country's in a state of civil war. But at least it's based on common sense and some kind of ordinary decencies. It's open and simple and people aren't afraid.

TOKUZAN: You seem to attach some sort of mystical importance to the absence of fear. But people will always fear something. They need to.

YORIMITSU: You can't have truth *and* fear. Absence of fear is the key to any sort of decent politics.

TOKUZAN: As I said, political power is a miracle, or—to use your word—a mystery. Sovereignty is a mysterious growth, Yorimitsu. The fountain head of a system of obedience. Where it exists—and it exists in the palace— it should not be damaged by the irresponsible shouting of empty slogans. Justice is a word of which you literally do not understand the meaning. Justice is a cobble stone, it is not a thought.

YORIMITSU: I think political power should have a human face. And I think sovereignty belongs to the people.

TOKUZAN: Really, Yorimitsu, I think you have forgotten which century you are supposed to be living in.

YORIMITSU: It's funny about you. I thought you were a political theorist. I thought you had some sort of ideals of your own, however mad or mistaken. But it seems to me that in the end you're just a gangster. There isn't a pin to choose between you and the General. Your Majesty.

TOKUZAN: And I'm afraid you idealise the peasantry because once, a long time ago, they cried your battle cries and threw their filthy caps in the air when you rode by. However, I did not come here to argue politics with you. Your views are puerile and of no interest to me. I came to discuss your position.

YORIMITSU: Is it open to discussion?

TOKUZAN: Reflection, let us say. It has seemed to me, especially of late, that you are living in a dream world. Of course it is hard for a prisoner not to console himself with dreams. But I would have expected a man as intelligent as you to be more of a realist. Your mind appears to be split into two halves. With one half of it you imagine yourself free, being a great leader and a great statesman. With the other half you must appreciate that there is absolutely no chance whatsoever of your realising your ambitions. You are completely trapped.

YORIMITSU: The bugles are blowing in the north. You too hear them in your sleep.

TOKUZAN: You will never hear them, Yorimitsu. How romantic you are. *That* has nothing to do with you. Oh you are not a negligible quantity—but you are important now merely as a piece of property. You no longer own yourself. Your people must surely appreciate by now that if there were any really important revolutionary movement in the north you would immediately be killed. So your dreams of power are strictly self-contradictory, they are nonsense. You can never have power. The forces that could bring you to power would merely ensure your death. You speak of truthfulness and justice. Be truthful enough with yourself to confront the realities of your situation.

[*Pause.* YORIMITSU *is silent. He slowly lowers his eyes.*]

And dismiss from your mind any idea that the future may improve your lot. If either the General or the Imperial family should fall from power, the other side would immediately execute you. I am sorry to be so grim, but I am afraid that our gentlemanly behaviour may have contributed to nourish your illusions.

That is what I wanted to say, and I advise you to reflect upon it. My advice to you, my dear Yorimitsu, and I mean it really kindly, is despair. Despair, despair, despair. You will never be released from here. Never, never, never.

[*They stare at each other as the stage darkens.*]

ACT ONE

Scene Six

The prisoner's cell. Night. The cell is rather dark. A second brazier has been installed. YORIMITSU *is doing his exercises, press ups and so on. He pauses a little breathless and feels his body. Is he putting on weight? He starts again. Distant sound of armed men. He stops and listens. The sound approaches his door and stops outside.* YORI-MITSU *retreats, waits. Enter the* SHOGUN. *Attendants rapidly arrange throne, cushions, etc. The* SHOGUN *motions them out.* YORIMITSU *kowtows. The* SHOGUN *bows. The* SHOGUN *sits cross-legged on his throne, the prisoner kneels. A moment of silence. Very faint ironical smiles. The atmosphere is very different from that of the last scene. A little later the audience will have realised that the two men like each other.*

YORIMITSU: Your excellency—has not honoured me with a visit—for a long time.

SHOGUN: Everything looks much the same in here.

YORIMITSU: I have been here since we last met. I haven't had the place redecorated. The only thing that changes is this. [*He indicates the vase.*] Chrysanthemums, then pine branches, myrtle and bay and yew. And later almond, and later cherry, symbol of the Samurai, and then flowers of spring from the emperor's garden. And I change too, growing older in captivity.

SHOGUN: And wiser, I trust, and less full of empty hopes.
    [YORIMITSU *looks hard at the* SHOGUN.]
    Yes, you seem quite comfortable in here. Flowers, braziers, books. How is your treatise on political economy getting along?

YORIMITSU: I am full of thoughts.

SHOGUN: I must say I envy you this quiet life of study and contemplation. I scarcely have time to open a book these days. By the way, that anthology of Chinese poetry

I lent you, could I have it back if you've finished with it?

YORIMITSU: Yes, it's here. [*He gets the book out.*] Thank you. It gave me great pleasure. I specially liked—

SHOGUN: I'm sorry, I have not come to chat—this time.

YORIMITSU: Funny, all those discussions on philosophy and literature we used to have, when everyone thought you were interrogating me about my subversive activities!

SHOGUN: Yes, that was real talk. Like that first evening in my tent.

YORIMITSU: Yes, I remember that evening.

SHOGUN: But I am afraid those days are over.

YORIMITSU: What have you come to tell me? Is it—? [*Gesture.*]

SHOGUN: No, not that. It's something which I would like to make very definite and very clear.

YORIMITSU: Go on—your excellency.

SHOGUN: Has it ever occurred to you that the conditions of your imprisonment might—change?

YORIMITSU: It occurs to me every day.

SHOGUN: And I don't just mean depriving you of your flowers.

YORIMITSU: I understand you perfectly, your excellency. I don't think you need go into details.

SHOGUN: But the details are important, my dear Yorimitsu. If a man can read and write, talk to people, get exercise and enough to eat, he can remain fairly healthy and sane in captivity for quite a long time. Perhaps not forever, but for many years if he is a person of character.

YORIMITSU: Go on, my friend.

SHOGUN: We are supposed to have become civilised, Yorimitsu. But how very primitive and barbarous we really remain in this little backward country. We are the greatest imitators in the world. We imitate the Chinese, we ape and copy and assimilate the superficial flowers of that great civilisation. But while they are genuinely cultivated people we are merely peasants who have put on silk robes and perfume without in any way changing our savage hearts. Cruelty is never far from us. It is a national characteristic. The great sword-masters of the Samurai, like your friend Okano who pays you visits, are artists, who will bow to a man one moment, cut his head off, with the utmost elegance, the next, and then go and drink a glass of sake and arrange sprays of peach blossom. That is what we are like. What I am like. What you are like.

YORIMITSU: Not me actually, but go on.

SHOGUN: So it is that a prisoner, who at one moment has books and friends and flowers, at the next moment, because the wind has changed, or somebody has the toothache, may find himself in solitude, in darkness, starving, chained to a wall, in a cell where he can neither stand up nor sit down. [*Pause*] And, of course, there can be, naturally, further elaborations.

YORIMITSU: So you've made some sort of bargain with the old fox, have you? It's come to that at last. I'm too dangerous as I am. I can live—but only degraded, broken, made into a wailing lunatic.

SHOGUN: Any man can be destroyed by torment.

YORIMITSU: I have seen it done.

SHOGUN: So I hope you won't feel that my hypothetical predictions are in any way disrespectful to you.

YORIMITSU: [*laughs*] So you've joined forces. You and Tokuzan. All right. When does it start?

SHOGUN: No, no, don't misunderstand me. There is no plot, as you seem to imagine, and what I have just been mentioning is, as I say, purely hypothetical. Such things could happen, even in this age of refinement, and even to an Imperial prisoner. What I really came to tell you was something else.

YORIMITSU: I smell fox. You're doing Tokuzan's dirty work for him. He was here this morning telling me to despair. Now you add this little thought for the day. You might have been somebody, Musashi, if you hadn't let yourself be corrupted by this rotten set-up. My father respected your father.

SHOGUN: My father was practically your father's vassal.

YORIMITSU: Your father was a decent man who lived in the open. He didn't have a secret police!

SHOGUN: I've got something else to say!

YORIMITSU: Say it and get out, and bring on the chains and the instruments of torture!

SHOGUN: Listen. I am sending you a visitor tomorrow. No, not the executioner or the torturer. A monk called Father Akita.

YORIMITSU: Akita. He was my father's teacher, in the last years, in the mountains.

SHOGUN: He is a very holy man. I know that you have thought seriously of embracing the religious life.

YORIMITSU: I see, I see, I see. That's what you were up to at the Midera monastery.

SHOGUN: I think you should regard this as a most important moment of choice. And it is a choice that cannot be postponed. You will never escape from here, Yorimitsu, never. You would be a prisoner here to the end of your days. Meanwhile the peach blossom comes after the almond, and the cherry after the peach. If you choose now to take the tonsure you can do so with a whole body and a clear mind. Later on you may not even have a mind. Situations do not go on forever, my dear friend, they become critical, and we are all in the grip of circumstances which lead us to do not what we would do but what we must do.

YORIMITSU: Oh get out! Here, take your book of poems. I don't know how you can even touch that book, living as you do. Or go to someone like Father Akita with your lousy schemes. And exhorting me to the religious life and threatening me with torture. You've become a rat.

SHOGUN: You have the spiritual pride of the cloister already. You should do well. You might become a prince of the church. If you had my place you would do as I do. You would have to.

YORIMITSU: Never, never, never.

[*They stare at each other.*]

SHOGUN: I am sorry that fortune has made us enemies.

YORIMITSU: Why did you stop coming to see me?

SHOGUN: I felt it unwise to become attached to what I might one day have to destroy. Reflect on that choice. Goodnight.

[*The* SHOGUN *bows low and the prisoner makes a gesture of hopelessness.*]

Curtain

END OF ACT ONE

ACT TWO

SCENE ONE

The apartments of the princess. The stage is divided by a screen. On one side sits the ex-emperor TOKUZAN, *on the other side the princess, with* KURITSUBO *and* AYAME *a little farther off. Branches lie in the foreground, waiting to be arranged.*

TOKUZAN: What about Prince Mitachi?

KEIKO: Too old.

TOKUZAN: What about Prince Tekuan?

KEIKO: Too young.

TOKUZAN: What about Prince Natuka?

KEIKO: Too small.

TOKUZAN: What about Prince Koyama?

KEIKO: Too fat.

TOKUZAN: What about Prince Hirota?

KEIKO: Too hairy.

TOKUZAN: Too hairy?

KEIKO: *Much* too hairy!

[*She is both amused and exasperated and obviously answering at random.* KURITSUBO *and* AYAME *desperately suppress giggles.*]

TOKUZAN: What about Prince Kawada?

KEIKO: Too tall.

TOKUZAN: Prince Kawada is about four feet eight.

KEIKO: In that case he's too small.

TOKUZAN: I think you must be getting rather mixed up, my dear. You saw Prince Kawada, in the distance I must admit, at the archery contest. In fact he won the archery contest. Don't you remember him now?

KEIKO: [*beating her brow with exasperation*] Oh yes of course I remember him now! He looks exactly like a monkey.

TOKUZAN: He is generally regarded as rather good-looking. And he is an excellent shot. Really, Keiko, you shouldn't

178

be in such a muddle about this important matter. You ought to keep a notebook.

KEIKO: A notebook!!!

[*The other two cannot stifle their amusement any longer. Unmistakable sounds of giggling.*]

TOKUZAN: Who's in there with you?

KEIKO: Kuritsubo and Ayame.

TOKUZAN: You girls really should try to behave like grown-up people. Keiko!

KEIKO: Yes, uncle.

TOKUZAN: Are you listening?

KEIKO: Yes, uncle.

[*She motions the other two away. They fall over among cushions, stifling their mirth.*]

TOKUZAN: Keiko, you are the Crown Princess. At the moment you are just a silly giggling schoolgirl.

KEIKO: Really, uncle!

TOKUZAN: But one day you will be a very important and powerful person. Your marriage is a matter of vital importance to the whole country. And I must warn you that if you don't soon make up your mind for yourself I shall have to make it up for you. I am afraid you are a very silly girl. All those court romances you read have put the most frivolous ideas into your head.

KEIKO: You mean frivolous ideas about loving the person you marry?

TOKUZAN: Precisely. Marriage has nothing whatever to do with love. Love is a temporary, irrational and ridiculously over-valued emotion and a very bad start for any marriage. Much better to regard it as a duty and make the best of it. Then you may even begin to discover some tolerably agreeable characteristics in your spouse. A marriage of romantic love leads to nothing but disillusionment and bitterness.

[KURITSUBO *is nodding her head in agreement.*]

Expect nothing from marriage, Keiko. Then you may

find in it some small traces of happiness, or at least the satisfaction of doing your duty. A woman's lot is inevitably a hard one and you must have the courage to face that fact from the very start.

KEIKO: [*who has been pulling faces*] I don't want to marry yet, uncle.

TOKUZAN: I am afraid that having had no parents to control you you have grown up with notions of having your own way which are to say the least, in a woman, distinctly un-Imperial.

KEIKO: I'm sorry, uncle.

TOKUZAN: I advise you to reflect seriously and be ready to make a choice soon. Otherwise you will have to abide by decisions made by others. Do you understand me, Keiko?

KEIKO: Yes, uncle.

TOKUZAN: All right, my child. There, I don't want to be vexed with you. Just try to be grown-up and brave and make up your mind, will you? Now I must go. I've spent far too long with you already. Goodbye, then.

KEIKO: Goodbye, uncle.

[*She listens to be sure he is really gone, then wails, bursting into tears.*]

AYAME: I think it's a shame!

KEIKO: [*through wails and tears*] Well, you said you'd marry anyone your mother chose.

AYAME: Yes, but I'm only me.

KURITSUBO: Modest little thing!

KEIKO: [*fiercely*] Well, I'm certainly *me* and I'm not going to marry any of those *puppets*. I know what they're like. I can see from the way they walk. Oh I'm so full of hope and love, I *can't* see it like uncle says, I can't just regard it as a dreary duty, I'd rather kill myself.

KURITSUBO: I think he talked a lot of sense actually. Love is just an adolescent's dream. If I were you I'd have Prince Mitachi. He's nearly seventy and he lives in a bath-chair and he wouldn't make you any trouble and he'd soon be dead.

KEIKO: And then I'd be a widow, and you know what it's like being a widow around here.

KURITSUBO: Oh I don't know. Some widows I can think of knock up quite a lot of fun.

KEIKO: [*wailing again*] I don't want fun I want—

KURITSUBO: All right, don't tell me, let me guess!

AYAME: Did you hear him say Prince Hirota? He's my suitor, the one who writes me letters!

KEIKO: He's writing to other women already!

KURITSUBO: Don't be silly, he isn't to know he's going to get you. They all write round to lots of girls just in case. They have to make contacts. The palace is full of pages carrying love letters, there's so many of them you don't see them.

KEIKO: Ach—it's as if we're for sale.

KURITSUBO: We are for sale!

AYAME: Oh poor Keiko. I'm so sorry about Prince Hirota. Fancy his writing to me!

KEIKO: [*calming down, thoughtful*] I don't want to marry— one of them—somebody ordinary. I wish there was some- one quite different and special—someone like—

AYAME: He writes on such lovely paper. My nanny says you can always tell a gentleman by his writing paper. [*She begins to finger the branches.*]

KURITSUBO: Come on, Keiko, cheer up!

AYAME: Let's arrange the branches, shall we? Bags I these ones. [*She selects three.*]

KURITSUBO: It's only matrimony, you know. You aren't going to be beheaded!

[KEIKO *shudders. Half-heartedly she joins the other two, select- ing branches to arrange. She looks pensive, kneeling slightly apart. Then she raises her hand to her face. Perhaps she has had an idea?*]

ACT TWO

Scene Two

The prisoner's cell. Afternoon. FATHER AKITA *sits cross-legged. The prisoner kneels. They have obviously been talking for some time.*

AKITA: Has it then taught you nothing, my son, to live for so long in the shadow of death?

YORIMITSU: I haven't felt the shadow, really.

AKITA: Most of what we think about death is an illusion. But it is a great sign. It signifies the vanity of all earthly striving.

YORIMITSU: I know. But no young man can see this. I can't see it any more than I can see that I am going to die. Even I, who have lived for five years with the threat of the axe, do not really believe in my heart that I am going to die.

AKITA: You must go far beyond your heart. Conceive that everything you know and feel now is a dream. Except for one pinpoint of faith. Something which speaks no word and sheds no light, but which burns and burns inside.

YORIMITSU: Yes. I have felt it burn, Father— I have felt it —hurt me—here. I have wanted these things, yes. But I am still young. My father had everything. He had a full life of action, he was a general, a great statesman, a great prince. And then when he was old he gave himself over to holiness.

AKITA: Your father had not enough time. To achieve the Buddha nature requires a lifetime of attention.

YORIMITSU: [*bowing to the ground*] I revere it in you.

AKITA: You may revere it anywhere for it is in all things. But to achieve enlightenment, to clarify the mirror so that what is seen is seen, what is shown is shown, takes years and years and years of devotion. Did your father never say anything about that to you when you saw him at the end?

YORIMITSU: Yes. He told me he had come to it too late.

AKITA: There is such a thing as being soiled by the world. You take the stain deeply, deeply as the years pass. It cannot be otherwise.

YORIMITSU: I know. Father, I'm sorry, I am trying to think but I can't put those other things out of my mind, what I was telling you earlier. If I do this thing under duress—

AKITA: You will not be doing it under duress. You will be doing it because you have recognised the most precious thing in the world and chosen it.

YORIMITSU: How do I know that I won't be doing it under duress. I fear the maiming of my body and my mind more than I fear death. I have seen brave strong men reduced to whimpering mindless tatters. And even if these threats are empty—and how can I know—I will have chosen partly out of fear. Or so it will appear to my friends. So it will appear at times to myself forever after. I will have disappointed my friends and rejoiced my enemies. The General will think that I did it out of fear.

AKITA: Yorimitsu, what does it matter what the General thinks! See the *scale* of these things. With one bound you must overleap obsessions of this kind—your pride, your motives, your reputation. Be great enough of soul to see how little these things matter. Magnanimity is the beginning of enlightenment.

YORIMITSU: I can't make this great bound.

AKITA: In the achievement of enlightenment it is a scarcely perceptible movement.

YORIMITSU: You see, I want to do some good in the world, Father. Nothing very grand. Just some simple good things for ordinary people.

AKITA: You cannot measure what good a dedicated life may do.

YORIMITSU: Yes, I know—but I want to do things which I *can* measure.

AKITA: Think, my child, think. [*He indicates the cell.*] Think where you are.

YORIMITSU: Yes, yes, I know, you said this before. I'm dreaming again. Father, I can't give up the hope of freedom, I can't.

AKITA: Perhaps you should. I am not siding with your enemies in saying this. You must face the full truth of your situation.

YORIMITSU: I know. Tokuzan was right. I've been thinking in a double way.

AKITA: And even if you were free—you imagine yourself helping people. You would be fighting for power. Consider the strength and nature of what opposes you. [*He indicates the palace.*]

YORIMITSU: You think it would be all intrigue and brutality in the end, like the rest of them.

AKITA: Intrigue and brutality and the shedding of innocent blood. Even by sitting here and hoping you may become the cause of bloodshed.

YORIMITSU: I've thought about that too.

AKITA: Society cannot be saved. It is a great beast. Almost all men are made victims by power. You have told me how envy and pride even now devour your soul.

YORIMITSU: Yes. I feel them, physically, like rats.

AKITA: And later, would it not be worse, in a life continually concerned with power?

YORIMITSU: Oh if only I could see the future! You speak in such riddles, Father. I don't think I'd be corrupted. And how do I know that your way is really of such supreme value? How do I know that the spiritual life is not just—empty?

AKITA: It is empty—empty, empty, empty. There is no way. There is only a ceaseless profitless preoccupation with the end. There is nothing for you to possess. All you will gain is with you already.

YORIMITSU: You mean—

AKITA: This and this and this. [*He touches things.*] To perceive purely, without illusion, without anxiety, without dream, without self. There is no other world, Yorimitsu. There is only this one, only most people cannot see it. Amida's paradise is here.

YORIMITSU: You speak to my ambition.

AKITA: That is wrong too. If your ambition hears my words they are not my words.

YORIMITSU: My swordmaster Okano speaks of being purposeless, of there being no me any more, and then action and vision would be—pure.

AKITA: It is so. When you are without self the Buddha nature in you is the real individual. Then action is spontaneous. And only then is it entirely right. You recognise and love perfection, Yorimitsu. Why not give yourself over to it entirely?

[*Pause.* YORIMITSU *is obviously moved, shaken.*]

YORIMITSU: [*last hope*] I suppose one couldn't learn to be enlightened by practising politics?

AKITA: No, because politics is neither an art nor a science.

YORIMITSU: I'm sorry, my mind is in an uproar.

AKITA: Make it still. Be quiet, my child.
"The lake-reflected swan knows this:
What is is not, what is not is."

YORIMITSU: I don't understand you, Father.
"For I am still
Only as the hawk is still:
Aloft, my searching will."

AKITA: What you call your will is an illusion too.

[*A sound of excited voices, approaching feet. The door flies open and* OKANO *rushes in. The blood-stained body of* NORIKURA *is carried after him.* OKANO *is incoherent with grief. His grief is terrible. Moment of confusion.*]

OKANO: [*weeping, almost inarticulate*] They did it. They provoked him. It was done deliberately. The guards did it. We were in the first courtyard. He began to draw his sword and they cut him down from behind. I tried to fight but—dozens of them—holding me—they took away my sword—oh my darling—I should have died with you, I should have died, I should have died, I should have died. Oh my darling one, my heart— [*He falls down beside the body moaning.*]

YORIMITSU: Done deliberately, yes. As a warning. To me.

AKITA: This is your work, my son. Let there be no more.

YORIMITSU: My work. I know.

AKITA: Come out of it, my son, come right out of it.

YORIMITSU: I don't know what it means. I don't know which way to go. [*He kneels slowly beside the body.*]

ACT TWO

Scene Three

The prisoner's cell. Night. Dim light. YORIMITSU *is alone. He is obviously distracted and miserable. He wanders about, touches his sword, leans his head against the wall below it, beats his fist on the wall. Listens. Sits down. Stands up. Kneels by the brazier and ruminates.*

[Muted gong. Enter a page with an official letter.]

YORIMITSU: Oh thank you. *[He sighs, pulls himself up.]* The Imperial Seal. They won't leave one alone even at night. It's probably some rubbish.

[The page is still kneeling by the door. The audience is by now so used to the coming and going of pages that it takes them a little time, perhaps as long as it takes YORIMITSU, *to realise that the page is the princess in disguise.]*

Ridiculous the way they do these things up. *[He opens it.]* Oh—my God—oh—heavens—

[With luck the audience might suppose it is his death warrant.]

Somebody has written me a love letter.

"So swift, so true, the dove

Flies like an arrow

To your heart, my love."

But no one is allowed to— How did this get through? I suppose the Imperial Seal—young fellow, who sent this letter? Who—?

*[*YORIMITSU *stares. The princess rises and moves back. Her very long hair, hidden under her cap, is dislodged and falls about her.]*

Who are you? *[Desperate whisper.]*

*[*KEIKO *is so frightened throughout this scene that she can hardly talk. She is also on the verge of tears. This dishevelled wild-haired terrified girl is very different from the soignée aristocrat of the earlier scenes.]*

KEIKO: I am Keiko—the Emperor's sister.

YORIMITSU: The Crown Princess! [*He looks at the door.*]

KEIKO: He's asleep.

YORIMITSU: But you shouldn't have—why—?

KEIKO: Don't be angry with me.

YORIMITSU: Oh I'm not— But why—?

KEIKO: I had to come. I love you.

YORIMITSU: Oh—my—dear—girl.

KEIKO: It's not a very good poem.

YORIMITSU: It's a wonderful poem. It's the best poem in the world. But you take such a terrible risk, coming—

KEIKO: I was so frightened, I thought I'd lost my way, I kept going on and on, and I thought my hair would come down or someone would speak to me, and—

YORIMITSU: You're wonderful. So brave—

KEIKO: I had to see you, I had to— I knew you were the only one— Forgive me, please.

YORIMITSU: Oh Keiko, you've come—to me—through all those awful corridors.

KEIKO: Please be kind to me. I've never talked to a man —like this—before.

YORIMITSU: Oh my dear, so lovely, so beautiful— But I'm just a prisoner, I'm nothing, nothing at all.

KEIKO: They aren't going to kill you, are they?

YORIMITSU: No, they're not going to kill me. Oh Keiko, you miracle, you came to me, to me!

KEIKO: I love you, I love you— Yorimitsu.

YORIMITSU: There's my brave girl!

[*They kneel facing each other and very cautiously and gently* YORIMITSU *takes her hand.*]

ACT TWO

Scene Four

The office of the ex-emperor TOKUZAN. TOKUZAN *seated.*
PRINCE HIRAKAWA *standing. In-trays, out-trays, etc.*

TOKUZAN: It has the great simplicity of an idea of genius.

HIRAKAWA: I just couldn't be more surprised, your
majesty.

TOKUZAN: I can't think why I didn't think of it before.
It's perfect.

HIRAKAWA: I congratulate you. And of course I'm delighted.

TOKUZAN: As it was I didn't even think of it myself.

HIRAKAWA: Who thought of it?

TOKUZAN: The princess thought of it.

HIRAKAWA: But whatever could have put it into her head?

TOKUZAN: Oh just the fantastical whimsy of a young girl.
As Yorimitsu is the only man she hasn't seen she thinks
he must be far more remarkable than the others.

HIRAKAWA: He is far more remarkable than the others!

TOKUZAN: And being in prison of course he's a romantic
figure.

HIRAKAWA: What an absolutely amazing plan. But there
must be some snag surely.

TOKUZAN: I thought that. But I can't see one. I've been
looking up the rules of the ordeal. [*He takes up a scroll.*]

HIRAKAWA: After all, Yorimitsu is a political prisoner.

TOKUZAN: [*looking at the rules*] It doesn't say the suitor
mustn't be a political prisoner.

HIRAKAWA: I suppose they never thought of that one!

TOKUZAN: He must be socially acceptable, of course.

HIRAKAWA: Well, Yorimitsu is certainly that.

TOKUZAN: From the north. That might have mattered a
generation or two ago, but now—

189

HIRAKAWA: Isn't he related to the Imperial family through his maternal grandmother?

TOKUZAN: Yes. I've been looking at his pedigree.

YORIMITSU's *pedigree is an immense scroll which unwinds across the entire stage.* TOKUZAN *and* HIRAKAWA *crawl about on hands and knees perusing it.*]

HIRAKAWA: [*whistling*] Phew! I say, look at that! And that!

TOKUZAN: Yes, he has some quite impeccable ancestors.

HIRAKAWA: Wait a moment. Have you told Yorimitsu?

TOKUZAN: No, not yet. You're going to tell him. Now.

HIRAKAWA: It's perfectly possible that he won't agree. He'll be suspicious.

TOKUZAN: You will persuade him that he has nothing to fear. And he will believe you.

HIRAKAWA: Well, *has* he nothing to fear?

TOKUZAN: Nothing. Come, come. It's an ideal way of ending the deadlock. You see, my dear Hirakawa, I have never ruled out the possibility of an alliance between Yorimitsu and the General.

HIRAKAWA: Yorimitsu is far too ambitious—

TOKUZAN: And you know your friend's views about the proper role of the Imperial family!

HIRAKAWA: Well—

TOKUZAN: You are not giving anything away.

HIRAKAWA: So you think this marriage would recruit Yorimitsu for the Imperial interest?

TOKUZAN: He is a man of honour.

HIRAKAWA: He won't agree. I'm sure he won't agree. He'll see too many strings, implications. It will look like a trap.

[*Muted gong. Enter a page with letters. They fall silent.*]

He would automatically become a member of the Imperial family, wouldn't he?

TOKUZAN: Yes. And a member of the Imperial family cannot be an Imperial prisoner. He would gain his freedom, a charming girl, political power. Why should he look further? The alternative is the prospect of endless imprisonment: a prospect which I suspect has been depressing our friend somewhat of late.

HIRAKAWA: Aren't you a little nervous at the idea of Yorimitsu at large, even married to the Crown Princess?

TOKUZAN: It would be a gentleman's agreement. He could perfectly well employ his talents without making trouble for us. He could even amuse himself unseating the General. The girl would be the seal of the agreement. And more than that. A clever woman has great power over her husband. My niece is a little goose at the moment but she has plenty of brains. I shall make something of that girl.

HIRAKAWA: You *do* look ahead!

TOKUZAN: But not a word of this to anyone else, Hirakawa. We'll call this Operation Arrow. Kindly refer to it in this way.

HIRAKAWA: All right. But—

TOKUZAN: Not a hint of this must reach the General. Not until we have to make it public just before the event. I've told Keiko to keep it absolutely secret.

HIRAKAWA: The General couldn't stop it, could he?

TOKUZAN: I don't know.

HIRAKAWA: Well, I'm silent. I'll go to Yorimitsu now. But I'm perfectly certain that he won't agree.

ACT TWO

Scene Five

The prisoner's cell. OKANO *is sitting bound up in his grief.* YORI-
MITSU *walks about, stretches out his arms. He is holding the
princess's letter. He is obviously ecstatically, mindlessly happy. He
listens absently to* OKANO's *grieving.*

OKANO: Yes, I ought to have died with him. To see him
killed before my face and not even—cut down and
slaughtered like an animal without a chance to fight—
his blood—flowing—and I— My sword taken away from
me. Disgraced, utterly utterly disgraced. I can never lift
my head. Forgive me, my darling. Oh I'll avenge this, I'll
have blood for this. Blood, blood.

YORIMITSU: What did this thing doesn't bleed. [*He indicates
the palace.*] I'm sorry—

OKANO: Ought I to kill myself, my lord?

YORIMITSU: Don't be a damn fool, Okano.

OKANO: I'll revenge this, somehow. I'll kill those swine.
For his blood, an ocean of blood. Oh my dear love—

YORIMITSU: [*making an effort*] Don't destroy yourself with
grieving, Okano, my dear friend.
[*Enter* PRINCE HIRAKAWA.]

HIRAKAWA: Oh, Yorimitsu. [*He sees* OKANO *who pays no
attention.*] Look, I've got something rather important to
tell you. No, it's nothing awful. Could he—er— [*He points
to* OKANO.]

YORIMITSU: Let Okano stay, he is my brother. Whatever
is it, Hirakawa?

HIRAKAWA: It's top secret.

YORIMITSU: Well, I'm not going to turn him out, especially
not now. Come on, you're bursting with something.

HIRAKAWA: Yorimitsu, you promise you won't be angry
with me?

YORIMITSU: No, I don't promise.

HIRAKAWA: It's a bit hard to explain really—I don't know what on earth you'll think of it—but please don't just say no at once—

YORIMITSU: Oh come on, come on, out with it.

HIRAKAWA: Well, a most extraordinary idea has been put forward.

YORIMITSU: Who by?

HIRAKAWA: By Tokuzan.

YORIMITSU: I can't imagine liking any idea of his. What is Tokuzan's idea?

HIRAKAWA: [*lowered voice*] That you should marry Keiko, the Crown Princess.

[YORIMITSU *turns away, hiding his ecstatic face from* HIRAKAWA. *After a moment he kneels, then lies prone upon the ground hiding his face.*]

Oh dear, I knew you'd hate it.

YORIMITSU: Go on about it a bit. I can just bear it.

[OKANO *is now listening.*]

HIRAKAWA: Look, this is absolutely secret, that's understood, isn't it. And—sssh. [*He points at the door.*] Well, I know it sounds awful, but— You see it's a way of ending the deadlock. You'd be set free of course—you see, Tokuzan has been afraid that you might make a deal with the General—and he thinks you'd be grateful—to the Imperial family I mean—he thinks it's a way of sort of—I suppose guaranteeing that you wouldn't do anything awful to them—I mean it would be like a sort of gentleman's agreement, wouldn't it?

OKANO: A very foxy plan!

HIRAKAWA: Tokuzan thinks you and he could sort of co-operate. He has the highest opinion of you—

OKANO: Ha! We sell ourselves to the Imperial family for the price of a girl. And what guarantees that my lord would be set free?

HIRAKAWA: That's quite certain.

OKANO: Tokuzan says so! There would be other traps and other ways of captivity. Why should we trust Tokuzan? Why should we trust you?

HIRAKAWA: [*ignoring* OKANO] Please think about it seriously, please. *Think*, Yorimitsu. It's a way out. And it may be the only way out.

[*Sobered a little by* OKANO's *outburst,* YORIMITSU *sits with his arms round his knees, regarding* HIRAKAWA *with bright intent eyes.*]

YORIMITSU: What do you think, Hirakawa? Would Tokuzan really let me go?

HIRAKAWA: Yes, I believe him.

YORIMITSU: And he thinks family ties and gratitude would prevent me from being too nasty to the Imperial family, assuming I became—a powerful man?

HIRAKAWA: Yes. Obviously Tokuzan would be glad to see you fight it out with the General. There's no need to mistrust the thing, because it does make such perfect sense. It's a genuine bargain.

OKANO: These are all lies, my lord. Now you are imprisoned by walls. Then you would be imprisoned by intrigues and compromise and Imperial slime. Tell him to go!

YORIMITSU: I'm getting a bit tired of the walls, actually, Okano. This would certainly be a change.

OKANO: You would be selling your friends to the Imperial interest.

YORIMITSU: Of course, Hirakawa, I would be doing Tokuzan a great favour, marrying this girl that I've never even seen. She may be ghastly. I'd expect a lot in return.

HIRAKAWA: Well, of course. And, naturally, about the future your word would be enough. Tokuzan would trust you if you trusted him. It's the ideal solution. Oh Yorimitsu, consent. Think, freedom—

OKANO: Do not consent, my lord.

HIRAKAWA: Be quiet, let him think!

[*Voices are raised.*]

OKANO: Now the issues are clean and clear cut. We can see where right is and where wrong is. Tokuzan wants to confuse everything and cover it over with his network of filth and lies. My dear lord, don't you see that if you go in with one side or the other you will lose your strength, you will destroy the purity of your cause? You must fight the whole system, not become part of it.

HIRAKAWA: How can he fight it in here?

OKANO: It would be a betrayal of the north. And it's a trap, it must be.

YORIMITSU: [*rising, exasperated*] Everything's a trap, life is a trap. And what's the use of a pure cause inside a prison cell?

OKANO: They would use it somehow as an instrument of your death. There is the ordeal of the three arrows, and if you fail you die.

YORIMITSU: [*thoughtful*] Even if I knew that—what is the method of death?

HIRAKAWA: Seppuku.

YORIMITSU: An honourable and significant end. At the worst that would be better than growing old in here.

OKANO: My lord, your life is not your own.

YORIMITSU: [*exasperated again*] It is now, Okano. I've spent five bloody years in here. I've earned the right to gamble with my own life.

OKANO: Do not do anything Tokuzan suggests.

YORIMITSU: He thinks he can use me. Well, we'll see.

HIRAKAWA: Then you agree, you agree?

YORIMITSU: Yes! Anything's better than this endless waiting.

HIRAKAWA: My dear! [*They embrace.*]

OKANO: Remember the terms of the ordeal. If you fail you have to take your own life.

YORIMITSU: Oh be silent, Okano!

[*By now they are all talking at once. Enter the* EMPEROR,

TENJIKU *and a rout of drunken noblemen. They come in laughing, carrying wine, etc. The* EMPEROR *has some flowers, almond blossom perhaps, which he waves and distributes amid general confusion.* YORIMITSU *and* HIRAKAWA *are immediately caught into the festive mood. Chatter, laughter, pouring of wine. The* EMPEROR *shouts "It's spring! It's spring!"* OKANO *departs silently.* YORIMITSU *looks round for him, finds he is gone and is momentarily troubled. Then he returns to the wild gaiety of the party.*]

ACT TWO

SCENE SIX

The apartments of the princess. Late evening. The screen is in place. Outside sits the EMPEROR. *Within are* KEIKO, KURITSUBO *and* AYAME.

EMPEROR: [*in a loud clear voice*] So I was going to go on this pilgrimage to this monastery—

KEIKO: Tai, whatever has come over you—

EMPEROR: It's a rather special sort of monastery—only uncle got his tame priest to declare every day this month inauspicious for travelling. [*Giggles from* KURITSUBO *and* AYAME.] Who's in there with you?

KEIKO: Kuritsubo and Ayame.

EMPEROR: Hiya, girls! Yoo hoo! [*More giggles.*]

KEIKO: Be quiet, Tai, you're awful!

EMPEROR: [*lowering his voice*] I say, Keiko, can you hear me?

KEIKO: Yes.

EMPEROR: I say, I've heard something.

KEIKO: What do you mean?

EMPEROR: I've heard something about—well—something about something to do with wheeee—ping! [*He simulates an arrow shot.*]

KEIKO: Ssssh! Who told you? Did uncle tell you?

EMPEROR: No, of course not! That old chappie told me, Father Akita, you know, the Queen Bee of Zen.

KEIKO: It's a secret!

EMPEROR: I know, but you see—
 [*Enter* TOKUZAN.]

TOKUZAN: I want to speak to you, Keiko.
 [*He jerks his head and the* EMPEROR *runs off.*]

KEIKO: Yes, uncle. Is everything—all right—for you know?

TOKUZAN: Yes. If anyone is with you please send them away.

197

[KEIKO *motions* KURITSUBO *and* AYAME *to go, and they depart.*]

Are you alone now?

KEIKO: Yes.

TOKUZAN: Come close to the screen, please.

KEIKO: Yes.

TOKUZAN: The ceremony will take place next Tuesday.

KEIKO: [*ecstasy*] Oh!

TOKUZAN: Now, Keiko, remember what I told you about keeping this absolutely secret. It must not come out until the very last moment. If certain people knew about it they might try to prevent it. Do you understand?

KEIKO: Yes, uncle.

TOKUZAN: Silence is a great virtue in a woman, Keiko. It is a great test of a woman. It is like the testing of a man upon the battlefield. Spiritual rewards come to those who can keep silent. Very much depends upon this matter, Keiko. Great affairs of state, of which you know nothing, depend upon it. This is not something to be silly about.

KEIKO: I am not silly about it, uncle. I have never in my life been more serious about anything.

TOKUZAN: That's right. Keep the virtue and the duty of silence before your face, my child. May Lord Amida bless you. [*He makes a gesture of blessing. Exit.*]

[*Enter* KURITSUBO *and* AYAME.]

KURITSUBO: May we come back again?

KEIKO: Yes, yes, come in, come in! Oh I'm so happy. I think I'm dying of happiness.

AYAME: I got another letter from Prince Hirota.

KEIKO: [*with the warm sympathy of the truly happy*] Did you? Bless the child. I'm so glad. I hope he writes you hundreds and hundreds of letters and you'll get married and live happily ever after. [*She dances about the room.*]

[KURITSUBO *is regarding the princess with curiosity.*]

AYAME: Mama says that we mustn't be in too much of a

hurry. She says we'll get much better offers than Prince Hirota. Nanny says all his estates are mortgaged.

KEIKO: Mortgaged, mortgaged—what a beautiful word!

KURITSUBO: What *is* it, Keiko?

AYAME: Oh dear, Nanny's just called for me, I must run. Goodnight, Keiko, goodnight, Kuri. See you tomorrow. [*Exit.*]

KEIKO: Tomorrow and tomorrow and tomorrow and— [*counting on her fingers.*]

KURITSUBO: Keiko, you're getting over-excited. You'll make yourself ill.

KEIKO: Oh I am ill, Kuritsubo, I am ill. Here. [*Holds her heart.*] I'm so sick with it, the most wonderful sickness in the world.

KURITSUBO: What are you talking about?

KEIKO: Love. Kuritsubo, feel my heart beating, feel it. [KURITSUBO *feels it.*] And look at my hands, they're trembling, I can't keep them still. I can hardly breathe the air, I'm faint with it, Kuritsubo. I'm in love.

KURITSUBO: In love? This is all nonsense, Keiko.

KEIKO: No, it's something new, something's happened. Oh you don't know what it's like, you can't know.

KURITSUBO: Was this the secret your brother was talking about?

KEIKO: Oh I can't tell you, I mustn't. But oh it's so wonderful—

KURITSUBO: Come on, Keiko, tell me, it's only me. You know I wouldn't tell anybody.

KEIKO: No, Kuritsubo, I really mustn't tell you.

KURITSUBO: Whoever can you be in love with? You really are a little bit mad, Keiko.

KEIKO: Yes, mad with joy, mad with love.

KURITSUBO: Please tell me. Don't be so unkind. I can keep a secret. And you've half told me already.

KEIKO: No, I mustn't.

KURITSUBO: Please, Keiko. I'm your best friend. Do tell me.

KEIKO: Well—you absolutely swear not to tell anyone?

KURITSUBO: I swear.

KEIKO: Not anyone at all?

KURITSUBO: Not anyone at all.

KEIKO: No, I won't tell you.

KURITSUBO: Keiko!

KEIKO: Oh I know I shouldn't, but I've got to tell somebody or I shall just go dotty with joy. I'm going to get married on Tuesday.

KURITSUBO: Oh! Who to?

KEIKO: Prince Yorimitsu.

[*This news is obviously a dagger in the guts to* KURITSUBO. *Absorbed in her own feelings, the princess does not notice.*]

KURITSUBO: But how can that be?

KEIKO: My uncle wants me to marry him.

KURITSUBO: Uh hu—I see—

KEIKO: They're going to set him free, and—oh Kuritsubo, I'm so happy, I love him so much.

KURITSUBO: But you've never seen him.

KEIKO: No, but I just know he's the most wonderful person in the world.

KURITSUBO: This is just silliness, Keiko, you may not even like him.

KEIKO: It's funny about love, Kuritsubo. You've never been in love so you don't know. I've thought about it so much in these last years and I've waited for it. Waiting for it to come was the only thing that gave any meaning to my life at all. But now that it has come—

[*She begins to undo her hair.* KURITSUBO *helps her.*]

—it's somehow quite different, it's *huge*. I can't explain. I thought it would be part of me, but I'm part of it. I feel so humble and grateful I want to kiss the feet of the world. And this sense of certainty—it's not like anything I've ever felt before. I thought I knew what it was like to know things. But this makes everything I thought I knew before seem just vague, like a dream. You see love isn't a dream, Kuritsubo, there's nothing cloudy about it. It's a great test of truth, it somehow *is* truth, truth itself, and it reveals the world. It makes you see the world without any mist, without any darkness, seeing everything as it really is— seeing it so coloured and so detailed and so absolutely *here*.

Kuritsubo, would you play some music to me, just a little. I know you don't like to play, but—just touch it a little. [*She hands* KURITSUBO *a zithern.*] I think I'm going to lie down and sleep now. I must try to rest. Perhaps I shall die of joy before Tuesday. [*She lies down.*]
[KURITSUBO *plays.*]
Funny how happiness can make you sleepy too. As if your whole mind had become so open and gentle, like something floating in the sea. It's so lovely—falling asleep when you feel happy—I think it's the nicest thing in the world.

[*The princess falls asleep. When* KURITSUBO *sees that she is sleeping, she hastily leaves the room.*]

ACT TWO

Scene Seven

The office of the SHOGUN. *Night.* LADY ROKUNI *seated.*
KURITSUBO *standing.*

ROKUNI: You say next Tuesday.

KURITSUBO: Yes.

ROKUNI: The procedure of this ordeal—do you know about it?

KURITSUBO: Only what everyone knows, about the three arrows.

ROKUNI: Is it arranged by priests or by members of the Imperial household?

KURITSUBO: I don't know.

ROKUNI: You did very well to come and tell me. No one saw you coming?

KURITSUBO: I wore this cloak which belongs to one of my servants.

ROKUNI: The palace is full of people wearing their servants' cloaks. Are you sure you were not followed?

KURITSUBO: Sure. I came the long way round.

ROKUNI: Good. You are not a fool. Use equal caution going back. You will not regret what you have done. The General knows how to reward his friends—discreetly. You may be able to help us again in the future. Just listen and watch. Even little things may be important. Arrangements will be made for you to keep in touch with us without making any dangerous journeys. We like to spare our friends embarrassment.

KURITSUBO: I'd rather not, Lady Rokuni. It was just this that I wanted to tell you.

ROKUNI: Come, child. You have done something very risky in coming here. Something which could be very damaging to you indeed if it came out. After all, you are in a

202

position of very special trust in the Imperial household. But be assured that nothing of this will reach any other ears—if you are prepared to give us that little bit of help in the future.

[*Slight pause while* KURITSUBO *digests this threat.*]

ROKUNI: Come, we are very kind and reasonable people to deal with. No one would be vexed with you if you had nothing to tell. Here, take this comb away with you, as a present of course, not a payment. It is Chinese, a great rarity. See what a pretty pattern of diamonds, making a lotus flower.

[KURITSUBO *tries to refuse the comb.*]

Take it, you fool, do you think something like this matters? Tell me one thing, and stop trembling, I'm not going to eat you.

KURITSUBO: Yes?

ROKUNI: Why did you come here to tell me this?

KURITSUBO: I just—wanted to help. I thought you might be interested.

ROKUNI: That is certainly a lie. Answer again.

KURITSUBO: The prisoner is my husband's best friend.

ROKUNI: That is better, but still not good enough. Again.

KURITSUBO: I saw Yorimitsu once.

ROKUNI: You don't want her to have him. You couldn't bear it.

[KURITSUBO *dumbly signifies assent.*]

That is good. That is best of all. Your secret thoughts are safe with me. Never be ashamed of what are called evil motives, my child. We human beings are entirely composed of such motives. In our hearts we are all nasty cruel children. Any so-called virtue is merely egoism with a false face, it cannot be otherwise. Our deepest wishes are relentlessly selfish and these deep springs are the strongest ones of all. See into yourself, see deeply. All that is needful is honesty and courage. Accept yourself and then be resolute. Any other path is that of a victim. Now go. One of our people in the Imperial household will make herself known to you.

[*Exit* KURITSUBO *wrapped in her cloak. We see her returning through the palace. Already regretting her treachery she begins to cry. Enters the* SHOGUN.]

SHOGUN: What is it, mother?

ROKUNI: I have discovered something extraordinary.

SHOGUN: What?

ROKUNI: Next Tuesday Prince Yorimitsu is going to marry the Crown Princess.

SHOGUN: That's impossible.

ROKUNI: No. It's improbable. It's brilliant. It has the beautiful improbability of the really brilliant move.

SHOGUN: How did you find out?

ROKUNI: A silly jealous girl told me, a lady-in-waiting to the princess.

SHOGUN: But has Yorimitsu agreed?

ROKUNI: Apparently, yes.

SHOGUN: He must be mad.

ROKUNI: Why? He's tired of being caged up. Perhaps he's afraid of—other things too. Why should he refuse?

SHOGUN: He's putting himself—somehow—into Toku-zan's pocket. I wouldn't have thought it of Yorimitsu.

ROKUNI: Of course Yorimitsu fondly supposes that once he is set free he will be able to outwit everybody.

SHOGUN: If he's set free—that marriage secures him for Tokuzan.

ROKUNI: So Tokuzan imagines. But I don't think these hypothetical speculations need trouble *us*.

SHOGUN: Why?

ROKUNI: Because the prisoner will never marry the princess.

SHOGUN: Why not?

ROKUNI: Because he will be dead. Next Tuesday.

SHOGUN: What do you mean?

ROKUNI: My son, this is the moment we've waited for, the

chance we've waited for. To make the Imperial family appear to kill the prisoner, to make the Imperial family in fact kill the prisoner.

SHOGUN: I don't understand.

ROKUNI: This ridiculous ordeal, this business of the arrows. You know that if the suitor succeeds he is immediately married and if he fails he is immediately condemned. Both fates are ready and prepared and present. Yorimitsu must fail. And before anyone can start thinking he must be dead. And the blame will belong to the Imperial family.

SHOGUN: But if this ordeal thing is entirely in their hands—

ROKUNI: Precisely! They will do our work for us!

SHOGUN: We don't even know how it's run.

ROKUNI: We don't know at the moment. But we have several days in which to find out.

SHOGUN: It won't do, mother—

ROKUNI: Why not? We have friends over there. We have one friend who is particularly close to the Imperial person.

SHOGUN: Tenjiku. Yes. A man I don't care for.

ROKUNI: But who has been extremely useful to us.

SHOGUN: Whoever fixed this up would be signing his own death warrant.

ROKUNI: Or someone else's. It should be quite easy to frame some stupid priest. Come, this plan has everything. Tokuzan has been brilliant. We will be dazzling. The Imperial family will do our work for us and Yorimitsu's followers will take revenge on them.

SHOGUN: I wonder—

ROKUNI: Everyone will believe it is Tokuzan's treachery.

SHOGUN: I don't like it.

ROKUNI: There is a strain of weakness in you, my child. That's—dangerous. I am going now to tell our people to —find out.

[*Exit* LADY ROKUNI. *Enter by another door* FATHER AKITA.]

AKITA: Forgive me for intruding, your excellency. I was wondering if I might now have your permission to return to my temple.

SHOGUN: No, no! You stay here in the palace—I want to talk to you!

[*Suddenly frantic, he seizes hold of him.*]

ACT TWO

Scene Eight

The office of the ex-emperor TOKUZAN. TOKUZAN *and* PRINCE HIRAKAWA.

HIRAKAWA: So you have made me betray my friend.

TOKUZAN: Don't be melodramatic, Hirakawa.

HIRAKAWA: I persuaded him. He trusted me.

TOKUZAN: You have not betrayed him, you have probably saved his life.

HIRAKAWA: I told him there was no trap.

TOKUZAN: You should have used your mind.

HIRAKAWA: You say there'll be a coach waiting—

TOKUZAN: And a strong guard. And of course Yorimitsu will be unarmed. I anticipate no difficulties. After the marriage ceremony has been performed tomorrow our young friend will be in a blissful daze. He and his bride will be escorted to the coach.

HIRAKAWA: And driven to the Summer Palace.

TOKUZAN: Which has already been put into a state of seige.

HIRAKAWA: He won't go.

TOKUZAN: Why should he suspect anything? Of course he'll go. He'll go anywhere at that moment so as to be alone with the girl. He is thirty-two years old, he has not seen a woman for five years. I am told Keiko is very beautiful. I've briefed her, without the details of course. I told her they were going to spend their honeymoon at the Summer Palace. It will just turn out to be a rather long honeymoon. Tee hee!

HIRAKAWA: You—

TOKUZAN: Be careful, Hirakawa.

HIRAKAWA: So you are going to go on keeping him a prisoner.

TOKUZAN: Why put it in that unpleasant way: He will be

207

—detained. He will live in luxury in the Summer Palace with a most delightful bride.

HIRAKAWA: I thought you said the rules forbade a member of the Imperial family to be an Imperial prisoner.

TOKUZAN: He will no longer be classified as an Imperial prisoner. He will be an official state guest.

HIRAKAWA: [*exclamation of disgust*] Aren't you afraid that his friends will rescue him?

TOKUZAN: I have taken a great many precautions. No, I am not. The Summer Palace is an excellent fortress. In many ways it is a more effective prison than the Imperial Palace. And you must keep this in mind too. Once Yorimitsu is married to the Crown Princess he will be discredited in the north.

HIRAKAWA: I don't think so.

TOKUZAN: The northerners detest the General, of course. But the General is just a temporary phenomenon. Powerful, important, but temporary. A jumped-up bully. But the Imperial family has gone on and on and on—and will go on and on and on.

HIRAKAWA: Yes. They've always had you on their necks.

TOKUZAN: They hate us. We are more deeply and more traditionally detested there. Their precious prince married to our girl! No!

HIRAKAWA: I didn't think of this.

TOKUZAN: Perhaps you should have reflected a little more before you went on your embassy to Yorimitsu. Perhaps he ought to have thought more carefully about the implications of what he was doing and about what was likely to happen. I will now confess to you that I was extremely surprised by his decision. He must have been a little dazzled by the prospect of liberation. He turns out to be less courageous and also less intelligent than I imagined.

HIRAKAWA: And you're going to go on keeping him in captivity!

TOKUZAN: Well, of course. Really, when you think about

it, is it likely that I would let that man run about free? I have got him on a chain and I propose to keep him on a chain. Your so-important friend will turn out to be quite a little person after all. Merely a tame stallion in the Imperial stud.

HIRAKAWA: I'm going straightaway now to tell him all about it!

TOKUZAN: Don't be naive, Hirakawa. When you leave here some of my men will escort you back to your rooms, where you will find that I have taken the liberty of stationing an armed guard.

HIRAKAWA: Is that a polite way of telling me that I am under arrest?

ACT TWO

Scene Nine

The prisoner's cell. Night. YORIMITSU *is wandering about sleepless with ecstasy. Perhaps he is writing a poem on a long scroll. Suddenly a shrouded figure comes through the door. It is the* SHOGUN. *No salutations this time. They stare at each other.*

YORIMITSU: Hello.

SHOGUN: You lunatic.

YORIMITSU: What are you talking about, Musashi?

SHOGUN: Yes, it smells different in here already. The smell of freedom. You are different.

YORIMITSU: Yes. So you know.

SHOGUN: It's general knowledge in the palace.

YORIMITSU: Have you come to congratulate me on my engagement?

SHOGUN: I think you're mad.

YORIMITSU: To trust Tokuzan?

SHOGUN: Yes.

YORIMITSU: You think he might take this chance to kill me.

SHOGUN: Yes.

YORIMITSU: In this respect, my dear fellow, my situation is the same as it ever was. Tokuzan could have killed me at any time. But he won't dare to take my life tomorrow for the same reason that he didn't dare to take it yesterday.

SHOGUN: You will be in very grave danger tomorrow, Yorimitsu.

YORIMITSU: Nonsense. It's all Tokuzan's bright idea, he thinks he's winning a friend! There's no danger involved. But what are you worrying about, Musashi? Wouldn't it suit you rather well if Tokuzan removed me from the scene?

SHOGUN: Don't go tomorrow. Put it off. Say you've changed your mind.

YORIMITSU: No!

SHOGUN: You just can't win, Yorimitsu, placed as you are,
you simply can't win. If you go through with this ordeal
you will choose the arrow that will end your life.

YORIMITSU: What *is* going on in your mind? Of course you
don't like the idea of me in the bosom of the Imperial
family. But your attempts to intimidate me are a trifle
crude!

SHOGUN: I am not deceiving you. If you go to the ordeal
tomorrow your death will almost certainly be brought
about.

YORIMITSU: Brought about. Who by? By Tokuzan? Or by
you? [*Pause*] I think you're bluffing, Musashi. You're just
trying to mystify me. What *are* you up to?

SHOGUN: Listen. I've got something else to say to you and
I want you to think about it—to *think* about it—now,
since there's no more time. Why not join forces with me.
Together we could rule the country from end to end. Together we could destroy the power of the Imperial family
forever. Once there was no threat of civil war we could
really *govern*, we could change things. You could carry
out your reforms. I know you have all sorts of ideas. You
could have a free hand.

YORIMITSU: A free hand—with you there!

SHOGUN: Why not? We've been idiots not to do this before.
In fact the idea came into my head on that very first
evening, only—we are rational men, we know each other,
we could trust each other.

YORIMITSU: Even if I could trust you, which I'm not sure
about, I couldn't trust your friends. And they would never
trust me. And my people from the north— No. We'd both
spend every day waiting to be assassinated. You couldn't
bring me into your set-up. I would want to change everything, everything from top to bottom. Only the highest
place will do for me, General. Your place.

SHOGUN: You are stupidly ambitious.

YORIMITSU: I want your place, my friend, not a seat in your organisation. How could I play second fiddle to you, or you to me. It's impossible, Musashi.

SHOGUN: And your ambition will be your death. You will be dressed up and led out as a helpless victim. This time tomorrow, Prince Yorimitsu, you will be dead. And the beautiful court dress which they have put upon you will be stiff with blood.

YORIMITSU: Your attempts to make my flesh creep are not succeeding very well. I don't believe you. There is indeed a different air in here. Free men and prisoners think differently. I am beginning to think like a free man. Already I can smell the mountains, I can smell the sea. You are shaking in your shoes at the thought of my getting out. You are trying to frighten me into hesitating. But I would never join forces with you, Musashi, never.

SHOGUN: You're prepared to join forces with that swine Tokuzan.

YORIMITSU: No. Once I'm free, I'll do what I please with Tokuzan.

SHOGUN: You will never be free, Yorimitsu. Even if you did survive tomorrow, Tokuzan would never release you.

YORIMITSU: I trust—those whom I trust—absolutely. [*Pause*] And even if there were danger I would walk into it open-eyed. If I survive tomorrow I shall get out of this net somehow. If I don't survive at least I won't be rotting in here year after year. And I shall have died honourably, at a significant moment in a significant way for something that has a meaning.

SHOGUN: Are you really so sentimental about your death scene?

YORIMITSU: I've had enough. Tomorrow will settle the business of my life one way or the other. Tomorrow either you will be rid of me, or you will have a free and very dangerous enemy.

SHOGUN: It's curious. I'd got sort of—used to you.

YORIMITSU: Like a pet in a cage.

SHOGUN: I suddenly feel, which I've never felt before, that you are young and I am old. I am sorry [*He half turns to go.*] One other thing, Yorimitsu. Though perhaps it doesn't matter now. Those things I said to you last time—about darkness and solitude—you know. I didn't mean them. That really was bluffing.

YORIMITSU: I don't think you know what you mean. You've lived too long in the palace. Goodbye, General. Tomorrow.

SHOGUN: Tomorrow, then. Goodbye.

[*As the* SHOGUN *returns to his rooms past sleeping sentries etc.,* LADY ROKUNI *is discovered conferring with the hooded figure of* TENJIKU. *After* TENJIKU *departs,* ROKUNI *composes herself in prayer. Enter to her the* SHOGUN.]

ROKUNI: It has been arranged.

SHOGUN: Where's Father Akita? I asked him to wait for me.

ROKUNI: I sent him away.

SHOGUN: [*slightly wild*] I'm afraid I am interrupting your devotions. Are you praying for success tomorrow?

ROKUNI: Prayer has nothing to do with the worldly life, my son.

[*The* SHOGUN *has had enough. Exit.* LADY ROKUNI *returns to her rosary.*]

ACT TWO

Scene Ten

The apartments of the Crown Princess. KEIKO *is being attired for her marriage by various ladies, including* KURITSUBO *and* AYAME. *It is an elaborate business. A curtained litter stands waiting.* KEIKO *is over-excited, nervous, near to tears, somehow deeply frightened.*

KEIKO: We're going to spend our honeymoon at the Summer Palace. The Summer Palace. It sounds so lovely. Whatever will it be like?

KURITSUBO: Very cold.

KEIKO: We'll be going in a coach. I've never been in a coach.

KURITSUBO: You'll need plenty of cushions.

KEIKO: Just the two of us together. [*Pause for ecstasy*] Over the mountains. It'll be—snowy—won't it?

KURITSUBO: Yes. Very snowy.

KEIKO: Will we see Fujiyama?

KURITSUBO: I don't know.

KEIKO: It is an auspicious day, isn't it? They're quite sure it's an auspicious day.

KURITSUBO: Quite sure.

KEIKO: I shall be so frightened at the ordeal.

KURITSUBO: There's nothing to be frightened of.

KEIKO: Kuritsubo, you've been so kind to me, and we've been friends for so long. We must meet often, we will meet, won't we, you and Ayame? And we'll make poems and play music like we used to do. Won't we?

KURITSUBO: Yes, of course.

KEIKO: Kuritsubo, you look so beautiful.

KURITSUBO: *You* look beautiful, Keiko.

KEIKO: What a lovely comb you're wearing in your hair.

[KURITSUBO *is silent. She feels remorse, self-pity, cynicism.*]

214

ACT TWO

Tonight. Oh it seems so far away—but it will come.
Kuritsubo—

KURITSUBO: Yes?

KEIKO: Kuritsubo, it is—pleasant—to be married, isn't it?
You know what I mean?

KURITSUBO: Very pleasant.

KEIKO: I feel so happy, but I just want to cry, it hurts so.
It's like having an arrow in one's side. It hurts, here. I
love him so much. And when one loves like this one can't
help being frightened too, in case anything should harm
him.

[KEIKO *knocks over a bottle of perfume. It spills upon the floor.*]
Oh. It's spilt. That's a bad omen.

KURITSUBO: Not so. "Your maiden hours
          So nearly at their end:
          You tread on flowers."

KEIKO: "The perfume on the floor streams dark.
     Why does it look like blood
     To my frightened heart?"

[*The ladies put the finishing touches to* KEIKO's *attire. She
climbs into the litter which is carried off.*]

ACT TWO

Scene Eleven

The stage is set for the ordeal. The EMPEROR, TOKUZAN, HIRAKAWA *and others sit impassively in two rows staring at the audience. The* SHOGUN *and his mother are also present, sitting separately. The princess's litter is on a dais. Three suitably attired* PAGES, *perhaps with shields representing the three birds, hold the arrows. Target and bow are also prominent. On the left side in the foreground are the marriage arrangements, with* FATHER AKITA. *On the right side in the foreground are the seppuku arrangements, knife, white sheet, etc.*

Enter PRINCE YORIMITSU *in court dress, unarmed, under guard, followed by* OKANO. YORIMITSU *kowtows to the* EMPEROR. *A sinister black-clad official who appears to be in charge of the ordeal turns out to be* TENJIKU.

TENJIKU: Let the suitor proceed to the ordeal: make his choice, and abide by the consequences. If he chooses rightly, the target will glow with a green light, signifying life. If he chooses wrongly, the target will glow with a red light, signifying death. If he chooses rightly the suitor will be married to the princess. If he chooses wrongly he will be required honourably and ceremonially to disembowel himself here in the presence of his judges in accordance with the revered custom of our land.

YORIMITSU: Your majesty, my lords, my lady. You all know who I am. You know what I have done and what has been done to me. With hope and with resolve, accepting my fate, I choose now the arrow of the dove. This expresses the deepest truth which I can really understand. The way of action corrupts the heart. The way of holiness mystifies the soul. But the way of love is innocent and human. I choose this certain good thing with a humble mind, laying aside all ambition. And, in accordance with

this choice, am ready now to live with happiness, or to
die with honour.

[*He shoots the arrow. A red light flares.* KEIKO *cries out. At*
TENJIKU'S *command the wedding preparations vanish. Solemn
rhythmical sound of wooden clappers. The sheet, etc., for the seppuku ceremony are brought to the centre of the stage.* YORIMITSU
bows to the EMPEROR, *to the litter and to the* SHOGUN. *He
takes off his robe, kneels, receives the glittering knife. The*
EMPEROR *has meanwhile been struggling with some sort of
indecision.* AKITA, *who has been watching him closely, suddenly
crosses the stage.*]

EMPEROR: [*incoherent*] Wait! Stop! Obedience! I mean—
Listen— [*He reads from a paper*]

"There are more ways than one to be a loser.

Prove worthy of your dove, dove-chooser.

Remain her happy prisoner, twice tried,

Or homeless be forever, if you lied."

TOKUZAN: What does this mean—your majesty?

EMPEROR: [*reading*] It is laid down—I am told— [*Looking
at* AKITA] It is laid down in the earliest records of the
ordeal that it is the Imperial privilege to decree that a
suitor who has failed the test of the arrow may proceed,
if he so desires, to a second and more extreme ordeal.
He may accept the terms of the second ordeal or, if he
finds them unacceptable, must enact the ceremonial and
honourable death which has already been allotted to
him.

YORIMITSU: What is this second and more extreme ordeal?

EMPEROR: The second ordeal tests the sincerity of the
choice which the suitor has made. You, Prince Yorimitsu,
have rejected the paths of action and of holiness, and have
chosen the path of love. The second ordeal, which is in
accordance with a known precedent, consists of this further choice. Either you may marry the princess, on condition that you remain a prisoner in the Imperial Palace
for the rest of your life, or you may leave the palace as a

free man on condition that you promise never to see the princess again and never to wed any other woman. If you accept the second ordeal and choose your freedom rather than your love, the princess will, in accordance with the rule, be required at once to enter a nunnery. If you reject the second ordeal your original fate remains, to give yourself a ceremonial and honourable death in accordance with the revered custom of our land. [*Pause*] Your decision must be made at once.

YORIMITSU: I don't believe this. It's another damned mystification. It's— It's to disgrace me and cheat me out of a proper honourable death. So, I have to choose between my love, my honour, and my cause— [*to* AKITA] Is this true?

AKITA: I don't know, my son. You will have to choose in the dark and you will have to choose now.

YORIMITSU: [*after a pause during which he has turned the point of the knife against himself*] This is no moment for making speeches or for asking anyone's forgiveness. I cannot choose servitude. And I have not got the right to choose death. My life is not my own. The world must be served. I accept the terms of the second ordeal—and I choose freedom. Now let us see what these promises are made of!

TENJIKU: [*to an* ATTENDANT] Kill him!

EMPEROR: No!

[*Confusion. Men attack* YORIMITSU. HIRAKAWA *and* OKANO *run forward with drawn swords. The* EMPEROR *signals to his* GUARDS *who also interfere. The* SHOGUN *rushes toward* YORIMITSU. *The* EMPEROR'S MEN *dominate the scene, arrest* TENJIKU *and restrain* TOKUZAN *who watches with cynical resignation. Amid the turmoil* OKANO *kills the* SHOGUN. *Sudden silence with the* EMPEROR *evidently in charge.*]

[*to* YORIMITSU] You see I—after all—

YORIMITSU: [*to* OKANO] Why did you kill him? He was trying to save me.

[OKANO *bows silently.* YORIMITSU *turns and leaps up to the litter. But* KEIKO *is dead. She has stabbed herself. He carries her body down.*]

HIRAKAWA: She is dead.

YORIMITSU: She killed herself when she thought I was going to die.

HIRAKAWA: Or when she heard you decide to give her up.

YORIMITSU: I shall never know.

EMPEROR: Quick. My men will take you to the gate. There are horses waiting.

YORIMITSU: Thank you. Goodbye, General. I suppose I would have made the mistake of mercy too. [*He turns to* KEIKO.] There's my brave girl.

EMPEROR: Quick, quick!

[YORIMITSU *and* AKITA *look at each other. Exeunt* YORIMITSU, HIRAKAWA *and* OKANO. *The* EMPEROR *goes to* KEIKO.]

I'm sorry, I didn't— How beautiful my sister was.

[*He weeps.* LADY ROKUNI *is mourning the* SHOGUN. *The last light shows* FATHER AKITA.]

FINAL CURTAIN

THE BLACK PRINCE

A play in two acts

Homage to

Josephine Hart
Stuart Burge
Ian McDiarmid

THE BLACK PRINCE

A play in two acts

Characters in order of their appearance

BRADLEY PEARSON, an unsuccessful writer
FRANCIS MARLOE, a defrocked doctor
ARNOLD BAFFIN, a successful writer
RACHEL BAFFIN, his wife
JULIAN BAFFIN, their daughter
PRISCILLA, Bradley Pearson's sister
CHRISTINE, Bradley Pearson's former wife
1st Policeman
2nd Policeman
Policewoman or 3rd Policeman

ACT ONE

Scene One

The sitting-room of BRADLEY PEARSON'S *flat. Suitcases ready for departure.* BRADLEY *sings merry songs of liberation (such as 'Linden Lea' or 'Over The Hills And Far Away'). He lifts the telephone.*

BRADLEY: Can I have a taxi, please, to go to King's Cross Station? Pearson. You know, Penrose Court. Straight away? Thank you.

[*The doorbell rings.* BRADLEY *goes to the door, returns with* FRANCIS.]

BRADLEY: Who are you?

FRANCIS: I'm Francis, your brother-in-law, *you* know—

BRADLEY: I have no wife, *ergo* no brother-in-law.

FRANCIS: She's back!

BRADLEY: Who's back?

FRANCIS: Your wife, Christine, my sister, *you* know—

BRADLEY: Christine is no longer my wife. I left her many years ago. Thank God.

FRANCIS: She's back from America, she's a widow, she's fearfully rich, don't you want to see her?

BRADLEY: No.

FRANCIS: I'm sorry I haven't been around, you see I've been unfrocked.

BRADLEY: I'd forgotten you were a priest. I'm afraid I've got a train to catch. I'm expecting a taxi.

FRANCIS: Not a *priest*! I'm a doctor—or I *was*—I've been struck off. Can't you remember me?

BRADLEY: No. [*Sudden thought*] She didn't send you, did she?

FRANCIS: No, she's anti-me—don't be cross, Brad.

BRADLEY: Don't call me 'Brad'!

FRANCIS: Sorry, Brad, you see I need money, and when she comes to see you—

BRADLEY: *What?*

FRANCIS: She really cared for you, like she loved you, she'll come.

BRADLEY: No she won't! I'm just leaving for the country.

FRANCIS: She's rich now, *you* know, merry widow style.

BRADLEY: I'll be away the whole summer. I'm going to write a *book*.

FRANCIS: She'll be after you, she'll want to show off, she'll come to gloat over you.

BRADLEY: 'Gloat'? What do you mean 'gloat'?

FRANCIS: I've always liked you, Bradley, I've always admired you, I've read one of your books.

BRADLEY: I haven't published any books!

FRANCIS: I forget its name, it was great—look, I'm in debt up to the neck, and when you see Christine you could—

BRADLEY: No!

FRANCIS: With Chris back, it's like a new start, all sins forgiven.

[*The doorbell rings.*]

BRADLEY: No! Go away!

[*The telephone rings.* BRADLEY *picks it up. He points* FRANCIS *to go to the door.* FRANCIS *goes.*]

Hello. Arnold, what's the matter? . . . *What?* . . . Impossible. . . You've killed her!? Don't be silly . . . You can't have killed her, you just can't have . . . Have you called a doctor? No? . . . What happened? . . . All right, I'll come round, I'll come at once . . .

[FRANCIS *returns.* BRADLEY *replaces the receiver.*]

FRANCIS: There's a taxi—What's up?

BRADLEY: The wife of a friend of mine has had a serious accident, I'm just going over—

FRANCIS: Can I come?

BRADLEY: No.

FRANCIS: I'm still a doctor in the eyes of God.

BRADLEY: —Yes—all right. Hold the taxi.

[*He automatically picks up his suitcases, then puts them down.*]

BRADLEY: [*as the scene changes*] Arnold Baffin. The famous writer. He always exaggerates. I discovered him, I encouraged him. Now he's a book-a-year man. I'm not envious, I'm just not that kind of scribbler.

ACT ONE

Scene Two

The sitting-room in ARNOLD BAFFIN'S *house. The room is in chaos, chairs overturned, books on the floor.*

BRADLEY: Oh my God.

ARNOLD: She was crying and screaming.

BRADLEY: Dr Marloe—Arnold Baffin. He happened to be with me when you rang up about your wife's *accident*.

FRANCIS: Are you *the* Arnold Baffin?

BRADLEY: Yes, he is.

FRANCIS: I do so admire your books, I've read several of them—

ARNOLD: Oh thank you.

BRADLEY: Arnold, just keep calm—

[RACHEL, *lying on a sofa, looks dramatically dead, head thrown back, arm drooping to the floor.*]

ARNOLD: [*distraught*] She just lies there and doesn't move and I can't bear to look at her—

BRADLEY: Arnold, sit down.

[FRANCIS *watches with interest.* ARNOLD *sits, head in hands.* BRADLEY *goes to* RACHEL, *kneels, takes her hand.*] Rachel, Rachel—it's me—Bradley. Oh dear. Her hand is so cold and—

ARNOLD: [*moaning*] Oh, let her be all right—

BRADLEY: Rachel—it's Bradley—she's moving, she's looking at me! [*Faint moan from* RACHEL] Listen, she made a sound!

ARNOLD: [*jumping up*] Oh darling, are you all right?

BRADLEY: Just keep away.

ARNOLD: I'm so sorry—oh my darling—

BRADLEY: Rachel, dear Rachel, don't worry, we'll make you better. [*To* FRANCIS] Look, you take over.

[BRADLEY *returns to* ARNOLD. FRANCIS *fusses over* RACHEL, *who is showing more signs of life.*]

ARNOLD: Is that chap a medical doctor?

BRADLEY: Yes.

ARNOLD: I thought he might be a doctor of literature. Look, let's have a drink. Oh God, I've been a bloody fool.

[*With shaking hand* ARNOLD *pours out whisky for himself. From now on* ARNOLD *begins to recover, perhaps regrets having panicked so soon and invited his friend into this domestic scene.*]

BRADLEY: What happened?

ARNOLD: We had a damn stupid argument about one of my books—she thinks, or says she thinks, they're all about *her*, all caricatures of *her*.

FRANCIS: [*coming forward*] First-aid kit? Hot water, basin, towels?

ARNOLD: [*pointing*] Kitchen. Is she OK?

FRANCIS: Hope so.

ARNOLD: I thought she was done for. Silly of me to panic. She gets this persecution mania—I said a few things and then we just couldn't stop, she began to scream and I can't *stand* that, and I pushed her and she clawed my face—here, see—and I slapped her and then she sprang on me like a tiger and I picked up this poker just to keep her away, like a barrier between us, I didn't mean to hit her, I mean, I didn't hit her, and then suddenly she was pouring blood—

[FRANCIS *appears, drying his hands on a towel.*]

FRANCIS: Nothing serious—a cut on the head, a lot of bruising, very nasty fall she must have had. I think her nose is OK.

ARNOLD: I'm so grateful—

FRANCIS: Bit of concussion and shock. You'd better get your own doctor. [*To* BRADLEY] She wants to see you, not him.

ARNOLD: Oh my sweetheart, don't be angry with me!

BRADLEY: You two clear off.

[FRANCIS *and* ARNOLD *depart.* FRANCIS *seizes the whisky bottle as he goes.* BRADLEY *goes to* RACHEL, *who has come forward.*]

There, my dear, there now, you'll be all right.

[RACHEL *is a sad sight, blood, black eye. She feels her nose carefully and round her eye. She is not crying now. She speaks in a fierce cold voice, not looking at* BRADLEY.]

RACHEL: No I won't be all right.

BRADLEY: Of course you will!

RACHEL: It's the shame, it's the disgrace—and he invited you round to see it!

BRADLEY: He was shaking like a leaf. He was afraid he'd hurt you.

RACHEL: Hurt me! He's taken my whole life and blackened it and stolen it and put it into his hateful lying books. *And* he discusses me with other women, everybody loves him and flatters him, he's surrounded by women. Be my witness, I shall never forgive him, never, never, never, not if he were to kneel at my feet for twenty years. If he were drowning I'd watch, I'd *laugh*.

BRADLEY: Rachel, please don't talk in this awful theatrical way. You don't mean it, don't say it! Of course, you'll forgive him!

RACHEL: I'm just as clever as he is—but I can't work, I can't think, I can't *be* because of him. I've never lived my own life at all, I've always been afraid of him, that's what it comes to. All men despise all women really, all women fear all men really. Men are physically stronger, that's what it comes to. They can end any argument! He's given me a black eye, just like any common drunken lout—

BRADLEY: I'm sure there were faults on both sides.

RACHEL: I'm a battered wife.

BRADLEY: But you hit him.

RACHEL: Ach! And he's hit me before! I never told him,

but the first time he hit me our marriage came to an end. He has taken away my life and spoilt it, breaking every little piece of it, like breaking every bone in one's body, every little thing ruined and spoilt and *stolen*.

BRADLEY: Rachel, don't talk like this, I won't listen.

RACHEL: He wouldn't let me take a job. I obeyed him, I've always obeyed him! I haven't any private things. He owns the world. It's all his, his! I won't save him at the end. I'll watch him drown, I'll watch him burn.

BRADLEY: Oh, Rachel—

RACHEL: And I won't forgive you either for seeing me like this with my face all bruised and my eyes running with tears.

BRADLEY: Rachel you're upsetting me!

RACHEL: And now you'll go and comfort him and connive with him and tell him all the dreadful things I've said.

BRADLEY: No I won't!

RACHEL: I fill you with disgust and contempt—a battered whimpering middle-aged woman. Now I'm going upstairs to bed. Just tell Arnold not to come near me. I'll come down later, I'll be as usual, I'll be myself. Myself, ha!

BRADLEY: [*as she goes*] Don't be cross with me, it's not my fault!

[RACHEL *departs. A distant door slams.*]

Poor old Rachel. And it's not the end of that either.

[*He turns to the audience.*]

My life before it was enlivened by these events had been a quiet one. Some people might call it dull. In fact, if one can use that rather beautiful and pungent word in an almost non-emotive sense, my life had been sublimely dull. A great dull life—spent working as a Tax Inspector. A great Danish philosopher once described the truly virtuous man as 'looking like an Inspector of Taxes'. More usually, and perhaps this is the point, a taxman is a figure of fun. The profession, like that of dentist, invites laughter. But this laughter is, I suspect, uneasy. Both taxman and dentist only too readily image forth the deeper horrors of human life; that we must pay for our pleasures, that our resources are lent, not given, and that our faculties decay even as they grow. My life since—all this [*gesture*] has been secluded, solitary. I have in my monastic enclosure become more happy, I hope more wise . . . This direct speaking is a kind of relief. It eases some pressure upon the heart, allowing the mind to pass like a light along a series of present moments aware of past images, unaware of what is to come. I am a writer, a serious writer, that is an artist. If someone complains, but you have published nothing! I reply: that is the essence. I am not a blocked writer, I am a perfectionist—a slave of the dark power which alone enables beauty to be truth. In art, as in lives of men, great things are lost because at the crucial moment, when the empowered imagination is poised for its final work, we let go, we think, 'that'll do', and we accept the second best. When is that moment? Greatness is to recognise it, to hold it, to extend it [*gestures*]. The most sacred command laid upon any artist is: wait. Writing is like getting married. Don't commit yourself until you are amazed at your luck.

[ARNOLD *and* FRANCIS *return, carrying bottles and glasses.*]

BRADLEY: She's gone to bed. She says please leave her alone, she'll be down later.

ARNOLD: God, what a relief. I expect she'll be down for supper. I'll cook her something special.

BRADLEY: All the same, it was a serious accident.

ARNOLD: He says she'll recover quickly. Have another drink.

BRADLEY: I haven't had one yet. [*To* FRANCIS] Well, we needn't keep you, thank you for helping.

ARNOLD: Oh, don't go, doctor!

BRADLEY: [*firmly*] Goodbye.

ARNOLD: I'm so grateful—do I owe you anything?

BRADLEY: You owe him nothing.

[FRANCIS *is very reluctant to go. He drains his glass.* BRADLEY *begins to shepherd him out.*]

FRANCIS: Better keep her in bed. [*To* BRADLEY] About what we said before—when you see Christine—

BRADLEY: I won't.

FRANCIS: Here's my address. [*He thrusts it into* BRADLEY's *hand.*]

BRADLEY: Goodbye, thank you.

[FRANCIS *departs.* ARNOLD *fills his own glass. They continue to drink during the conversation which follows.*]

Do you really think she'll come down to supper?

ARNOLD: Yes, she never sulks for long. These rows aren't real warfare, we love each other. My hand is trembling—look at the way that glass is shaking—it's quite involuntary—isn't it odd?

BRADLEY: You'd better get your own doctor in tomorrow.

ARNOLD: Oh I shall be all right tomorrow. You know I think she was shamming a bit to frighten me.

BRADLEY: Do you mind if I tidy up?

[BRADLEY *puts chairs upright, returns books to the bookcase.*]

ARNOLD: We're happily married. I'm not a violent person. But marriage is a long journey. Of course we argue. Every married person is a Jekyll and Hyde really. You know, Rachel is a real nagger. She can go on and on saying the same thing over and over, I mean repeating the same sentence.

BRADLEY: Then she should see a psychiatrist.

ARNOLD: That shows you've no idea! Half an hour later she's singing in the kitchen.

BRADLEY: She said you discussed her with other women. You're not playing around?

ARNOLD: No, I'm a model husband! Why shouldn't I talk

231

to women, I have to have friends, I can't give way on a point like that—it could be a very serious sacrifice—and if a sacrifice would make you mad with resentment you oughtn't to make it!

BRADLEY: Naturally I won't mention this business to anybody.

ARNOLD: [*glancing at* BRADLEY, *a bit annoyed*] Oh—well—suit yourself. Why did you chuck that doctor out so quickly? He said he was your friend.

BRADLEY: Did he! Well, he's not!

ARNOLD: He said something about Christine—wasn't that your wife?

BRADLEY: Ex-wife. He's her brother.

ARNOLD: How awfully interesting! Isn't she in America? She married an American. I wish I'd met her.

BRADLEY: She's in London now, she's a rich widow.

ARNOLD: So you'll see her?

BRADLEY: No, why should I? I don't like her.

ARNOLD: Hurt pride?

BRADLEY: Hurt pride! No, *I* left *her*.

ARNOLD: Well, resentment.

BRADLEY: Hatred, my dear Arnold, pure mutual hatred.

ARNOLD: I don't believe in hatred, I think it's terribly unusual really. I should be dying with curiosity if I were you. So the doctor is her brother—

BRADLEY: He's not a doctor, he was struck off.

ARNOLD: Ex-wife, ex-doctor! What did he do?

BRADLEY: I don't know, I don't like him either.

ARNOLD: You mustn't be so censorious. I rather liked him actually, I asked him to come round and see us.

BRADLEY: Oh no—!

ARNOLD: You ought to be interested in people and know details about them, justice demands details. Curiosity is a kind of charity.

BRADLEY: I think curiosity is a kind of malice.

ARNOLD: That's what makes a writer, knowing details.

BRADLEY: It may be your sort of writer, it doesn't make mine!

ARNOLD: Here we go again!

BRADLEY: Malicious sketches and lists of things one happens to have noticed isn't art!

ARNOLD: I never said it was—I don't draw directly from life!

BRADLEY: Your wife thinks so.

ARNOLD: Oh—! [*Dismissive gesture*]

BRADLEY: Journalistic reportage isn't art, and neither is semi-pornographic romantic fantasy! Art is truth, art is imagination, it's metamorphosis, without that you have either senseless details or egotistic dreams.

ARNOLD: [*raising his voice*] All right!

BRADLEY: Art comes out of endless restraint plus silence.

ARNOLD: If the silence is endless there isn't any art!

BRADLEY: One must wait for what's perfect—

ARNOLD: I publish things without waiting for them to be perfect because I know they'll never be perfect, anything else is hypocrisy—that's what it means to be a professional writer. Why not just think of yourself as someone who very occasionally writes something, who may in the future write something? Why make a life drama out of it?

BRADLEY: Are you suggesting I'm some sort of amateur?

ARNOLD: I know I'm second rate, I live with continual failure, every book is the wreck of a good idea! But there's no point in moaning about it—if you publish a book it must look after itself. I don't think I'd write better if I wrote less, I'd just be less happy. [BRADLEY *grimaces*] I enjoy writing, it's a natural function. The alternative is to be like you, finish nothing, publish nothing, have a grudge against the whole world, and feel superior to people who try and fail!

BRADLEY: How clearly you put it, my dear fellow.

[*Enter* JULIAN. *She is wearing a track-suit and carrying a cassette player with headphones.* BRADLEY *and* ARNOLD *exchange signals.*]

JULIAN: Hello Bradley.

ARNOLD: Hello darling. You haven't seen your mother have you? I'll just pop up, she's not well. [*He goes.*]

JULIAN: They were quarrelling so I left the house. Have they calmed down?

BRADLEY: Yes of course.

JULIAN: Don't you think they quarrel more than they used to?

BRADLEY: No!

JULIAN: I'm so glad you're here, I want to ask you something. [*She tears up a letter.*]

BRADLEY: What are you doing?

JULIAN: It's a love-letter from my ex-boyfriend.

BRADLEY: Have you parted company?

JULIAN: Yes, here goes the last I hope. [*She puts it in the waste paper basket.*] That's better. I want your advice about something.

BRADLEY: What?

[*Enter* ARNOLD.]

Or is it a secret?

ARNOLD: She's asleep.

JULIAN: I've decided to become a writer, and I want you to help me.

[*Groans from* BRADLEY *and* ARNOLD]

BRADLEY: [*pointing to* ARNOLD] There's the expert!

JULIAN: Fathers can't teach—and anyway I think I'm going to be your kind of writer, not Daddy's kind.

BRADLEY: [*amused*] What is my kind?

JULIAN: The slow kind.

[BRADLEY *and* ARNOLD *laugh.* JULIAN *skips out.*]

ARNOLD: Bradley—we mustn't be enemies, we *mustn't* be—Not just because it's nicer to be at peace, but because we could do serious damage to each other—we know exactly what hurts the other most.

BRADLEY: [*rising to go*] I couldn't damage anybody. I just want to get my book written.

ARNOLD: [*who has also risen*] By the way, here's my latest novel, with the usual affectionate inscription. Someone told me you were reviewing it? [BRADLEY, *accepting the novel, politely signifies assent.*] Why don't you come to lunch next week? Rachel would love to see you.

BRADLEY: Would she? Next week I shall be over the hills and far away. I've left the old Tax Office, I'm a free man!

ARNOLD: Of course, that cottage by the sea where you're going to write your great book. Where is it?

BRADLEY: That's a secret!

[*To the audience.*]

I had at various times tried quite hard to reflect rationally upon the value of Arnold's work. I think I objected to him most because he was such a 'gabbler'. He wrote very carelessly, of course. But the gabble was not just casual and slipshod, it was an aspect of what one might call his 'metaphysic'. Arnold was always trying, as it were, to take over the world by emptying himself over it like scented bath water.

ACT ONE

Scene Three

At BRADLEY'S *flat.* BRADLEY *is on the phone.*

BRADLEY: Can I have a taxi, please, to go to King's Cross Station? Pearson. You know, Penrose Court. Straight away? Thank you.
[*The front doorbell rings.*]
Damn!
[BRADLEY *goes to the door and admits* PRISCILLA. *She walks in, and starts to cry.*]
Priscilla! What's the matter? For God's sake—what is it?

PRISCILLA: I've left my husband.

BRADLEY: Bloody Roger—I'm not surprised. Yes, I am surprised! Don't be silly, you can't have left him, you've had some little tiff—it's the hot weather.

PRISCILLA: My marriage is over, my life is over, I'm dead, I'm dried up, I'm *shrivelled* with misery and grief, years and years of misery and grief.

BRADLEY: Priscilla, I'm terribly sorry, but I am just at this moment leaving London. I've just rung for a taxi.

PRISCILLA: You're my brother, you've got to help me, someone's got to help me. I don't know how a human being can be so unhappy all the time and still be alive [*sob*]. Roger has become a devil, he wants to kill me, he tried to poison me.

BRADLEY: Oh nonsense—

PRISCILLA: Living with someone who hates you drives you mad. He said I was mad and he'd have me certified. I put up with it because there was nothing else to do.

BRADLEY: Priscilla, there *is* nothing else to do! Roger's a very selfish nasty man, but you'll just have to forgive

236

him! You can't leave him, you haven't anywhere else to go.

PRISCILLA: I got rid of the child because he said he couldn't afford it and then I couldn't have another.

BRADLEY: Please, not that old story! Look, I've got a train to catch.

PRISCILLA: I've never felt well since, never. I think I've got cancer. Can I have a drink? I've started drinking. That's another thing he holds against me.

[BRADLEY *brings a sherry bottle and glass, pours out some.* PRISCILLA *takes off her shoes, then her jacket and skirt.* BRADLEY *watches with dismay as she begins to settle herself on the sofa.*]

Could you put a rug over me?

[BRADLEY *puts a rug over her.* PRISCILLA *sips the sherry, then petulantly returns it to* BRADLEY.]

No, don't touch me, I can't bear to be touched, I feel like a leper, I feel my flesh is rotting. I wish I was a corpse, a dead one not a living one. He cut down my magnolia tree, the garden was *his* garden, the house was *his* house, I gave him my life. Oh, I'm so *frightened*.

BRADLEY: My parents kept a stationer's shop in Croydon. My sister Priscilla and I slept under the counter. No, of course we didn't, we can't have done— but I remember it all the same. Some people just have rotten lives. Why did God love Jacob and hate Esau? Answer me that one! Take Priscilla for instance. My mother certainly hated Priscilla. Well, she hated me too, but I hated her so it didn't signify.

Priscilla, listen, I'm going away—you can't stay here!

PRISCILLA: Roger hated the sight of me, he said so. And I used to cry in front of him, I'd sit and cry for hours with sheer misery, and he'd just go on reading the paper.

BRADLEY: You make me feel quite sorry for him!

PRISCILLA: Oh I know I've lost my looks—

BRADLEY: As if that mattered!

PRISCILLA: So you think I look horrible? Ach—I made a home for that man, I tried and tried, when he shouted at me I asked him to forgive me! I kept trying to make everything nice for him, to keep the house nice and now I've left it all behind, all my things, my nice *things*, my fur coat, my pearls, my amber necklace, and my little ornaments, the little animals I had, my Chinese vases and the silver looking-glass—all my nice things, all gone.

BRADLEY: They're perfectly safe at home!

PRISCILLA: No they're not! There is no home. Please, please, could you go and fetch them. He'll destroy them all out of spite. I'm a fool, I just ran out—I hate Roger, I hate him, I'd like to stick a red-hot knitting-needle into his liver.

BRADLEY: Priscilla!

PRISCILLA: I read it in a detective story. You die slowly in terrible agony.

BRADLEY: Do stop this!

PRISCILLA: You don't understand, you don't see the *horror*, no wonder you can't write books, you've had an easy life, you've never had this sort of pain, oh the pain, if you only knew what it's like to be me, to want to spend hours and hours just screaming with pain—

[PRISCILLA *begins to utter little hysterical moaning cries.*]

BRADLEY: Oh shut up! You can't stay here!

PRISCILLA: I'll kill myself—that's best—they'll say she's better dead—she had too much pain—and now it's over—she's dead, she's DEAD.

[*The doorbell rings.*]

BRADLEY: Oh God, the taxi—

[BRADLEY *goes to the door.* PRISCILLA *produces a bottle of pills from her handbag and swallows handfuls of them with gulps of sherry.* BRADLEY *returns.*]

Now just stop all this—

PRISCILLA: [*calm*] Don't worry—I've just eaten all my sleeping pills.

BRADLEY: I don't believe you—

PRISCILLA: Eaten them all—see? [*She shows the empty bottle.*] Now you can go away. Just leave me alone—and I'll go to sleep—and forget it all—forever—it's the end, it's the *end*.

[*She drops the bottle on the floor and covers her face with the rug.*]

BRADLEY: Oh God—Priscilla!

[*He rushes to and fro. Lifts the telephone. Fumbles with telephone directories.*]

BRADLEY: Now you've made me miss my train.

[*The doorbell rings.* BRADLEY *returns with* FRANCIS.]

FRANCIS: I hope you don't mind my coming.

BRADLEY: No, I don't!

FRANCIS: *What?*

BRADLEY: My sister has just taken an overdose of sleeping pills—she's under that rug.

[FRANCIS *removes the rug and inspects* PRISCILLA *who moans slightly.*]

FRANCIS: Try to get her sitting up. What did she take? Can you find the bottle?

BRADLEY: It was here just now—

[*During what follows* FRANCIS *carries on a sort of struggle with* PRISCILLA *who is moaning and throwing herself about.*]

FRANCIS: Ring up Middlesex Hospital and ask for Casualty. How many did you take? Tell me what you took.

[PRISCILLA *gags.*]

[*The doorbell rings. Enter* ARNOLD *and* RACHEL. *They are in their best clothes and look like a model pair in an advertisement except that Rachel has a slightly black eye. They stand together and click their heels and salute, smiling at* BRADLEY.]

ARNOLD: You left the door open so we came in. We thought we'd come and parade ourselves, it's such a lovely warm day. We want to show you how all right we are, and wish you *bon voyage* and best of luck with the book!

BOTH: [*in unison*] *Bon voyage* and best of luck with the book!

BRADLEY: My sister Priscilla has just attempted suicide. [*Exclamations of appalled sympathy.*]

FRANCIS: Where's the bottle?

BRADLEY: I've got to find the bottle. [*He starts crawling about the floor.*]

ARNOLD: What bottle? We'll help! [*They all help.*]

FRANCIS: Ring up the hospital!

BRADLEY: Rachel, could you do it? Ring the Middlesex Hospital and ask for Casualty and tell them—

RACHEL: Yes—yes—

PRISCILLA: Help me, help me to die.

FRANCIS: You're not going to die.

[RACHEL *seizes the telephone book from* BRADLEY. *During the following exchanges her voice continues semi-audibly, sometimes covered by the other speeches. An effect of everyone talking at once.*]

ARNOLD: Francis, my dear old friend, always where the action is!

RACHEL: Casualty please, yes, urgent.

PRISCILLA: [*in background*] Help me—help me to die—oh help me to die.

RACHEL: Someone has taken an overdose of sleeping pills.

[*Enter Julian.*]

JULIAN: What's happened? Dad, what's happened?

ARNOLD: [*searching*] The bottle, the bottle.

JULIAN: [*to* BRADLEY] Is someone hurt?

BRADLEY: No, yes, my sister, that's my sister. We've got to find the bottle!

JULIAN: Oh dear! What bottle?

PRISCILLA: Can't you please just let me die?

ARNOLD: [*finding the bottle*] Is this it?

[FRANCIS *comes forward and takes the bottle.*]

FRANCIS: Brad! Some salty water.

[BRADLEY *goes to fetch it.*]

RACHEL: I can't hear— [*To the others*] Be quiet! [*Shouting to* BRADLEY] When did she take them?

BRADLEY: [*off*] Just now.

RACHEL: Just now. Yes—yes—

PRISCILLA: Bradley, you won't leave me, will you, you'll go and get my things—

RACHEL: 23 Penrose Court—you know—yes—

PRISCILLA: I haven't anyone but you, you won't leave me alone, will you—

BRADLEY: [*off*] Of course not.

RACHEL: That's right, we're quite close.

PRISCILLA: I'm so unhappy—

[BRADLEY *returns.*]

BRADLEY: Stop jumping about, can't you *rest*?

PRISCILLA: *Rest!*

RACHEL: [*finishing call*] Yes—thank you so much. [*To* FRANCIS] I'm so grateful to you.

FRANCIS: [*pleased*] Not at all, it was a pleasure. [*The doorbell rings.*]

RACHEL: It can't be the ambulance already.

PRISCILLA: Don't leave me!

ARNOLD: I'll go.

[ARNOLD *and* RACHEL *go out to the front door.* FRANCIS *returns to* PRISCILLA. BRADLEY *comes forward, holding his head.*]

JULIAN: Bradley, I'm so sorry. Poor Priscilla, oh dear, old age is so awful.

BRADLEY: [*raised eyebrows, curtly*] Yes. Isn't it. [*Distractedly he tidies the scene, folds the rug, picks up* PRISCILLA'S *skirt and shoes.*]

JULIAN: But she'll be all right, won't she?

BRADLEY: Yes, yes.

JULIAN: Bradley, I'm sorry to be a bother, can I ask you something?

BRADLEY: [*distracted*] What?

JULIAN: Could you do something for me?

BRADLEY: Oh God, why does this have to happen!

JULIAN: Could you talk to me a bit about *Hamlet*?

BRADLEY: *Hamlet?*

JULIAN: I don't mean now. What about Tuesday at eleven, here. You see it's my set book for my exam. It's such a *confusing* play—Do you think Gertrude was in league with Claudius to kill the king?

BRADLEY: No.

JULIAN: I thought perhaps she was having an affair with Claudius before the king died?

BRADLEY: No.

JULIAN: You don't think that all women at a certain age feel an urge to commit adultery—?

BRADLEY: No.

[*Sounds of ambulance.* RACHEL *returns. She helps* FRANCIS *to get* PRISCILLA *to her feet and propel her towards the door.*]

RACHEL: Ambulance.

PRISCILLA: Nobody loves me, nobody cares about me. My mother hated me, my father hated me. They broke my back, they broke my bones.

BRADLEY: God, I hope she'll be all right.

PRISCILLA: [*at door*] I don't exist, I've never existed. I'm nothing—nothing—

[*Her wails die away outside, as* RACHEL *and* FRANCIS *lead her out, wrapped in a rug.*]

BRADLEY: Wait a moment, what about her clothes!

[*He rushes to* JULIAN *carrying* PRISCILLA'S *jacket, skirt, shoes.* JULIAN *goes with them. During this confusion* ARNOLD *has returned, unnoticed by* BRADLEY, *with* CHRISTINE.]

BRADLEY: [*to* ARNOLD]
What's the matter with you?

[BRADLEY *notices* CHRISTINE.]

Christine!

[CHRISTINE *looks youthful and smart. She speaks with a slight American accent.*]

CHRISTINE: Bradley—after all these years, the same old Bradley, I thought you might be old and grey, but you're *young*—isn't he young—

RACHEL: Francis has gone with her, she'll be fine.

CHRISTINE: And poor old Priscilla, I remember Priscilla—oh the poor thing. Isn't it just a cry for help, Rachel?

[*enter* JULIAN.]

And this is your lovely daughter. Hi Julian!

JULIAN: Hi.

BRADLEY: [*utterly confused*] But—do you all know each other?

CHRISTINE: Yes, we do!—We met on the doorstep. Say, I like your friends. I've read all his books [*indicating* ARNOLD], isn't that great? [*To* ARNOLD] I wrote an essay on you when I was a mature student.

ARNOLD: You must come round and see us.

RACHEL: Yes, do come!

[ARNOLD *and* RACHEL *are thoroughly amused by this scene, so far.*]

CHRISTINE: I'd love to—I don't have any friends in London now, I don't know anybody except him [*indicating* BRADLEY] and my delinquent brother—*he* came round to my place yesterday asking for money and now it turns out he's a friend of you-all—it's a small world, that's for sure. Bradley—[*she stares at him with appreciation, head on one side*] well, well, it's like old times—

ARNOLD: May we offer Christine a drink?

[*He does so, getting glasses from the cupboard and seizing the sherry bottle.*]

JULIAN: Bradley, I have to go. Tuesday will be OK, won't it? [*Exit.*]

CHRISTINE: Brad, you're all of a tremble!

BRADLEY: [*to* CHRISTINE] Will you please leave my house?

CHRISTINE: Bradley, please don't take that tone. I've been thinking about it all—I come in peace.

ARNOLD: Bradley, relax, you've got to face it, it's got to happen—

CHRISTINE: It's happening. I'm all of a tremble too. I'm in a state of shock. You know I pictured this meeting a thousand times, I dreamt about it, I thought I'd faint! And now—it's a blessed miracle. Brad, dear, do say something—say something kind and good!

BRADLEY: I have written you a letter. Here it is.

[*He hands the letter to* CHRISTINE *who reads it.*]

CHRISTINE: Well, it's not very polite!

[*She hands the letter to* ARNOLD.]

ARNOLD: [*reading*] 'I do not under *any circumstances* wish to see you. Do not, prompted by curiosity or morbid interest attempt to . . . In the long years of our merciful separation I have forgotten you . . .'

CHRISTINE: Of course he hasn't!

[*She peers at the letter too.*]

ARNOLD: [*touching her sleeve and reading on*] 'I was relieved to be rid of you, I do not like you. But since your memories of me are doubtless as disagreeable as my memories of you . . .'

CHRISTINE: But they're not disagreeable, that's what I came to say! You mustn't be scared.

BRADLEY: I am not scared!

CHRISTINE: Well, you're all sort of excited—isn't he excited?

ARNOLD: [*very amused*] Oh Bradley, what a writer you are, it's a real writer's letter! Listen to this.

BRADLEY: Shut up!

CHRISTINE: Jesus, I shall get the giggles—I always do

when I'm shit scared. You know this man makes me laugh! [*she indicates* ARNOLD] Oh Lordie!

[ARNOLD *is laughing quietly over* BRADLEY'S *letter.* CHRISTINE *begins to giggle. He and* CHRISTINE *go off into crazy laughter.*]

RACHEL: [*now uneasy*] Bradley, I'm sorry. Don't worry about Priscilla. Come on, Arnold, we must go too.

ARNOLD: I'm going to stay with Bradley, I think he needs a friend!

CHRISTINE: I could look after Priscilla. I know all about suicide, My God, I did a course. I'll go see her.

BRADLEY: Oh no you won't.

CHRISTINE: Don't get so het up, man. Let's talk.

BRADLEY: I refer you to my letter.

CHRISTINE: [*to* ARNOLD] You say something to him.

[ARNOLD, *much amused, makes despairing gestures.* CHRISTINE *laughs. She turns to* BRADLEY.]

Come now. I'm glad to see you. I thought you'd be glad to see me. I pictured your eyes all warm and smiling. Was I crazy? Maybe it's just that I'm happy now. I get a buzz from the whole world, I love everything. I wake in the morning and I cry Hallelujah! [*Turning to* ARNOLD] Am I awful? You see I'm free now, I'm a free lady. Like in Zen when you get enlightenment.

ARNOLD: Satori! I know all about Buddhism.

CHRISTINE: [*to* ARNOLD] I guess I went through Zen like a knife through butter. I'm into real philosophy now— Goodness Ethics.

ARNOLD: Aren't all ethics goodness ethics?

CHRISTINE: [*counting on her fingers*] Oh no—there's Duty Ethics, and Virtue Ethics, and Welfare Ethics—But Goodness Ethics is the new Christianity. God is out, he's right out, he's finished. That leaves Jesus, sort of like Buddha, you can have him for free, no need to believe in all that old stuff. [*She points upward.*] It's all here and now! You take Jesus as your Saviour, and Jesus equals Goodness, so you just *love* Goodness, like in Plato!

RACHEL: Plato!

ARNOLD: That sounds wonderful, we must discuss it, I'm so interested in religion.

CHRISTINE: [*to* BRADLEY] He's laughing at me, but it's all true!

BRADLEY: You came here to exhibit your self-satisfaction, your fancy American accent and your money, and now that you have done so will you kindly understand that I do not want to see you.

CHRISTINE: What's wrong with being rich? It's a quality, it's attractive. Rich people are nicer, they're less nervy, they're serene. Look, I come back here and I come straight to you. Think about that. I'm not an emotional kid looking for kicks. I'm a middle-aged well-balanced woman. I can see into my motivation. I was years in deep analysis back in Illinois. I want real happiness. I want friendship, I want to know all sorts of people, I want to help people. I guess it would help us if we could discuss our marriage, so we could sort of redeem the past.

BRADLEY: You make me sick—

CHRISTINE: Say, have you been analysed?

BRADLEY: *Analysed?!*

CHRISTINE: Lie down, relax, and talk about yourself to a nice wise Jew, it's great. That's what you need! [*To* ARNOLD] Don't you agree?

BRADLEY: And leave my friends alone!

CHRISTINE: Oh come on, Brad, you don't own your friends. You're getting jealous already! [*To* ARNOLD] He always was a jealous man. [*To* BRADLEY] How many books have you published? I thought you'd be a real author by now. We had a literary guy from England to our Writers' Circle, but he hadn't heard of you.

Say, it's great to meet Arnold Baffin though. You still in the old Tax Office?

ARNOLD: He's retired.

CHRISTINE: I've got some dandy tax problems. I thought maybe you'd help me. [CHRISTINE *to* ARNOLD.] He never should have been in that office, he ought to have been out seeing the real world, no wonder he can't write. I've seen plenty and I'll see plenty more. I always wanted to be an authoress, I did a course in creative writing and—

BRADLEY: [*pointing to the door*] Will you get out?

CHRISTINE: Bradley, don't be unkind to me—don't you think I might be a different person now?

BRADLEY: I am not interested in anything you might have become.

ARNOLD: Of course he's interested! Bradley don't be so pompous and vindictive!

[BRADLEY *gestures towards the door.*]

CHRISTINE: All right, buster, if that's the way you want it. I thought maybe we could have some fun together, you and me. I'm a rich woman now, I'm going to be happy and I'm going to make other folks happy. I've been looking at you, Bradley Pearson, and you're not a happy man.

BRADLEY: I may not be happy, but I'm not for sale. Go away I hate you. I just simply hate you.

CHRISTINE: Bradley, hatred's bad, it's negative.

[BRADLEY *points again at the door.* CHRISTINE *makes a wry face and a helpless gesture. She repeats the gesture to* ARNOLD. *She waves to* RACHEL, *who is sitting on the sofa.*]

Bye!

[CHRISTINE *goes out.* ARNOLD *galvanised, starts to go after her, then turns back.*]

ARNOLD: Bradley—

[BRADLEY *regards him grimly.* ARNOLD *with a quick glance*

at RACHEL *runs out after* CHRISTINE. *Silence while* BRADLEY *and* RACHEL, *not looking at each other, breathe deeply.*]

RACHEL: [*still sitting at the back*] Well, that was an interesting scene.

BRADLEY: Hatred is terrible, it's degrading—

RACHEL: I don't think it's degrading, it's a natural phenomenon. It's a source of energy.

BRADLEY: [*absorbed in his rage and misery*] That woman gets right inside me, it's like swallowing a knife. But no one seems to want to believe that I really do hate her!

RACHEL: I believe it. I know hatred.

BRADLEY: She's the only person I hate. Because of her I know about hatred, and I don't like it. Being infuriated with Arnold is something quite different. God, I must calm down! I've written a nasty review of his new novel, I can't decide whether to publish it. [*He takes the review from his pocket and reads.*] Listen to this. 'Arnold Baffin's new novel provides his many admirers with what they want, the mixture as before. Hero, stockbroker, forty, decides to become a monk, enters monastery. Heroine, sister of Abbot, intense lady returned from East, tries to convert hero to Buddhism. Boring ill-informed discussion of comparative religion. (Oh for a little light relief!) Abbot (Christ figure of course) is killed by immense bronze crucifix falling on his head. Is it an accident? etc. etc. [*skipping*]. Mr Baffin is a fluent prolific writer, this facility, which he mistakes for imagination, is his worst enemy. A good writer needs the courage to destroy and to wait. Judging by his output, Mr Baffin is incapable of either destroying or waiting. Only a genius can afford "never to blot a line". We must ask of this book, not whether it is entertaining, but whether it is a work of art. The answer is, alas, no. Naturally the film rights have already been sold!'

RACHEL: [*peering at the review*] It's perfectly horrid, it's spiteful, you can't publish that!

[BRADLEY *makes as if to crumple it up, then restores it to his pocket.*]

RACHEL: Actually you're in love with Arnold, everybody is, you're a masochist, you like it when he puts you down.

BRADLEY: I do not!

RACHEL: He's very fond of you. So is Julian. She admires you because you're so unlike Dad, she says she's been trying to attract your attention for years. I wish you'd see her sometime. She's awfully unhappy, poor child.

BRADLEY: It's an unhappy age, always falling in love. Thank God I'm past it.

RACHEL: Are you? I see you as all set to fall in love all over again with Christine.

BRADLEY: [*controlled*] Rachel, dear, don't make me *scream*!

RACHEL: She's awfully clever and attractive. I think Arnold's fallen for her already.

BRADLEY: No!!

RACHEL: What do you imagine he's doing now? He's sitting with her in some pub, then he'll give her lunch, then they'll go back to her flat, and he'll make her tell him everything about your marriage.

BRADLEY: Let me not be mad, not mad, sweet heavens!

RACHEL: [*cool, tormenting him*] Arnold makes people talk, he's everybody's father confessor. She'll be dying to tell him the details of how awful it was.

BRADLEY: If Arnold were to . . . with Christine . . .

RACHEL: I know, you'd kill him. Perhaps we need to *imagine* things like that to stop us actually murdering our nearest and dearest. Calm down, Bradley, remember you're a quiet timid man. It's all in your head.

BRADLEY: I live in my head.

[BRADLEY *suddenly seizes* ARNOLD'S *new novel which is lying on the table and tears it to pieces.*]
Sorry.

RACHEL: [*kicking the pieces away*] Don't worry, I enjoyed that. Really, about Arnold and his women, I'm a bit relieved, it helps me to feel free. Let's have a drink.

BRADLEY: I'm always drinking these days. I don't usually. God, and there's poor Priscilla, I must ring up—

[RACHEL *pours a drink for herself and* BRADLEY.]

RACHEL: Bradley, sit down.

[*They sit side by side.*]

BRADLEY: I thought you might hate the sight of me because I came—you know, on that day—

RACHEL: No, it makes me feel closer to you. I've always wanted to know you better, but I've felt shy. You're a *difficult* man.

BRADLEY: [*gratified*] Am I?

RACHEL: I imagine it's a long time since you made love to a woman.

BRADLEY: Yes. [*Pregnant pause*] Look, I really must ring the hospital—

[*He is reaching for the telephone when it rings.*]

Yes—[*to* RACHEL] It's Francis. Yes, Francis. She's all right, no danger at all—Thank heavens for that—Yes, I'll fetch her things—she's made a list, has she!—Good—Thank you—I'll be along. [*He replaces the receiver.*] I think I'd better—go and see her—

[BRADLEY *is clearly uncertain about whether he wants to sit down again beside* RACHEL, *or to run away to see* PRISCILLA. RACHEL *firmly pats the sofa and he returns to his seat.*]

RACHEL: Bradley, I knew she'd be all right. Do you mind if I kiss you? I've always wanted to give you a real kiss, not just a social kiss. [*She kisses him*] Bradley—dear—

BRADLEY: Thank you. But—look—I'm a lone wolf—

RACHEL: I've only kissed you! You *are* racing ahead! Or do you think women of my age have a sudden urge—?

BRADLEY: Like Gertrude. No.

RACHEL: Who's Gertrude?

BRADLEY: Old flame of mine. I just mean I don't want any muddle.

RACHEL: You mean like falling in love with *me*?

BRADLEY: [*calm*] No. It's just that I've got work to do. I've got to be alone. I'm going to write a book I've been waiting all my life to write.

RACHEL: Don't be so solemn about your book, it won't do it any good! You musn't think of yourself as a writer, like Arnold, you must just write. You need *more life* and that's what I need too. Now hold my hand, that's right, I won't harm you, Bradley, it's all *simple*. I need love, I need more people to love, I need you to love. I think you need me to love. I've been so tired—and motionless—I must move, I must have new feelings. That won't hurt Arnold, he'll be glad—I've become a dull wife. Listen, concentrate, you're good for me, you're the only person with whom I'm not acting a part!

BRADLEY: I'm glad—but—

RACHEL: We may even have found a key to happiness— one can't really be happy until one's over forty. My dear, don't look like that, I don't mean dramas or adventures or crises, we must just come closer, you must let me love you.

BRADLEY: But do you mean something secret? I don't like secrets.

RACHEL: No, Arnold will know, everyone will know, that we care for each other a bit specially—but—well—any close friendship is secret too. You do love me a bit, don't you?

BRADLEY: Of course, I always have, but I can't exactly define—

RACHEL: Don't define! That's the point!

BRADLEY: Rachel, I don't want to feel guilty, it would interfere with my work.

RACHEL: [*little laugh*] Oh, you're such a puritan! [*She slips off her jacket.*]

BRADLEY: I'm terrified of being tied to anything just now, I've got to write this book and I've got to be *worthy* of it.

RACHEL: Bradley, I do admire you, you're so much more serious about writing than Arnold is. But why can't you write? It's because you're *repressed*, I mean in a spiritual way.

BRADLEY: In a spiritual way—perhaps—but—

RACHEL: You need to exercise your freedom, it's getting old and stiff, like mine. More freedom, more love, is what your book needs. [RACHEL *removes* BRADLEY'S *tie.*] Now kiss me again, just to prove you can. [BRADLEY *kisses her.*]

BRADLEY: We must know what we're doing. I don't want to behave badly.

RACHEL: Who says anything about behaving badly?

BRADLEY: [*pulling back a little*] You're not doing this to spite Arnold?

RACHEL: No. You're not just doing it to spite Christine?

BRADLEY: Don't be crazy. Anyway I'm not doing anything.

RACHEL: Aren't you?

BRADLEY: Could he have an affair with Christine?

RACHEL: I don't know, it doesn't matter. On that awful day—when he brought you in—as a witness—I might have hated you. But it's the opposite, I've *decided* it's the opposite. I've known you so long, and now—you've got a special role, like a knight with a charge upon him, my knight, my precious chivalrous knight.

BRADLEY: You mean courtly love?

RACHEL: Yes.

ACT ONE

[*As the conversation continues* RACHEL *is pulling off* BRADLEY'S *jacket, undoing the buttons of his shirt. She slips off her blouse.*]

BRADLEY: Rachel, courtly love isn't like this.

RACHEL: Are you afraid of Arnold?

BRADLEY: Yes.

RACHEL: You mustn't be. I must see you unafraid. That's what being my knight is about. It will set me free, and it will set you free too. I've always seen you as a free spirit, a holy man, a wise man.

BRADLEY: Well, I think this is most unwise. Moreover, I don't want it! We're both conventional middle-aged people.

RACHEL: I'm not conventional. That's what I've just discovered.

BRADLEY: Well, I am. I'm pre-permissive. And you are my best friend's wife. Please do not start anything.

RACHEL: It's started. I do enjoy arguing with you.

BRADLEY: You know where arguments like this end.

RACHEL: Yes.

[*They sit apart, staring at each other.*]

ACT ONE

Scene Four

BRADLEY *alone. He comes forward to the audience.*

BRADLEY: I received a letter from Arnold. [*Reading*] 'My dear Bradley, I have got into a mess and feel I must lay the whole matter before you. Christine and I have fallen in love. I know you don't believe in romantic love, but I assure you it exists. Of course I care for Rachel, but there is such a thing as simply getting tired of someone, our marriage is lifeless, almost a pretence. I have to look elsewhere. Of course I won't abandon Rachel, but I must have Christine too, and if that means running two establishments, well thank God I can afford it. I rely on you to help Rachel through this. Christine too needs something from you, your blessing on our relationship. Do you think you could see her soon and just say it's OK? Please? Arnold.'

[*During the reading* BRADLEY'S *flat becomes visible. He is holding* ARNOLD'S *letter. Enter* JULIAN. *She carries a copy of* Hamlet.]

BRADLEY: [*surprised*] Julian!

JULIAN: You left the door open. It's terribly hot in here. You've forgotten. I've come for my *Hamlet* tutorial. You said Tuesday was OK.

BRADLEY: Did I? Oh dear.

JULIAN: How is Priscilla?

BRADLEY: Better. She's coming back here.

JULIAN: Poor old thing, she must be *ages* older than you. Bradley, how nice to see you, you're so good for my nerves. Everybody irritates me like mad except you. Have you a moment?

BRADLEY: Yes, yes.

[*They sit down opposite to each other at the table.*]

254

ACT ONE

JULIAN: Bradley, this is fun!

BRADLEY: Nothing's happened yet, it may not be fun.

JULIAN: I'll ask questions and you answer—all right? I've got a whole list! [*She waves the list.*]

BRADLEY: All right, get on with it. I haven't got all day.

JULIAN: [*reading from the list*] Why did Hamlet delay killing Claudius?

BRADLEY: Because he was a dreamy scrupulous young intellectual who wasn't likely to commit a murder just because he imagined he'd seen a ghost. Next question.

JULIAN: But isn't the ghost a real ghost?

BRADLEY: Yes, but Hamlet doesn't know that.

JULIAN: But there must have been another reason why he delayed, isn't that the point of the play?

BRADLEY: I didn't say there wasn't another reason.

JULIAN: What is it?

BRADLEY: He identifies Claudius with his father.

JULIAN: Oh, so that makes him hesitate because he loves his father and so can't kill Claudius?

BRADLEY: No, he hates his father.

JULIAN: But wouldn't that make him murder Claudius?

BRADLEY: No. After all he didn't murder his father.

JULIAN: I don't see how identifying Claudius with his father makes him not want to kill Claudius.

BRADLEY: He doesn't enjoy hating his father. It makes him feel guilty.

JULIAN: So he's paralysed by guilt? He never says so. He's fearfully priggish and superior. Look how nasty he is to Ophelia.

BRADLEY: That's part of the same thing.

JULIAN: How do you mean?

BRADLEY: He identifies Ophelia with his mother.

JULIAN: But I thought he loved his mother.

BRADLEY: Yes, that's the point.

JULIAN: How do you mean, that's the point?

BRADLEY: He is furious with his mother for committing adultery with his father.

JULIAN: Wait a minute, I'm getting mixed—

[JULIAN *is trying at intervals to take notes.*]

BRADLEY: Claudius is identified with Hamlet's father on the unconscious level.

JULIAN: But you can't commit adultery with your husband, it isn't logical.

BRADLEY: The unconscious mind knows nothing of logic.

JULIAN: You mean Hamlet is jealous? You mean he's in love with his mother?

BRADLEY: That is the general idea. A tediously familiar one, I should have thought.

JULIAN: [*after a pause*] Oh—that.

BRADLEY: That.

JULIAN: I see. [*Scribbling in notebook*] I say, this is awfully interesting. Why couldn't Ophelia save Hamlet?

BRADLEY: Because, my dear Julian, pure ignorant young girls cannot 'save' complicated neurotic over-educated older men from disaster, however much they may kid themselves that they can.

JULIAN: All right, I'm ignorant and young but I do not identify myself with Ophelia!

BRADLEY: Of course not. You identify yourself with Hamlet, everybody does.

JULIAN: I suppose one always identifies with the hero.

BRADLEY: In great works of literature, not necessarily. Do you identify with Macbeth or Lear?

JULIAN: Well, no—

BRADLEY: Or with Achilles or Agamemnon or Raskolnikov or Fanny Price or Madame Bovary or—?

JULIAN: Wait, I haven't heard of some of them.

BRADLEY: *Hamlet* is unusual because it is a great work of literature in which everyone identifies with the hero.

JULIAN: Please—I want to catch up with my notes about Hamlet thinking his mother was committing adultery with his father—Gosh, it is hot today—do you mind if I undress a little?

[JULIAN *kicks off her shoes, pulls up her skirt, takes her jacket off, revealing a dress with narrow shoulder straps.*]

For this relief much thanks.

BRADLEY: Do you mind if I take my jacket off? You'll see my braces.

JULIAN: How exciting!

[BRADLEY *takes off his jacket and unbuttons his shirt a little. As he does so he frowns.*]

BRADLEY: Of course Hamlet is Shakespeare.

JULIAN: Bradley, was Shakespeare homosexual?

BRADLEY: Of course.

JULIAN: Oh I *see*, so Hamlet's really in love with Horatio—

BRADLEY: Silence, girl. Life is serious, art is gay. Wittgenstein. Now if the greatest genius elects to be the hero of one of his plays, is this an accident?

JULIAN: No.

BRADLEY: So this must be what the play is about.

JULIAN: What?

BRADLEY: Shakespeare's own identity. When is Shakespeare at his most cryptic?

JULIAN: The Sonnets?

BRADLEY: Shakespeare is at his most complex and secretive when he's talking to himself. How is it that *Hamlet* is his most famous play, the best-known work of literature in the world?

JULIAN: I don't know, you tell me.

BRADLEY: Because Shakespeare by the sheer intensity of his meditation on the problem of his identity has produced a new language, a rhetoric of consciousness. Words are Hamlet's being as they are Shakespeare's.

JULIAN: Words, words, words.

BRADLEY: What work of literature has more quotable lines?

JULIAN: To be, or not to be: that is the question.

BRADLEY: Since my dear soul was mistress of her choice.

JULIAN: Oh what a rogue and peasant slave am I.

BRADLEY: For at your age the heyday in the blood is tame, it's humble, and waits upon the judgement. [*He is dismayed at happening upon these lines.*] Something too much of this.

JULIAN: Oh what a noble mind is here o'erthrown.

BRADLEY: *Hamlet* is a monument of words, Shakespeare's most rhetorical and longest play. See how casually, with what easy grace he lays down the foundations of modern English prose.

JULIAN: What a piece of work is man—

BRADLEY: How noble in reason, how infinite in faculty, in form and moving how express and admirable, in action how like an angel, in apprehension how like a god! *Hamlet* is a work endlessly reflecting upon itself, not discursively but in its very substance, a Chinese Box of words as high as the Tower of Babel, a meditation upon the redemptive role of language. *Hamlet* is words and so is Hamlet. He is as witty as Jesus Christ but whereas Jesus speaks, Hamlet is speech. He is the tormented, sinful consciousness of man seared by the bright light of art, the god's flayed victim dancing the dance of creation. Shakespeare is prostrating himself before the author of his being, the god of love and art, the black Eros, the Black Prince, before whose countenance the unworthy shrivel like moths at a flame. Self-immolation, pure love, here invent language as if for the first time, changing pain into poetry and orgasms into thoughts. Shakespeare, *Hamlet*, enacts the purification of words, the deification of speech—we are redeemed because speech itself is ultimately divine—

JULIAN: I played Hamlet once.

BRADLEY: What?

JULIAN: I played Hamlet once, at school, I was sixteen.
[*She smiles.* BRADLEY *staring at her does not. She giggles.*]

BRADLEY: The show is over.

JULIAN: Please—that was marvellous what you were saying—I want to write it down.

BRADLEY: That stuff won't do for your exam. So you played Hamlet once. Describe your costume.

JULIAN: Oh the usual. All Hamlets wear the same, unless they're in modern dress.

BRADLEY: Do what I ask please.

JULIAN: What—?

BRADLEY: Describe your costume.

JULIAN: Well, I wore black tights and black velvet shoes with silver buckles, and a sort of black slinky jerkin with a low neck and a white silk shirt and a big gold chain and—What's the matter, Bradley?

BRADLEY: Nothing.

JULIAN: I enjoyed it ever so much, especially the fight at the end.
[JULIAN *poses a little, not looking at* BRADLEY, *imagining herself as Hamlet.* BRADLEY *stares at her.*]

BRADLEY: Here, thou incestuous murderous damned Dane!

JULIAN: Yes—yes—! Look, could you just tell me—

BRADLEY: Enough, enough. How are your parents?

JULIAN: You are a *tease*! They're all right. Dad's out at the library all day scribbling. Mum stays at home and moves the furniture about and broods. It's a pity she never had any education, she's so intelligent.

BRADLEY: Don't be so bloody condescending.

JULIAN: Sorry, that sounded awful, perhaps I'm awful, perhaps all young people are rather awful.

BRADLEY: Lay not that flattering unction to your soul.

JULIAN: I wish someone would write a really long nasty review of one of Dad's books, it might do him good.

BRADLEY: So you want to be a writer.

JULIAN: Yes, but not like that. And I won't call myself Julian Baffin!

BRADLEY: Perhaps you'll be married then—and have— a different name—Julian, I think you'd better go.

JULIAN: [*rising*] I've enjoyed this ever so much. Could we meet again? I don't want to be a nuisance. May I ring you?

BRADLEY: All right. Off you go.

JULIAN: You won't forget about me?

BRADLEY: Go, go! Out!

   [JULIAN *goes, leaving her copy of* Hamlet *behind on the table.* BRADLEY *picks up the book and holds it to his face. Then he falls on his knees.*]

Oh my God!

   [*He falls prone.*]

[*Blackout*]

END OF ACT ONE

ACT TWO

Scene One

Music. BRADLEY *is revealed sitting in a chair, upright, quiet, composed, his hands folded, breathing deeply. He looks utterly serene, deeply happy.* PRISCILLA'S *things are in evidence.* BRADLEY *muses softly.*

BRADLEY: So. I am still alive. A thunderbolt struck me. But I am not destroyed. I am not desperate. I am not driven mad. I am driven sane. Lucid, truthful, redeemed. Saner than I have ever been. Stronger, wiser, better. I am setting my life in order. I have fetched Priscilla from the hospital and brought her here. I have brought back her things, all the things she wanted, her fur coat, her amber necklace, her silver looking-glass, her Chinese vases, her little animals. I shall look after Priscilla. I shall see Roger and Christine and Rachel and Arnold. I shall make peace in the world. It's all quite easy now.

[*The bell rings.* BRADLEY *goes, returns with* CHRISTINE.]

BRADLEY: Christine!

CHRISTINE: [*defensive, holding up her hand*] Don't explode! I know you hate the sight of me!

BRADLEY: I don't—I don't—I'm glad to see you!

CHRISTINE: [*surprised, inspecting* BRADLEY] Oh, are you? You look all different. What is it?

BRADLEY: I've just been over to Roger's place and got the things Priscilla wanted—

CHRISTINE: Something's happened to you—you're beautiful, you're young. What have you been taking?

BRADLEY: Oh, draughts of pure unilateral love—when you hope for nothing and you're just glad that something else *is*—like this vase.

[*He brings out a ghastly vase of* PRISCILLA'S.]

Isn't it marvellous?

CHRISTINE: I don't know, but you've certainly improved.

BRADLEY: The world is so beautiful—and if you can only stop thinking about yourself and think of somebody or something else, the beauty is everywhere, it crowds upon you, like swarms of golden bees. I am under a vow of eternal silence, but I am filled with love and on that I can live forever.

CHRISTINE: Bradley!

BRADLEY: He never told his love but let concealment— oh blessed concealment, womb of art, now wrapped in my cloak of darkness I shall write.

CHRISTINE: Dearie me! Say, are you crazy?

BRADLEY: Yes. No. I have achieved the higher sanity— absolute unselfish love—it's unnatural, it's terrifying, it takes you—out of yourself—what's good, what's real is suddenly *somewhere else*—over there—and you can *see* the whole world, everything that is, real and clear and beautiful and full of light, like you've never really seen it before—you're happy, you're free, you're pure in heart, you love everything! And it's all there, all the things in the world, except for the one thing that used to obscure the view—yourself—you have no self. The disappearance of the ego is the secret of salvation. I am saved! Because I love, and I want nothing in return. The only thing that can destroy the self is absolute love.

CHRISTINE: Are you in love with Jesus?

BRADLEY: Yes, yes, Jesus too!

CHRISTINE: My Zen teacher used to talk about destroying the ego, but I never could, I guess I never wanted to. I think you'd better find that analyst.

BRADLEY: Chris, you were right about Priscilla, it was just a cry for help.

CHRISTINE: Wait a minute. Did you notice something?

You called me 'Chris' like in the old days. Who says
there ain't no miracles?

BRADLEY: I must tell you—I went over to get this
stuff and Roger, you know, her husband, has got his
secretary installed.

CHRISTINE: Oh my God.

BRADLEY: Apparently she's been his mistress for years,
she's called Marigold and she's pregnant—they were
drinking champagne! No wonder he wanted to get rid of
Priscilla.

CHRISTINE: Poor Priscilla—she always wanted a child.
Better not tell her just yet.

[CHRISTINE *has been turning over* PRISCILLA'S *things.
She finds some of them rather touching.*]

CHRISTINE: Oh, look.

BRADLEY: By the way, I'm expecting Francis.

CHRISTINE: You mean that foul crook Marloe—!

BRADLEY: Oh come!

CHRISTINE: What's got you? You're all dewy and spiritual like a cat with kittens. Bradley, did you get a letter
from Arnold?

BRADLEY: Yes—that's all right—I bless you—I bless
you!

[BRADLEY *waves his hand. He is now laying out* PRIS-
CILLA'S *possessions as listed in Act One, Scene Three, ready to
surprise her.*]

CHRISTINE: Well—good—thanks. There's something I
want to say, and want you to say, that you forgive me,
that there's peace between us. When our thing went
wrong I thought I'd be a cynic forever. When I was
in America the thing that really kept me going was
money—not painting or pottery or creative writing or
analysis or Zen—only money was real. And I was
damn good at it, I'm a business woman. But I always
felt there was more to life, something higher, like a
spiritual dimension. I used to dream we were recon-

ciled, you know, at night in real dreams. And then I'd wake up and remember how we'd parted in that awful crazy hatred. My God! And I felt when I was coming back here that I was coming for you, to you. And now— you know something—I feel you're open to me—I can walk straight in and there's *welcome* written on the mat. Brad, say those good words, say you forgive me, say we're reconciled, say we're real true friends.

BRADLEY: Of course I forgive you, of course we're reconciled, of course we're friends, you see how easy it is.

CHRISTINE: Yes, you're beautiful, you look like a god-damned saint. I never stopped thinking about you. After all, we were married in church, with my body I thee worship and all that jazz. You're a good man, Bradley Pearson. Let us open our hearts to each other.

BRADLEY: Chris, dear, I—

CHRISTINE: Kiss me, Bradley, the kiss of peace.

[*They kiss.* PRISCILLA, *in a dressing gown, enters and witnesses the scene. She suddenly sobs aloud.*]

CHRISTINE: [*going to* PRISCILLA *and kissing her.*] Priscilla, darling am I glad to see you better.

BRADLEY: Look what I've brought you—

PRISCILLA: Oh, my fur coat.

BRADLEY: —And all the things you wanted.

PRISCILLA: My Chinese vases, my silver looking-glass. My little animals [*Doorbell.*] My amber necklace, my pearls.

[*Enter* FRANCIS.]

BRADLEY: Francis!

PRISCILLA: My ducks!

BRADLEY: Priscilla, here's your friend the doctor. Chris, you must be kind to Francis, he's been so good. Hasn't he, Priscilla? Isn't he a good egg?

PRISCILLA: [*hugging Francis*] He is, he is!

ACT TWO

BRADLEY: Chris, say a kind word, you know how—he's your brother, he's my friend—I decree a season of good will!

CHRISTINE: Bradley's gone mad, he's become a saint!

FRANCIS: Chris, don't be cross with me, dear—

CHRISTINE: [*amused*] All right, come here, you rogue! [*They shake hands.*]

BRADLEY: I'm so glad. Look, Priscilla, everyone's friends! Let's have a party, we'll celebrate. Give him a cheque, Chris, he's broke, give him a cheque, give him a cheque!
[BRADLEY *is becoming hysterical with euphoria. He produces sherry, hands drinks around.*]

CHRISTINE: [*laughing*] All right, all right! [*She produces her cheque book.*]

FRANCIS: [*peering*] I say, could you make it five hundred? [*Enter* RACHEL, *who looks with surprise at the festive scene.*]

BRADLEY: Rachel, my dear, I'm so glad you've come. We're giving a party, we're giving a party for Priscilla!

RACHEL: *Priscilla!* You're looking so well. What a lovely coat!

CHRISTINE: Yes, isn't it just lovely.

PRISCILLA: It's silver fox. Look, it's monogrammed!

RACHEL: [*amiable*] Hello, Christine.

CHRISTINE: [*bad conscience*] Hello, dear Rachel.

BRADLEY: Rachel, tell Arnold I'm going to read all his books again with a humble open mind!

RACHEL: Is Bradley drunk?

CHRISTINE: No, he's just become good, maybe we should all try it!

BRADLEY: Here's to Priscilla! Health and happiness!

ALL: Priscilla, health and happiness!
[*Francis, clowning around, puts on some earrings and a hat.*]

FRANCIS: Bradley, won't you sing to us? Chris, you remember how Brad used to sing?

CHRISTINE: Yes, come on, Bradley.

265

BRADLEY: We'll all sing.
Great Tom is cast,
And Christ Church bells ring
One, two, three, four, five, six
And Tom comes last.
[BRADLEY *sings first alone, then conducts the others to sing in round. The round soon gets hopelessly mixed up and they go on singing and laughing. The scene darkens a little. Music, a cacophonous medley of the tune joins the voices, the voices fade as the singers are lost in darkness.*

BRADLEY *is left alone, holding his head. The horror of the situation has reached him at last. The music gradually changes, the stage lightens.*]

ACT TWO

Scene Two

JULIAN *enters.*

JULIAN: I left my book.
[BRADLEY *hands it to her. Another pause.*]
BRADLEY: I'm just going away. So I must say goodbye.
JULIAN: I—I felt I wanted to talk to you again. [*She puts the book down.*]
BRADLEY: [*laconic, abrupt*] So sorry. I'm off to the country. I'll be away some time. Francis is coming to look after Priscilla.
JULIAN: I'm sorry you're going. I wanted to thank you.
BRADLEY: That's kind of you. Now I'm afraid I have a train to catch. [*He looks at his watch.*] I mustn't keep you. [*He goes to the telephone.*]
JULIAN: Don't be cross with me.
BRADLEY: I'm not cross with you.
JULIAN: [*upset, near to tears*] Yes, you are. You're being cold, and hostile. You know how much I like and admire you. I just wanted to see you.
BRADLEY: Thank you for coming. I'm sorry to be in such a hurry. I just can't see you—I—I don't want to see you.
JULIAN: Why? There must be a reason. [*Pause*] And I think I know what it is.
BRADLEY: [*handing her* Hamlet] Don't forget your book.
JULIAN: Bradley, I know—because of the way you looked at me last time, and the way you're behaving now.
BRADLEY: If you want me to gratify your vanity by a display of my feelings you will be disappointed.
JULIAN: You are displaying your feelings.
BRADLEY: Why have you come here to bother me?

267

JULIAN: I wanted to be sure. Don't you want to talk about it?

BRADLEY: No, of course not. There's nothing to talk about.

JULIAN: This concerns me too. I'm upset too. You have upset me. You speak as if there was no one involved but you.

BRADLEY: There is no one involved but me. You're just something in my dream!

JULIAN: I'm not, I'm real, I'm here. Don't you care what I think?

BRADLEY: [*bitter amusement*] My dear Julian, of course I don't care what you think! Now please run along, there's a good girl. I'm just going to ring for a taxi.

JULIAN: No you're not.

[*They stare at each other.*]

BRADLEY: You're a criminal.

JULIAN: Don't you think that you can hurt me—don't you think that I can suffer?

BRADLEY: Suffer? You?!

JULIAN: You're just concerned about yourself. All right, I'm concerned about myself. You started it. You can't just stop it now when you decide.

BRADLEY: The fact that I may imagine myself to be in love with you does not preclude my knowing that you are a *very silly girl*. This thing is not a toy, your curiosity will be unsatisfied and your vanity unflattered. And I hope that, unlike me, you will *keep your mouth shut*.

JULIAN: Don't be like that, please talk to me. Don't you want to talk to me about your love?

BRADLEY: No. I imagined talking to you about it. But that was in the fantasy world. I can't talk love to you in the real world. What do you want me to do—praise your eyes?

JULIAN: Has telling your love made your love end? It hasn't, has it?

268

ACT TWO

BRADLEY: No. But it has no speech—any more—its tongue has been cut out.

JULIAN: You talk as if there was nobody here but you.

BRADLEY: There is nobody here but me.

JULIAN: So you don't want to know what I feel.

BRADLEY: I know what you feel. You are amused and pleased because an older man is making a fool of himself.

JULIAN: How old are you Bradley?

BRADLEY: [*slight hesitation*] Forty-two.

JULIAN: [*slightly shaken*] Oh—forty-two—well, I don't all that old. Bradley, don't be so horrid to me. [*She reaches out a hand.*]

BRADLEY: I may be a fool, but that's no reason for you to be a bitch.

JULIAN: To a nunnery go, and quickly too—

BRADLEY: [*pointing to the door*] Farewell!! [*He goes to the telephone.*]

JULIAN: It doesn't occur to you that I might return your love.

BRADLEY: [*removing his hand from the telephone*] No.

JULIAN: I've known you all my life, I've always loved you. I was so happy when you came to see my father and I could ask you things and tell you things—so many things weren't real at all until I'd told you them—you were a sort of touchstone of reality to me. If you only knew how much I've always admired you. When I was a little child I used to say I wanted to marry you. Do you remember? All right, you don't! You've been my ideal man for ever and ever. This isn't just a silly child's thing, it's real deep love, of course it's a love I haven't questioned or thought about or even named until quite lately—but now I have questioned it and thought about it—now that I'm grown up. You see, my love has grown up too. I've so much wanted to be with you and know you properly—since I've been a woman.

Why do you think I wanted to discuss *Hamlet*? I did want to discuss *Hamlet*, but I much more wanted your affection, your attention, I wanted to *look* at you. I've *longed* to touch you and kiss you in these last years, only I didn't dare to, I never thought I would. I've been thinking about you all the time—I love you, I love you.

BRADLEY: I'm not accusing you of insincerity, just of not having the faintest idea what you're talking about. *Don't touch me!*

[JULIAN *advances.* BRADLEY *retreats. She seizes his sleeve. He wrenches it away. She stands before him. They stare at each other. Then he quietly takes her into his arms and they embrace, eyes closed, without kissing. Then* BRADLEY *thrusts her away.*]

You little devil.

JULIAN: I love you.

BRADLEY: Don't talk lying rubbish.

JULIAN: Why do you think it's impossible? Do you think I'm a child, or that you're so unlovable?

BRADLEY: Both. Oh Julian, I intended to lock this thing up until it died of starvation. And now—we mustn't do this. You are younger than you think, I am older than you think.

JULIAN: I'm in love with you. I've been *trembling* since I last saw you. I had to come and see you. I feel absolutely shattered and yet I feel absolutely calm. I feel like an archangel. Oh, please kiss me, please. [*They kiss, briefly.*]

BRADLEY: God. let's sit down.

[*They sit down on the sofa.*]

JULIAN: We aren't doing anything wrong.

[JULIAN *begins to unbutton* BRADLEY'S *shirt.* BRADLEY *removes her hand. Perhaps he is uneasily reminded of a recent similar scene.*]

BRADLEY: We mustn't be together, we mustn't see each other—

JULIAN: I so want to touch you, it's so marvellous, it's a privilege. [*She gently touches his face, drawing her fingers down.*]

BRADLEY: You're mad.

BRADLEY: Bradley—dear—don't be afraid. We'll just get to know each other slowly and quietly, tell each other the truth and tell each other everything and look—and look—and—

BRADLEY: All right, Julian, we'll talk—we've got to talk each other out of this!

JULIAN: If we talk—we'll talk each other—deeper in— deeper and deeper—in.

BRADLEY: [*panic*] You mustn't feel tied, there's no tie, there's no connection, we musn't define this, we mustn't use words like 'love'—

JULIAN: Don't be silly—

BRADLEY: I'm terrified.

JULIAN: I'm not. I've never felt braver in my life. I haven't said anything to my parents of course, I couldn't till I was sure, but I'll tell them now.

BRADLEY: *What?* What'll you tell them?

JULIAN: That I love you and I want to marry you.

BRADLEY: Julian—it's impossible—this is a dream— it's even a lie—

JULIAN: Bradley, it's true, it's truest, it's the test of all truth.

BRADLEY: I'm too old.

JULIAN: Lots of girls prefer older men—you don't just want a love affair and then goodbye?

BRADLEY: No!

JULIAN: Real love is forever.

BRADLEY: Yes, I know—but, Julian, don't—I'd rather you didn't tell your parents.

JULIAN: You think they won't like it?

ACT TWO

SCENE THREE

BRADLEY'S *flat.* ARNOLD'S *house.* BRADLEY *and* ARNOLD *are talking by telephone.* RACHEL, *with* ARNOLD, *is listening on the extension.*

ARNOLD: Bradley, get back to reality. You're in some sort of dream world. You're nearly sixty. Julian is twenty. She said at the start that you'd told her your age and that she didn't mind, but you can't mean to take advantage of a sentimental child who is flattered by your attentions—

BRADLEY: She's not a child.

RACHEL: She's a child!

BRADLEY: I didn't want her to tell you.

ARNOLD: You asked her to deceive her parents?

RACHEL: I think he's really in love with Christine, and he's subconsciously transferred it to Julian.

ARNOLD: *Is* it Christine?

BRADLEY: No! I don't care *what* Christine does! Thank you for your letter, by the way!

ARNOLD: All right. You find Julian attractive. But if you felt randy about her, why the hell didn't you keep it to yourself, instead of annoying and upsetting her?

BRADLEY: She's not annoyed or upset.

ARNOLD: She was this morning.

BRADLEY: Then you upset her. You evidently don't know what it is to be in love. Now I come to think of it, you've never really described it in any of your beastly novels!

ARNOLD: What *you* imagine about your vile feelings and lusts is your affair. Julian is certainly not in love.

RACHEL: [*seizing the telephone*] You haven't been to bed with her, have you?

ARNOLD: Of course he hasn't, he's not a criminal!

BRADLEY: I haven't. Please don't get angry—you're frightening me—I'll leave her free—she *is* free—but I can't say I won't see her.

ARNOLD: If you pester her now, you'll make an *emotional situation*, that's what you want, and that's what I won't allow. Now I hope you'll have the decency to leave London at once!

BRADLEY: You don't understand. I am not proposing to go away.

ARNOLD: What do you propose to do?

BRADLEY: Stay here, see Julian a bit—get to know her— since it appears we love each other—

ARNOLD: Bradley! I warn you! I will take any measures to stop this.

BRADLEY: Don't be so angry, I haven't done anything wrong.

RACHEL: [*taking the telephone*] Yes, you have. You spoke to her about your feelings. And you permitted yourself to *have* such unspeakable feelings!

BRADLEY: Rachel—

RACHEL: [*softly*] You have behaved horribly, and I will never forgive you.

[RACHEL *disappears*, ARNOLD *continues*.]

ARNOLD: By the way, that letter I wrote you, there's no need to do anything about it just now.

BRADLEY: I wasn't going to.

ARNOLD: It's not unusual for men of your age to want to sow some unsavoury wild oats. I'm going to take Julian away and you won't know where she is. I'm going to hide her until you come to your senses.

[*Enter* JULIAN.]

BRADLEY: Oh, so you're going to hide her . . . and I won't know where she is . . . oh dear.

ARNOLD: Hello . . . hello . . .

[BRADLEY *replaces the telephone, embraces* JULIAN.]

JULIAN: Oh Bradley, whatever shall we do?

BRADLEY: [*his joy fading*] I don't know. [*He points to her suitcase.*] What's that?

JULIAN: I've left home—oh it's been such a *nightmare*.

BRADLEY: I gather they weren't pleased.

JULIAN: I was a perfect idiot. I told them all about it last night in a triumphant sort of way—I've never seen my father so angry, he got quite violent, he shook me—

BRADLEY: Oh my dear child—

JULIAN: And then I lay on my bed and couldn't stop crying. And later on they said they'd rung you and you'd agreed it was all nonsense and you'd said you were going away.

BRADLEY: That wasn't true, of course.

JULIAN: I knew it wasn't, and I wouldn't promise not to see you and then the row started again and my father was shouting and my mother was crying and I *screamed*, and—I just didn't know ordinary educated middle-class people could behave like we behaved last night!

BRADLEY: That shows how young you are! I wish it wasn't open war—you *can't* be certain, you ought to be locked up—it'll end in tears.

JULIAN: Then this morning they were pretending to be nice and reasonable, and I said I quite understood and I'd got over it, and then I crept out the back way.

BRADLEY: Oh my heroine, but darling, what do we do now? They'll be here.

JULIAN: We'll run.

BRADLEY: But where to?

JULIAN: Anywhere, to a hotel.

BRADLEY: We can't go to a hotel, we haven't anywhere to go. MY GOD, YES WE HAVE! We can go to my cottage, my secret cottage beside the sea!

[BRADLEY *rings up.*]

Can I have a taxi, please, to go to King's Cross Station?

Pearson. You know, Penrose Court. Straight away? Thank you.

[*Enter* PRISCILLA, *she is dressed ready for departure, with handbag and fur coat.*]

PRISCILLA: Hello, Julian. Bradley, I've decided to go back to Roger. You were quite right. We should forgive each other and be reconciled. Could you send my things on after me?

[BRADLEY *conducts* JULIAN *and suitcase out and returns.*]

BRADLEY: Priscilla, you can't go back, you can't!

PRISCILLA: Why not!

BRADLEY: [*frantic, almost shouting*] Because Roger has got somebody there, he's got a mistress, they've been together for years, they've settled in the house, it's their house now, you can't go back any more! Oh God, I'd forgotten all about you—Francis said he'd come—Roger's mistress is there—she's called Marigold and she's pregnant.

[PRISCILLA *sits down. She speaks very slowly.*]

PRISCILLA: She's pregnant. You mean Roger and his mistress have taken it all over, it's theirs now?

BRADLEY: Yes!

PRISCILLA: Did you see them?

BRADLEY: Yes—she's young and beautiful, they're happy, they're in love—

PRISCILLA: I was thinking of Roger all alone, all by himself, trying to cook something in the kitchen, missing me, wanting me, and feeling sorry he'd been so bad—

BRADLEY: He's not sorry! They're singing and drinking champagne! You can't go back, Priscilla, it's too late!

[*The doorbell rings. Julian returns.*]

Julian, hold the taxi.

JULIAN: Is Priscilla all right?

BRADLEY: Yes, of course.

[JULIAN *goes out.*]

PRISCILLA: You're on their side. Everyone is on their side. God is on their side. You'd forgotten all about me.
[*Enter* FRANCIS.]

BRADLEY: Oh it's you, thank God. Francis said he'd stay here and look after you. I'm just going away. I'll ring you later.
[BRADLEY *rushes to his suitcases.*]

PRISCILLA: Bradley, don't go away, don't leave me!

FRANCIS: What about the money? The *money*?

BRADLEY: I'll give you a cheque. [*He tears out a cheque and gives it to* FRANCIS. *To* PRISCILLA] You'll be all right, Francis is here.
[*The doorbell rings.*]

FRANCIS: [*frantic, waving the cheque*] Brad, sign the cheque! Sign it, quick, just sign it!

JULIAN: It's the taxi.
[BRADLEY *scribbles his signature.*]

PRISCILLA: Bradley—!

BRADLEY: Coming!

PRISCILLA: Don't go, don't leave me. I'll kill myself!
[BRADLEY *rushes out with suitcases.* FRANCIS *gloats over the cheque, finds the sherry bottle and pours out two glasses.* PRISCILLA *is crying. He sits with an arm around her, offers her a glass which she thrusts away.*]
[*More softly*] I'll—kill—myself.

FRANCIS: No, you won't. It's a bad world. I don't like it either. It's a bloody rotten lousy cruel old world. Full of tears, oh the oceans of our tears. All we can do is try to cheer ourselves up. Come on!
[*She accepts the glass.*]

ACT TWO

Scene Four

Sitting-room at BRADLEY'S *cottage. A brilliant scene, large windows, sunlight.* BRADLEY *is heard singing his liberation song. Enter* JULIAN, *then* BRADLEY, *carrying towels, also stones, shells, bits of wood.* JULIAN *is holding a sheep's skull.* BRADLEY *and* JULIAN *have been transformed into outdoor seaside people,* BRADLEY *in shorts,* JULIAN *in bathing costume with colourful robe. They have been swimming, then exploring the beach.* JULIAN *holds up the skull.*

BRADLEY: *Memento mori.*

JULIAN: What? It's a sheep's skull, isn't it? Look, it's so smooth and shiny, like ivory. The sea has made it into a work of art.

BRADLEY: It's a symbol of death, a beautiful beautiful symbol.

[*In spite of his words,* BRADLEY *is clearly very happy.* JULIAN *begins to arrange the stones.*]

JULIAN: Stop it, darling. We've been swimming, we've been in paradise.

BRADLEY: We've become angels, not saints, angels.

JULIAN: We can hear the sea. Listen. [*No sound*]

BRADLEY: No we can't, it's too calm—and it depends on the wind.

JULIAN: We heard it last night. Didn't we hear it last night?

BRADLEY: We did, we did!

JULIAN: This has been the happiest day of my life. A long perfect day. Don't worry about Priscilla. We'll have her to live with us.

BRADLEY: We won't be living anywhere. There isn't any future. Don't think I'm complaining. He lives eternally who lives in the present.

JULIAN: Of course there's a future! I've bought brown bread, and toothpaste, and a saucepan, and an axe for chopping wood.

BRADLEY: Yes. But they're like the fossils religious people said God planted when he created the world in 4000 BC to give us an illusion of the past.

JULIAN: Bradley—

BRADLEY: We have an illusion of the future.

JULIAN: Don't talk in that silly way, it's a way of lying!

BRADLEY: We have no language in which to tell the truth about ourselves.

JULIAN: I have, I'm going to marry you! We're free, we aren't married to anyone else. Think what a bit of luck that is! And you're going to write a great book. Look, here are your notebooks!

[*She displays them.*]

BRADLEY: So white, so pure . . .

JULIAN: Bradley, you're tormenting me, you say bad things on purpose.

BRADLEY: Perhaps, but I must *move* a little, even cause pain, if I am to apprehend you at all. Yet I feel so connected with you, I *am* you, I've never *been* another person like this before—

JULIAN: We've only just found each other.

BRADLEY: We found each other millions and millions of years ago.

JULIAN: Then we're safe.

BRADLEY: I don't doubt your love, my darling, I'm grateful for it on my knees. [*He kneels and kisses the hem of her robe. She raises him.*] It's just that whatever miracle made us will automatically also unmake us. We are for breaking. Smash is what we're for.

JULIAN: You say these awful mechanical things because you're afraid to be happy.

BRADLEY: Yes, I fear the gods.

JULIAN: Look at these beautiful shells and stones, this

piece of wood with the funny pattern on it, they prove something.

BRADLEY: Priscilla thought her fur coat and her amber necklace and her pearls proved something.

JULIAN: We'll look after Priscilla and make her happy. Darling, don't reject happiness. I'll keep you here till you learn it!

BRADLEY: It's not my subject. I'm no bloody good, that's the trouble.

JULIAN: I know what's worrying you, it's last night, and this afternoon.

BRADLEY: Well, yes. That was a failure. I mean I was a failure.

JULIAN: You weren't a failure. You held me in your arms and I was perfectly happy—I've never been so happy in my life.

BRADLEY: It's like not being able to write, the god isn't there, he just isn't there.

JULIAN: He'll come—and you'll be able to write too. Dear heart, don't grieve, it will all come right.

BRADLEY: God, how I love you. But it's no good, I'm old, I'm older than you think.

JULIAN: Nonsense, look at yourself, you're young, you're beautiful. Bradley Pearson, will you marry me?

BRADLEY: Julian—

JULIAN: Will you marry me, yes or no?

BRADLEY: You're quite mad! I am your slave, and whatever you go on wanting will be the law of my being.

JULIAN: Then that's settled and you can stop boring me about your age!

BRADLEY: For all that beauty that doth cover thee is but the seemly raiment of my heart, which in thy breast doth live, as thine in me. How can I then be older than thou art?

JULIAN: Is that a quotation?

BRADLEY: It's a damn rotten argument.

[*Silence. Pause. They embrace. The scene darkens a little, faintly reddish glow, twilight. They now speak softly, enchanted.*]

JULIAN: Bradley, it's midsummer. Shall we go down and look at the sea?

BRADLEY: A midsummer night's dream—no—stay here, my sovereign lady.

JULIAN: How absolutely we've come home. Haven't we?

BRADLEY: Yes. If we can only stay here a bit longer, we're safe—forever—perhaps. [*Pause*] Look, there's the evening star.

JULIAN: We're inside a huge magic palace which reaches as far as the stars, as far as the outer galaxies, as far as—

BRADLEY: Dangerous places, magic palaces.

JULIAN: You mean they tend to vanish? But we're magic too—it's our magic. Wherever we are is magic.

BRADLEY: Julian, thank you for this perfect time. Nothing can damage this or take it away, ever, it's something eternal.

JULIAN: Sing to me, Bradley, I've heard you sing for other people, you've never sung just for me.

BRADLEY: [*sings*] Full fathom five thy father lies,
Of his bones are coral made,
Those are pearls that were his eyes,
Nothing of him that doth fade,
But doth suffer a sea-change
Into something rich and strange.
Sea-nymphs hourly ring his knell
Hark! now I hear them,
Ding-dong bell.
Hark! now I hear them,
Ding-dong bell.

[*Pause after the end of the song. The scene darkens a little more.*]

JULIAN: Thank you. All's well. [*She rises, ready to go into the bedroom.*] Come soon.

BRADLEY: Yes.

ACT TWO

[*Left alone,* BRADLEY *goes to the table where his writing materials are laid out. He picks up a notebook.*]

Yes. Love is the discovery of what one has always known. Art is the discovery of what one has always known—and which alone is true—*locked* into place by the dance of viewless atoms and the vast revolutions of the cosmos. I thought my poor sad patience would have to live its whole life without reward. But now—my love releases my art, my art enables my love. Like a magician who has waited ten thousand years for the juxtaposition of two stars, I have waited for this moment.

[*He raises his hands in prayer and triumph, then moves restlessly, tormented by joy and fear. He finally goes towards the bedroom door. The telephone rings.* BRADLEY *leaps to pick it up. He speaks softly throughout the conversation.*]

Hello. Yes, it's me. Who's that? . . . Francis! How did you know where I was? . . . What? What's the matter? Has Arnold found out? . . . Francis, what is it? . . . *What* about Priscilla? . . . Oh God—Oh no—what—? . . . Sleeping pills . . . It can't be, it's another false alarm, she can't be dead . . . Oh—No, it's my fault. Oh God . . . All right, stop moaning. Tell me how you found out where I was . . . I see. Does Arnold know I'm here? . . . No one knows but you? Hold on, just keep quiet for a moment, I want to think.

[BRADLEY *covers the mouthpiece. He looks at the bedroom door. Silence. He uncovers the mouthpiece.*]

Look—don't tell anybody where I am or that you got in touch . . . No, I can't come back . . . Yes, yes, she's my sister, but I can't come back yet. I will come . . . It was only an accident that you found the estate agent's letter. You must consider that this telephone call did not happen . . . Roger can fix the funeral. Do whatever you'd do if you couldn't find me! . . . Oh—why did you leave her alone? . . . Oh stop—do as I tell you. There's nothing we can do for Priscilla. She isn't there any more.

[BRADLEY *puts down the receiver, sits with head in hands, moans quietly. After an interval* JULIAN *emerges from the bedroom. She has put on her Hamlet gear, black tights, black jerkin, gold chain, white shirt, etc. She poses, holding the sheep's skull in one hand.* BRADLEY, *after a moment, lifts his head and sees her.*]

JULIAN: Oh! that this too too solid flesh would melt, thaw and resolve itself into a dew.

BRADLEY: What are you doing?

JULIAN: What do you think? Don't I look like the Prince of Denmark? Don't stare so. What's the matter?

BRADLEY: Nothing.

JULIAN: I brought this stuff to please you. Bradley, you're frightening me. What is it?

BRADLEY: Nothing.

JULIAN: I'll take it off—don't be cross—

BRADLEY: [*rising*] I'm not cross.

JULIAN: [*still frightened*] Bradley, darling—

BRADLEY: Oh—Julian—

[*He seizes her, tries to pull off her jerkin, gets entangled in the chain.* JULIAN *struggles to help him to remove the jerkin, unbutton the shirt.*]

JULIAN: Don't be so rough, you're hurting me!

BRADLEY: [*sobs*] It's the god—oh how terrible—oh Julian—

[*He buries his face in her hair, then picks her up and carries her into the bedroom. The music of the song is heard, first soft, then triumphant, then dying away into the sound of the sea as the stage becomes dark.*]

ACT TWO

Scene Five

Darkness. Then a terrible knocking at the door. Silence. Then more knocking. BRADLEY *in dressing-gown with electric torch, emerges cautiously from the bedroom, followed by* JULIAN *in nightgown.*

JULIAN: [*whispering*] What is it?

BRADLEY: I don't know.

JULIAN: Who can it be?

BRADLEY: You stay inside.

JULIAN: Keep quiet and don't put the light on, they'll think there's no one here. Oh I'm so frightened.
[*The knocking begins again. A metal object is pounding the panels of the door, there is a sound of splintering wood.*]

BRADLEY: Stay in the bedroom and lock the door.

JULIAN: No, no, Bradley, don't let them in!

BRADLEY: Stay in there!
[*He pushes* JULIAN *back into the bedroom and shuts the door. He turns up lights. The door bursts open. Enter* ARNOLD. ARNOLD *puts the axe he is holding on the table.*]

ARNOLD: [*almost speechless with rage and emotion*] Is Julian here?

BRADLEY: Yes.

ARNOLD: I've come to take her home.

BRADLEY: She won't go. How did you find us?

ARNOLD: Francis told me. And about the phone call.

BRADLEY: What phone call?

ARNOLD: He telephoned you last night and told you about Priscilla. You couldn't drag yourself away from your love-nest, even though your sister had killed herself!

BRADLEY: I'm coming to London and Julian is coming with me—we're going to be married.

ARNOLD: The car is outside. I want my daughter.

BRADLEY: No.

ARNOLD: Where is she?

[*He moves towards the bedroom door.* BRADLEY *picks up the axe. He opens the door and speaks through it.*]

BRADLEY: Your pa is here. Don't worry. We'll just explain the situation and see him off.

[JULIAN *enters. She is dressed, jeans, shirt.*]

ARNOLD: [*controlling himself*] My dear—

JULIAN: Hello.

ARNOLD: I've come to take you home.

JULIAN: This is home.

ARNOLD: You can't stay with this man. Here's a letter from your mother. Please read it. [JULIAN *automatically takes the letter.*] We've been so terribly worried—how could you be so cruel, staying here—and after what's happened to poor Priscilla.

JULIAN: What about Priscilla?

ARNOLD: [*triumphant*] Hasn't he told you?

BRADLEY: Priscilla is dead. She killed herself with an overdose of pills.

ARNOLD: He knew last night. Francis told him by telephone.

BRADLEY: That's correct.

JULIAN: You didn't tell me—and we were—in there—

ARNOLD: Aah!

BRADLEY: There was nothing I could do for Priscilla. But for *us*—I had to stay—it wasn't indifference.

ARNOLD: Lust is the word. Don't you see what he is?

JULIAN: [*in tears*] Bradley, how awful, how could you, oh poor poor Priscilla—and we wanted to make her happy!

ARNOLD: He is totally callous. His sister dies and he won't leave his foul love-making.

BRADLEY: I was going to tell you, and then we'd go to London. Please *listen*. I felt if we could only stay a little longer—here—alone—we'd be bound together forever. Do you understand? We needed this piece of time, *this* piece of time. I said nothing because of *you*, because of our love—

JULIAN: Oh Bradley—

BRADLEY: We'll go back now, together, and—oh I'm so much to blame!

JULIAN: It was my fault, because of me. Otherwise you'd have been with Priscilla, she begged you to stay. It's happened because of us—why didn't you say when Francis phoned?

ARNOLD: The sexual gratification of an elderly man. *Think!* He's thirty-three years older than you.

JULIAN: No he isn't, he's only forty-two.

ARNOLD: [*triumphant laughter*] He told you that, did he? He's fifty-three.

JULIAN: He can't be.

ARNOLD: Look him up in *Who's Who*.

BRADLEY: I'm not in *Who's Who*.

JULIAN: Bradley, how old are you?

BRADLEY: Fifty-three.

ARNOLD: When you're thirty he'll be a pensioner. Isn't that enough? Let's go, Julian, you can have your cry in the car.

JULIAN: Are you really fifty-three?

BRADLEY: Yes, Julian.

ARNOLD: Can't you see he is?

JULIAN: Yes I can—now.

BRADLEY: You said you didn't mind what age I was.

ARNOLD: Come along, Julian.

BRADLEY: You can't *go* suddenly just like this, I've got to talk to you properly—

ARNOLD: I am very upset and very angry and I am trying hard to be reasonable. I will not leave without you. Consider your mother's feelings. *Read her letter.*

[JULIAN, *distracted, tears open the envelope and holds the letter.*]

BRADLEY: I want to explain to you—

JULIAN: How can you explain!

[*She begins to read the letter.* BRADLEY, *still holding the axe, bars the door.*]

BRADLEY: My darling, don't leave me, don't leave me, I shall die—I can't let you go, I'll go mad, stay with me—

ARNOLD: Can't you see it's *over*? You've had a caper with a silly girl and now it's *finished*, the spell is broken.

[JULIAN *is clearly upset by the letter.*]

BRADLEY: Julian, we haven't lost each other, have we? I'm so deeply sorry I lied about my age, I did it instinctively—but it doesn't really matter, does it? And about Priscilla, I *had* to stay with you and be with you— I've done everything because I love you.

[JULIAN *in tears.*]

My darling, my love, let's sit down and talk quietly together, we'll talk about how it will be, how we'll be happy, and we'll go to sleep in each other's arms and everything will be all right.

JULIAN: I can't stay here—I must go home with my father.

ARNOLD: Thank God.

BRADLEY: Don't go—stay with me!

[BRADLEY *moves forward.* ARNOLD *seizes* JULIAN *and pushes her out of the door.* BRADLEY *rushes after them shouting, 'Julian, Julian'.*]

ACT TWO

Scene Six

BRADLEY'S *flat. The sunny weather is over. The window is dark.* FRANCIS *and* CHRISTINE, *with umbrellas and mackintoshes. They gradually take off macs, shake umbrellas. They are in mourning. They exchange glances, looking at the door.* PRISCILLA'S *things are visible, untidily piled together.*

CHRISTINE: Who was the poetry by that the man read? [*Getting no answer, louder.*]
It was such a lovely service. Who was the poetry by?
BRADLEY: [*off*] T. S. Eliot.
CHRISTINE: Was he Priscilla's favourite poet? [*No answer.*]
FRANCIS: Brad, I'll stay with you here if you like.
CHRISTINE: He'd better come round to my place.
FRANCIS: He'll want to stay here because of—you know—might turn up.
CHRISTINE: You could stay here and—Bradley, you'd better come over and stay at my house for a while. Francis could hold the fort here.
BRADLEY: [*off*] No thanks.
CHRISTINE: You need looking after. [*No answer.*] I'll pack Priscilla's things and send them back, you needn't worry.
FRANCIS: Can't Brad keep them?
CHRISTINE: No. That swine Roger actually came up to Bradley at the funeral and said of course he was Priscilla's heir and not to forget the silver fox! [*She holds it up.*] I guess it'll just fit Marigold.
[CHRISTINE *begins to sort and tidy the pile of clothes and ornaments. Enter* BRADLEY. *He sits on the sofa.*]
BRADLEY: [*tonelessly*] There's another bag under the stairs.

FRANCIS: I'll get it. And I'll put these in the kitchen.

[FRANCIS *goes out carrying umbrellas and macs. While he is away* CHRISTINE *approaches* BRADLEY.]

CHRISTINE: [*softly*] Brad. It's your old Chris—I do so much want to help.

[BRADLEY *smiles faintly, does not take her extended hand.* FRANCIS *comes back with the bag.* CHRISTINE *begins to pack it, wrapping ornaments carefully up in clothing. Francis sits down beside* BRADLEY, *trying to attract his attention.*]

FRANCIS: Brad, I wasn't out for long, I swear, I just met this chap in the pub like I said, and he kept on talking.

BRADLEY: Yes. You told me.

FRANCIS: Then later on I tried to wake her up—

BRADLEY: You told me.

FRANCIS: I don't see how I can go on living—Brad, you do forgive me, don't you?

BRADLEY: Yes, yes.

CHRISTINE: Oh brace up, Francis, stop whining, leave the poor sod alone. What did Rachel say when you went round?

BRADLEY: She said Julian was away somewhere with Arnold.

FRANCIS: I'll look for her, I'll find her!

BRADLEY: He's holding her by force, she's a prisoner, as soon as she escapes she'll come here.

[FRANCIS *and* CHRISTINE *look at each other and shake their heads. Poor* BRADLEY *is deluded. The doorbell rings.* BRADLEY, *galvanised into frantic activity, rushes to open it. It is* RACHEL.]

BRADLEY: Rachel!

CHRISTINE: Why it's Rachel. Hello Rachel I hope you're well.

BRADLEY: Rachel . . .

RACHEL: Hello Christine.

BRADLEY: . . . where's Julian?

RACHEL: Bless you, I'm so glad you're looking after her.

CHRISTINE: Thanks, dear.

BRADLEY: Where's Julian?

CHRISTINE: Come on Francis, let's be somewhere else.

FRANCIS: I want to stay here.

CHRISTINE: Francis, come on!

[*They depart.*]

RACHEL: [*calm, dignified*] I wanted to tell you how sorry I am about Priscilla.

BRADLEY: Rachel, *where's Julian?*

RACHEL: On holiday, with Arnold, I told you!

BRADLEY: She can't be, she's a prisoner, where is she?

RACHEL: I should imagine somewhere in the Lake District.

BRADLEY: The Lake District!

RACHEL: They went off by car. Julian loves a trip.

BRADLEY: A trip!

RACHEL: Here are the letters you sent her, by the way, I haven't opened them. [*She hands* BRADLEY *several letters.*]

BRADLEY: She'll come back to me as soon as she can get away.

RACHEL: Bradley, she left you of her own free will. Poor old thing, you look terrible, you look a hundred. Calm down, it's all your fantasy.

BRADLEY: You didn't think so when Julian said she loved me.

RACHEL: Your Julian is a fiction, it's all a mistake. You make me sick! Not so long ago it was *me* you were kissing passionately! Remember?

BRADLEY: Nothing happened. I made it perfectly clear I didn't want it. I can imagine you may feel resentful—

RACHEL: Resentful! I was just feeling sorry for you. And if nothing happened it wasn't because you didn't want it to! Our liaison was entirely for your benefit.

BRADLEY: There was no liaison!

RACHEL: Well, I suppose it didn't last long. No wonder Julian could hardly believe it.

BRADLEY: [*staggered*] You told Julian?

RACHEL: Yes, of course. I told Arnold at once how you'd sprung upon me, he was most amused. He suggested I write a letter to Julian about our relationship. He thought it might be an effective argument!

BRADLEY: [*appalled*] That letter—

RACHEL: Naturally she came running back to hear all about it, so I told her.

BRADLEY: What did you tell her?

RACHEL: Everything, it would have been wrong to conceal it.

BRADLEY: Oh God!

RACHEL: Bradley, one is responsible for one's past actions and you can't blot them out by entering a dreamworld, you can't make yourself into a new person over night, however much in love you feel you are. Do you really imagine you would be the final resting-place of a young girl's passion? Her final choice?

BRADLEY: *What did you tell her?*

RACHEL: I think you're having some sort of nervous breakdown. I told her about us.

BRADLEY: What did she say?

RACHEL: What could she say, poor child, she was crying like a maniac.

BRADLEY: What?

RACHEL: She got me to repeat it, give the details, swear it was all true and she believed me.

BRADLEY: What did she say? Can't you remember anything she said?

RACHEL: She said 'If only it had been longer ago.' I suppose she had a point.

BRADLEY: You misled her, you lied to her!

RACHEL: Bradley, don't shout! She'd already seen it was a silly mistake. You're a lonely frustrated man, and you

may have misunderstood my little attempt to help you.
I'm afraid happily married couples sometimes make
victims of people they're sorry for. Arnold and I tell
each other everything, we laugh about it, we're very
happy together.

BRADLEY: [*dazed*] I thought Arnold was going off with
Christine, he told me he was—

RACHEL: Don't be crazy!

BRADLEY: My mind's going—I thought he wrote— [*He
goes to his desk and takes out* ARNOLD'S *letter and reads from
it.*] 'Christine and I have fallen in love—'
[RACHEL *snatches the letter and reads it.*]

RACHEL: You did this on purpose.

BRADLEY: I'm sorry, I didn't know what I was doing, I'd
forgotten about it. He doesn't mean it.

RACHEL: God, you're vile, vindictive!

BRADLEY: You said you and Arnold told each other
everything.

RACHEL: You're a dangerous horrible person, living in a
dream, breaking everything, wrecking all the happiness
you can't have. No wonder you can't write, you aren't
really here at all. Julian looked at you and made you
real for a moment, I made you real for a moment
because I was sorry for you. Now all that's left of you is a
crazy spiteful ghost. I shall hate you forever. You kept
this letter as a weapon against me.

BRADLEY: Honestly, Rachel, I haven't given you a single
thought!

RACHEL: Aaaaaaaaarrgh!
[RACHEL *turns away and runs out screaming. Her screams
gradually die away. Red light on stage.*]

BRADLEY: [*litany*] I'll make a wager with the god. I'll give
it up.
Let these blank pages not be written on.
Forget my prayers, let there be no book.
Only let Julian come back again.

I here unmake all that I meant to do.
All that I ever begged for I hereby surrender.
Only let her come back, and end this pain.
[BRADLEY *tears up his notebooks. The telephone rings, he rushes to it in a frenzy. He shouts.*]
Julian! . . . Oh, it's Rachel . . . Is Julian there? . . . What? Is Julian all right? . . . What's the matter . . . You've done *what*? I can't hear . . . Yes, yes, I'll come round.
[BRADLEY *rushes out.*]

ACT TWO

SCENE SEVEN

The sitting-room at ARNOLD'S *house. The room is wrecked as in Act One, Scene Two. Chairs overturned. The bookcase shows a conspicuous gap.* ARNOLD'S *books have been torn up and scattered on the floor. The periodical with* BRADLEY'S *review of* ARNOLD'S *latest novel lies upon the table.* ARNOLD'S *body, sprawling on the sofa, is reminiscent of* RACHEL'S *in Act One, Scene Two.* RACHEL *is sitting moaning. Enter* BRADLEY.

RACHEL *points towards* ARNOLD. BRADLEY *kneels to look.*

BRADLEY: Oh my God!

RACHEL: [*whisper*] He's dead.

BRADLEY: Yes—I think so—oh Rachel—
[BRADLEY *rises. He picks up the bloodstained 'murder weapon', the familiar poker, which is lying nearby.*]
You did it—with this—

RACHEL: He's dead—he's dead.

BRADLEY: What happened?

RACHEL: I was so angry, I started to tear up all his books, he tried to stop me. I hit him—we were arguing, shouting—I didn't mean to—he started screaming with pain—I couldn't bear it—I hit him again just to stop him screaming.

BRADLEY: [*with poker, frantic*] We must hide this, you must say it was an accident—oh what shall we do—he can't be dead—Arnold! Arnold! Did you ring for the doctor?

RACHEL: He's dead—I killed him—

BRADLEY: Did you ring the doctor—ambulance—police?

RACHEL: No.

BRADLEY: It was an accident—he fell and hit his head—

293

that's what happened—I'll clean this up and—no fingerprints—

[BRADLEY *takes a handkerchief from his pocket, carefully cleans blood and finger prints off the poker, and pockets the handkerchief again. He keeps hold of the poker.*]

I hope that disposes of—we ought to clear up this mess—Rachel, I'm going to telephone—remember it was an *accident*.

RACHEL: It's no good—no good— [*She rocks to and fro in anguish.*]

BRADLEY: [*confused, distraught*] You must say it was an accident—or—or—self-defence! He hit you first, and you—Rachel, please *think* what you're going to *say*!

RACHEL: Oh my darling, oh my love, oh my love—

BRADLEY: [*dials 999*] Hello, emergency, someone badly hurt, ambulance, police—Milford House, Kent Gardens—my name is Pearson—yes—yes—Rachel, they're coming, remember, it's not your fault—oh—! [*He picks up the poker which is now once more stained with blood.*]

It's all bloody. God, I ought to—clean all this up— [*Still holding the poker he tries ineffectively to tidy the scene. Sound of police sirens.*]

Rachel, for God's sake think what you're going to tell them!

[*Enter three policemen. They observe the scene, inspect the body. One, moving in and out of the room, occupies himself with* RACHEL, *who sits sobbing incoherently.*]

I'm afraid there's been an accident. I think he's dead. He fell and hit his head. He's Arnold Baffin, the writer. This is Mrs Baffin.

IST POLICEMAN: And who are you?

BRADLEY: My name is Bradley Pearson, I'm a writer too.

2ND POLICEMAN: [*at body*] Stove his head in.

[*The* 2ND POLICEMAN *takes the poker from* BRADLEY.]

2ND POLICEMAN: Thank you, sir.

BRADLEY: You won't find any fingerprints on that except mine. Oh dear, there's more blood on it, I dropped it on the floor.

[BRADLEY *takes out his bloodstained handkerchief and wipes the end of the poker. The* 1ST POLICEMAN *takes the handkerchief from him.*]

[*The* 2ND POLICEMAN *has picked up the periodical from the table and shows it to the* 1ST POLICEMAN.]

1ST POLICEMAN: Did you write this article, 'Arnold Baffin, The End, We Hope.'

BRADLEY: Yes, but that's not my title. I wouldn't have used that title, the editor put it on, editors are always doing that.

1ST POLICEMAN: [*pointing to the books on the floor which the* 2ND POLICEMAN *has been examining*] Who tore up these books?

BRADLEY: I did—I mean—[*more softly*] no, not these ones actually—

[*The* 3RD POLICEMAN, *tending* RACHEL, *has been at the door, talking to those outside.*]

3RD POLICEMAN: Mrs Baffin, we've just got your daughter on the phone, would you like to speak to her?

BRADLEY: Julian!

RACHEL: He killed my husband!

3RD POLICEMAN: Come along now.

RACHEL: He murdered him!

3RD POLICEMAN: Don't worry, we'll look after you.

RACHEL: [*sobbing as she goes with the* 3RD POLICEMAN.] He's dead, he's dead.

3RD POLICEMAN: Come along, we'll help you, gently now.

[*He leads* RACHEL *out.*]

1ST POLICEMAN: I think you'd better come along with us, Mr Pearson. It is my duty to warn you that anything you say may be used as evidence against you.

BRADLEY: You don't think I killed him? I didn't kill him, I didn't! He was my best friend.

[BRADLEY *stands appalled, silently apprehending his situation.*]

1ST POLICEMAN: Come along please, Mr Pearson.

EPILOGUE

BRADLEY: The Great British Public absolutely loved my trial. Everyone including my lawyer, believed I had killed Arnold. *Writer slays friend out of envy.* Of course I never stood a chance. Arnold's books, supposedly torn to pieces by me, were brought into court in a tea-chest and fingered by the jury. I think that was what impressed them most. As for Rachel, all she had to do was dress in black and mop her eyes. There was a reverent sigh whenever she entered the box. It never entered anyone's head that she could have any motive for killing her husband. Marriage is a very private place.

RACHEL: I do not want to be unkind, even to the murderer of my husband, but since Bradley Pearson's fantasy life has achieved some notoriety I feel that I must speak. Bradley was not an artist—he was an unhappy disappointed man who pretended to be an artist. He claimed to be a perfectionist but he never wrote things and tore them up. I'm sure he never tore up anything except my husband's books. We all regarded him as an absurd little man, a figure of fun, someone one couldn't mention without smiling. He must have realised this. That's a shocking thought that a man might commit a serious crime just because people laughed at him. He was obsessively envious of my husband—and he knew that my husband really despised him. That must have caused him continual torment. Of course the romance with my daughter was pure fantasy. He was actually deeply in love with me. How far that unrequited passion led him to commit such a terrible deed it is not for me to say.

BRADLEY: My life sentence gave general satisfaction. It was a mean contemptible crime, to kill your friend out of envy of his talents. And poor Priscilla, rising from the grave, pointed her accusing finger. My 'callous indif-

ference' to her death, which the defence said proved me
insane, in effect proved me a monster. Perhaps you will
say that the judgement was not entirely unjust. Of
course—my extreme love—for that girl—did in some
sense occasion the deaths of both Arnold and Priscilla.
We cannot altogether evade responsibility for the
chains of moral failure which bring about the evil which
we protest that we never intended.

FRANCIS: It is not for me to dispute the sentence passed
upon my friend Bradley Pearson—but as a man of
science it is my duty to explain his conduct. We have
here the classical symptoms of the Oedipus Complex.
Male children love their mothers and cannot forgive
them for having sex with their fathers. So, many adult
men detest women. It's as simple as that. Bradley is
obviously a homosexual as I demonstrate in my forthcoming book *Hamlet, or The Case of Bradley Pearson*.

He appeared to be in love with a girl—but look! He
falls in love when he imagines her as a man, he achieves
sexual intercourse when she is dressed as a prince.
And who is Bradley's favourite author? The greatest
homosexual of them all, William Shakespeare! What
is Bradley's favourite fantasy? Boys pretending to
be girls pretending to be boys. And who is this girl
anyway? The daughter of Bradley's rival, friend,
enemy, *alter ego*, Arnold Baffin. Artists adore themselves, their relations with other people are always
unhappy. Bradley was blessed, or cursed, with only one
genuine attachment. Perhaps I should not instance his
affection for myself as evidence of his sexual tendencies.
But may I take this opportunity of saying to my old
friend—I was aware of his feelings, and I valued them
highly.

CHRISTINE: I want to say how very sorry I am for poor
Bradley. He didn't mean to kill his friend, he did it in
some sort of mad brainstorm. His memory of our

marriage isn't all that clear either—we never hated each other, I just got bored! I wasn't surprised to find he'd got nowhere and done nothing, I was even a bit pleased—isn't that awful? I wanted to help—I guess it was just curiosity really. When I turned up all rich and joyful of course he fell for me all over again and I had to throw him out a second time—and that's what made him go crazy. All his family were a bit off, his mother was a monster, and his sister could have used some electric shocks. And his mania about art, as if it were religion! We can live without art I should think— what's so special about art? Maybe it's some consolation if you *imagine* you're an artist. I hope Bradley's not too miserable in prison. Perhaps it's a blessing to be insane if it makes you think you're happy when you're not.

JULIAN: I find it difficult to identify myself with the child who imagined she loved Bradley Pearson. Perhaps there was such a child, and perhaps it was me. I never read Pearson's writings. There was something impressive there, a lifetime of trying and failing. It seems brave to go on trying. It also seems stupid. I am a writer myself now, a poet. I favour a small but perfect product. Pearson was wrong to picture some god as the ruler of art. Art is cold. Especially when it portrays passion. Erotic love never inspires good art. Love is concerned with possession. Art is concerned with truth. Pearson was not cool enough. He wanted to be the victim of a dark power, but there is nothing there. Art has no master.

BRADLEY: [*sitting*] The soul, seeking its survival, looks into the darkness. I lost my Julian. But I wrote my book. [*Takes book out of table-drawer and stands.*] I have changed my beloved into art. I have preserved her inside this frame. [*Gesture to indicate the prison, the theatre.*] This is her immortality—from this embrace she cannot escape. So speaks the artist. And yet, my dear, dear girl, however passionately my thought has worked upon your image, I cannot really make myself believe that I invented you. At the last you evade me; art cannot assimilate nor thought digest you. I do not know or want to know anything of your present life. Yet elsewhere, I realise, you are, you laugh, you cry, you walk in the sunlight, read books, perhaps write books, lie down in someone's arms. May I never deny this knowledge, or forget that it was a real person that I loved so much. That love remains, altered but undiminished, a great pure love with a clear memory. It causes me remarkably little pain. Only sometimes at night when I think you live now and are somewhere, I shed tears.

FINAL CURTAIN

THE SERVANTS AND THE SNOW

First performed September 20th 1970 at the Greenwich Theatre, London

Cast

PETER JACK	*William Marlowe*
BASIL	*Philip Bond*
ORIANE	*Adrienne Corri*
GRUNDIG	*Godfrey Jackman*
HANS JOSEPH	*Esmond Knight*
FREDERIC	*Bill Stewart*
FATHER AMBROSE	*Llewellyn Rees*
MARINA	*Maxine Audley*
MIKEY	*Christopher Reynolds*
MAXIM	*Tom Conti*
PATRICE	*Shay Gorman*
GENERAL KLEIN	*Shay Gorman*
Servants	*Timothy Heald,*
	Robert Lister, Malcolm Ransom

Directed by Alan Vaughan Williams

THE THREE ARROWS

First performed October 17th 1972 at the Arts Theatre, Cambridge

Cast

PRINCE HIRAKAWA	*Matthew Long*
PRINCE TENJIKU	*Tenniel Evans*
PRINCE YORIMITSU	*Ian McKellen*
TAIHITO, the Emperor	*John Tordoff*
GENERAL MASASHI, the Shogun	*Frank Middlemass*
LADY ROKUNI, mother of the Shogun	*Margery Mason*
KEIKO, the Crown Princess	*Marion Diamond*
KURITSUBO, lady-in-waiting	*Caroline Blakiston*
AYAME, lady-in-waiting	*Sheila Reid*
FATHER AKITA	*Robert Eddison*
OKANO, Samurai	*Jack Shepherd*
NORIKURA, Samurai	*Juan Moreno*
TOKUZAN, the ex-emperor	*Ronnie Stevens*
Pages and soldiers	*Andrea Addison,*
	Annette Badland,
	Hamish Patrick,
	Moira Redmond,
	Saul Reichlin,
	John Vine.

Directed by Noel Willman

THE BLACK PRINCE

First performed April 25th 1989 at the Aldwych Theatre, London

Cast

BRADLEY PEARSON	*Ian McDiarmid*
FRANCIS MARLOE	*John Fortune*
ARNOLD BAFFIN	*Simon Williams*
RACHEL BAFFIN	*Sarah Badel*
JULIAN BAFFIN	*Abigail Cruttenden*
PRISCILLA	*Norma West*
CHRISTINE	*Deborah Norton*
1st POLICEMAN	*Peter Yapp*
2nd POLICEMAN	*Christopher Mitchell*
POLICEWOMAN	*Norma Streader*

Directed by Stuart Burge
Designed by Ultz
Lighting by Gerry Jenkinson
Music by Ilona Sekacz
Performed by The Stephen Hill Singers

HIGHSMITH #45230

Printed
in USA